Safeguarding Children

A Shared Responsibility

HEDY CLEAVER
Emeritus Professor, Royal Holloway, University of London

PAT CAWSON
Research Consultant; former Head of Child Protection Research, NSPCC

SARAH GORIN
Senior Research Officer, NSPCC

STEVE WALKER
Principal Consultant, Children and Young People's Services with the Improvement and Development Agency

WILEY-BLACKWELL

A John Wiley & Sons, Ltd., Publication

This edition first published 2009

Crown Copyright © 2009. Reproduced with the permission of the Controller of Her Majesty's Stationery Office.

Wiley-Blackwell is an imprint of John Wiley & Sons, formed by the merger of Wiley's global Scientific, Technical, and Medical business with Blackwell Publishing.

Registered Office

John Wiley & Sons Ltd, The Atrium, Southern Gate, Chichester, West Sussex, PO19 8SQ, UK

Editorial Offices

The Atrium, Southern Gate, Chichester, West Sussex, PO19 8SQ, UK

9600 Garsington Road, Oxford, OX4 2DQ, UK

350 Main Street, Malden, MA 02148-5020, USA

For details of our global editorial offices, for customer services, and for information about how to apply for permission to reuse the copyright material in this book please see our website at www.wiley.com/wiley-blackwell.

The right of Hedy Cleaver, Pat Cawson, Sarah Gorin and Steve Walker to be identified as the authors of the editorial material in this work has been asserted in accordance with the Copyright, Designs and Patents Act 1988.

Library of Congress Cataloging-in-Publication Data

Safeguarding children : a shared responsibility / Hedy Cleaver ... [et al.].
      p. cm.
    Includes bibliographical references and index.
    ISBN 978-0-470-51873-1 (cloth) – ISBN 978-0-470-51874-8 (pbk)
    1. Social work with children.   2. Family social work.   3. Child welfare.
  4. Children.   I. Cleaver, Hedy.
    HV713.S224   2009
    362.2–dc22
                                                                    2008022821

Typeset in 10/12pt TimesTen by Aptara Inc., New Delhi, India.
Printed and bound in Singapore by Fabulous Printers Pte Ltd

Safeguarding Children

THE NSPCC/WILEY SERIES
in
PROTECTING CHILDREN
The multi-professional approach

Series Editors: Christopher Cloke,
NSPCC, 42 Curtain Road,
London EC2A 3NX

Jan Horwath,
Department of Sociological Studies,
University of Sheffield,
Sheffield S10 2TU

Peter Sidebotham,
Warwick Medical School,
University of Warwick,
Coventry CV4 7AL

This NSPCC/Wiley series explores current issues relating to the prevention of child abuse and the protection of children. The series aims to publish titles that focus on professional practice and policy, and the practical application of research. The books are leading edge and innovative and reflect a multidisciplinary and inter-agency approach to the prevention of child abuse and the protection of children.

All books have a policy or practice orientation with referenced information from theory and research. The series is essential reading for all professionals and researchers concerned with the prevention of child abuse and the protection of children.

Contents

List of Contributors

Mary Armitage Integrating Processes Manager, Children Leeds.

Arnon Bentovim Consultant Child and Adolescent Psychiatrist, Director, London Child and Family Consultation Service; Honorary Consultant Great Ormond Street Children's Hospital and the Tavistock Clinic; Honorary Senior Lecturer, Institute of Child Health, University College London.

Pat Cawson Research Consultant; former Head of Child Protection Research, NSPCC.

Hedy Cleaver Emeritus Professor, Royal Holloway, University of London.

Ruth Gardner Senior Research Fellow, University of East Anglia/NSPCC.

Sarah Gorin Senior Research Officer, NSPCC.

Jenny Gray Professional Adviser, Safeguarding Children Policy Team, Department for Children, Schools and Families.

Anna Gupta Senior Lecturer in Social Work, Royal Holloway, University of London.

Jan Horwath Professor of Child Welfare, University of Sheffield.

Margaret A. Lynch Emeritus Professor of Community Paediatrics, King's College, London.

Megan McNeill-McKinnell Former Adviser and Advocate for Family Rights Groups.

Wendy Rose Senior Research Fellow, The Open University.

Steve Walker Principal Consultant, Children and Young People's Services with the Improvement and Development Agency.

Carolyne Willow National Coordinator, Children's Rights Alliance for England.

Preface

> I am 14. My step-father hits my mum and me, and I am scared that one day he will start hitting my younger brothers, or hit my mum so hard she won't survive. I don't know what I should do, or who I should talk to, but I know I can't live like this anymore. The only adult I really know and who I trust is my school nurse; she always smiles and is quite chatty. Someone who I know I couldn't talk to is my form teacher; she doesn't seem interested in us unless we are her favourite students. She never makes jokes or smiles. I guess I just generally feel I couldn't walk up to her and tell her all of this because I don't think she cares about me.
>
> Written by Anya, aged 17 (not her real name), who contributed to a consultation exercise with young people held by the Children's Rights Alliance for England and the NSPCC, Autumn 2003

In 1974, the report on the death of 6-year-old Maria Colwell, killed by her stepfather, led to the setting up of formal inter-agency structures designed to prevent harm to children (Department of Health and Social Security, 1974). Thirty years later, following the death of another child at the hands of her carers, that of 8-year-old Victoria Climbié (Cm 5730, 2003), these inter-agency structures have been placed on a statutory footing by the Children Act 2004, which requires local authorities in England and Wales to set up Local Safeguarding Children Boards. In the intervening period, many inquiries and serious case reviews have highlighted the same problems: practitioners on whom children should be able to rely have not noticed that they were distressed; not listened to their complaints or appeals for help, and instead have focused on the needs and accounts of the parents and other adults around them. Sometimes – as with Maria and Victoria – the abuse described in the reports has led to children's deaths; sometimes to abuse or neglect of children living at home, in boarding schools, foster care, residential homes or young-offender institutions.

The inquiries and reviews demonstrated that practitioners who failed to assist abused or neglected children were not, for the most part, guilty of deliberate malice or negligence. Instead, they were too often responding inappropriately to pressures on resources, or caught up in dysfunctional organisational and professional traditions, or in loyalties to colleagues that inhibited reporting of poor practice. At times they were accepting, without question, common stereotypes such as assumptions that 'emotionally disturbed' or 'troublesome' children were untruthful, the 'rule of optimism' that things would improve in the child's life even though there was no objective evidence to support this belief, or that respectable professional 'pillars of the community' could not possibly be predatory paedophiles. Stereotypes of what happens in unfamiliar minority ethnic cultures have led practitioners to misjudge children's and carer's behaviour or wrongly decide a child was safe and happy. Sometimes, practitioners suspected that children were being abused or neglected but simply did not know how to go about safeguarding them, or had reports of their worries discounted by colleagues or managers. This reader aims to give practical help in overcoming these obstacles to the effective safeguarding and promoting of children's welfare by

- setting out the evidence from research, inspection and inquiries which underpins use of the practice guidance given in the *Framework for the Assessment of Children in Need and Their Families* (Department of Health, Department for Education and Employment and Home Office, 2000), *Working Together to Safeguard Children* (HM Government, 2006a) and *What To Do If You're Worried a Child Is Being Abused* (HM Government, 2006b);
- giving practical suggestions drawn from the evidence on 'what works' in safeguarding and promoting children's welfare and on managing some of the dilemmas that face practitioners in their everyday work;
- pointing the way to further help from government guidance, research, practice materials and the Internet.

In all of the inquiry reports, a key message emerges: observe and listen to children. We were clear that our starting point in this reader had to be children's perspectives on what made them feel safe and what would enable them to tell practitioners of their distress and ask for help if they were being abused or neglected. At the start of our work, a 2-day consultation with young people who had experienced the child protection process at first hand was held by the Children's Rights Alliance for England (CRAE) and the NSPCC. One of these young people was Anya, whose account of living with domestic violence is given above. Asked to write down for us what adults could learn from this, Anya wrote:

> If an adult is worried about a child – for example, if they think they are being abused – then it is important that the adult talks to the child directly. How to talk to the child depends on the age and how well the adult knows the child. A child may be trying to tell the adult (such as a teacher) that they are in danger deliberately, perhaps by mentioning they don't want to go home. If this is the case, a direct question such as 'Why?' may be enough to allow the child to open up and talk.

Anya gave three important points for adults to remember:

- It is important the adult not only tells the child what will happen (such as whether children's social care needs to be involved) but also asks the child what they want to happen; as far as is possible, this should be followed.
- It is also vital that the child is aware that all the adults involved in (for example) the ensuing police investigation or child protection conference are there to help the child – and furthermore, that what the child is doing (by telling them) is the right thing.
- The child also shouldn't think that the adult doesn't believe them.

We have therefore incorporated these messages in the choice of issues covered and in the way in which essential messages are presented.

HOW TO USE THE READER

The structure of the reader is intended to support and complement the materials in the training pack *Safeguarding Children: A Shared Responsibility*. Each chapter is written so that it is complete in itself and can be used independently for specific training courses or sessions. Each chapter incorporates basic principles of good practice: listening to children, knowing the child or the child's situation, informing those involved about what is happening or will happen, respecting diversity, and consulting and seeking advice when faced with complex, uncertain or unfamiliar situations. Some topics are touched on in all or most chapters, with cross-referencing to other chapters that deal with the topic in greater detail.

RESPECTING DIVERSITY

An early issue to be decided by the editors was whether to include separate chapters on diversity issues, particularly on those affecting children from minority ethnic communities and disabled children. We concluded that this would not be helpful to readers. The basic principles of good practice in safeguarding and promoting children's welfare are the same in all work with children and families, and practitioners should maintain awareness of and sensitivity to diversity in all their work. Consequently, throughout the text we identify where specific needs linked to ethnicity or disability arise.

THE STRUCTURE OF THE READER

There are two separate but complementary parts to the reader. Part I focuses on the themes and principles which underpin all work when safeguarding and promoting the welfare of children; Part II focuses on the processes set out in the *Framework for the Assessment of Children in Need and Their Families* (Department of Health, Department for Education and Employment and Home Office, 2000) and the government guidance *Working Together to Safeguard Children* (HM Government, 2006a).

Part I: Themes and Principles of Safeguarding covers questions of principle that underpin all practice to safeguard and promote children's welfare. The starting point is the focus on children. In Chapter 1, Carolyne Willow looks at the barriers that prevent practitioners from hearing and seeing children's distress, and the changes that must take place in adult attitudes and behaviour if children are to be truly at the heart of safeguarding practice.

For most children, the route to safe care and positive developmental outcomes is through support to their parents or carers. In Chapter 2, Ruth Gardner and Hedy Cleaver explore the complex issues of working with parents, especially when the threat to children's safety and welfare is thought to come from the parents' own behaviour. They discuss the challenges that practitioners face in dealing sensitively with parents and the importance of being open and honest about their concerns and about the consequences of taking particular actions to safeguard children's welfare.

Ways of using the strengths of the extended family and the resources of the local community are considered by Anna Gupta and Megan McNeill–McKinnell (Chapter 3). They stress the importance of practitioners assessing the availability of family resources, rather than simply assuming that extended families will or will not be able to give support, and the difference that the provision of small amounts of help in accessing local services can make to a struggling family.

When children live apart from their families – in boarding schools, foster homes, children's homes or in custody – practitioners face the same difficult task that parents face in responding to children's need for safety and guidance at the same time as meeting their developmental needs for privacy, exploration and growing independence. In Chapter 4, Pat Cawson outlines some of the strategies that assist children living away from home to be safeguarded from harm inflicted deliberately or unwittingly by peers, staff or foster carers, or by unscrupulous adults who exploit children through trafficking or prostitution.

Jan Horwath (Chapter 5) provides a navigation guide for routes through the thorny maze of practical and organisational problems that can beset inter-agency and multi-disciplinary working, highlighting essential rules for collaboration in the interests of children and practice that is truly professional in the best sense of the word.

Part II: The Process of Safeguarding takes the practitioner through the stages of safeguarding and promoting a child's welfare from the point at which someone first worries that a child's health or development may be being impaired, or he or she may be experiencing abuse or neglect due to the formation and conclusion of long-term plans. In Chapter 6, Margaret A. Lynch examines the signs that first cause practitioners to worry about the safety and welfare of a child, including the appearance and behaviour of children and parents, and the absent child who does not turn up for school or for expected health checks. She discusses the issues that arise with different age groups – from infancy to adolescence.

Mary Armitage and Steve Walker (Chapter 7) look at the ways in which practitioners can get help and advice prior to referring a child because of concerns about their welfare, in what are often difficult and uncertain circumstances. These include approaching colleagues, managers, specialists, professionals and other agencies. The practical requirements for gathering and recording information to assist the making of a referral are outlined.

In Chapter 8, Hedy Cleaver sets out the requirements for assessing the needs of children in order to decide whether they are 'children in need' and, if so, whether they are or may be at risk of suffering significant harm. She addresses the action that should be taken when there is a need for immediate intervention to safeguard a child from a potentially life-threatening situation. She discusses the contributions that different practitioners make to the assessment process and how this information contributes to a plan.

We move into longer term planning and decision making in Chapter 9 when Steve Walker takes us through the process from the initial strategy discussion to the formulation of a clear plan to safeguard a child. He stresses the importance of contingency planning, in a context where the course of events may not be totally predictable or under the practitioner's control. Arnon Bentovim (Chapter 10) describes the range of interventions that can be used when a child living with the family has suffered significant harm – to prevent children from suffering further harm and to bring about the necessary changes that will enable them to return to live with their families safely or, if necessary, to be placed successfully with new families. He outlines the different approaches to therapy with abused children and the work that can be done to support and develop parenting skills.

Finally, in Chapter 11, Wendy Rose considers the importance of monitoring and reviewing throughout the process – from initial contact with a child about whom there are concerns until work with the child and family is brought to a close – and the significance of good enough endings.

We could not cover every aspect of safeguarding and promoting children's welfare in one book, but we hope it is useful for practitioners and volunteers working in all types of services that have contact with children. The duty to safeguard and promote children's welfare applies to all children, irrespective of the circumstances in which they are living, playing or being educated, and to all ages from birth to 18. Most teenagers would not see themselves or be seen by others as 'children' but to reduce the use of cumbersome language by constant repetition of 'children and young people' the text uses the word 'children', as defined in the Children Acts 1989 and 2004, to refer to the entire age group.

HEDY CLEAVER
PAT CAWSON
SARAH GORIN
STEVE WALKER

REFERENCES

Children Act 2004 Chapter 31, http://www.opsi.gov.uk/acts/acts2004/20040031.htm (accessed 14 September 2008).

Cm 5730 (2003) *The Victoria Climbié Inquiry Report. An Inquiry by Lord Laming*, The Stationery Office, London, www.victoria-climbie-inquiry.org.uk (accessed 14 September 2008).

Department for Children, Schools and Families (2007) *The Children's Plan. Building Brighter Futures*, The Stationery Office, London, http://www.dcsf.gov.uk/publications/childrensplan/ (accessed 14 September 2008).

Department of Health, Department for Education and Employment and Home Office (2000) *Framework for the Assessment of Children in Need and Their Families*, The Stationery Office, London, http://www.dh.gov.uk/en/Publications andstatistics/Publications/PublicationsPolicyAndGuidance/DH_4003256 (accessed 14 September 2008).

Department of Health and Social Security (1974) *Report of the Committee of Inquiry into the Care and Supervision Provided in Relation to Maria Colwell*, HMSO, London.

HM Government (2006a) *Working Together to Safeguard Children: A Guide to Inter-Agency Working to Safeguard and Promote the Welfare of Children*, The Stationery Office, London, http://www.everychildmatters.gov.uk/socialcare/safeguarding/workingtogether (accessed 14 September 2008).

HM Government (2006b) *What To Do If You're Worried a Child Is Being Abused*, Department for Education and Skills, London, www.everychildmatters.gov.uk/socialcare/safeguarding/ (accessed 14 September 2008).

Acknowledgements

We owe thanks to the many people who contributed to this book. There are too many to name everyone individually but special thanks are due to the following:

- The young people who took part in the NSPCC/CRAE workshop, who played a valuable part in putting us on track about issues important to children.
- *Safeguarding Children — A Shared Responsibility* is produced in conjunction with a training resource pack. Both were developed by a consortium led by the NSPCC, including Children Rights Alliance (England); Family Rights Group; North Lincolnshire Social Services and Housing; Oxfordshire ACPC; Promoting Inter-Agency Training (PIAT); and Royal Holloway, University of London. All contributed ideas and assistance to the editors and authors.
- The Advisory and Steering Groups included representatives from social care, education, health, police and youth justice services, the voluntary sector, academia and several government departments. Many individuals helped in developing ideas and by giving us useful documents and contacts.
- The work was funded by the Department for Children, Schools and Families, and we would like to thank the staff from the Department who assisted us.

A number of individuals gave exceptional assistance in reviewing or preparing the final text:

Judith Masson, Professor of Law at Bristol University, read and commented on the text from a legal perspective, and saved us from numerous mistakes.

Jenny Gray, from the Department of Children, Schools and Families, read and commented on all drafts and was alongside us throughout the whole enterprise.

William Baginsky, from the NSPCC Training and Consultancy, produced the CD version of the reader and gave invaluable assistance in keeping, the text up to date in the context of major changes in government guidance and the organization of services, occurring over the period during which the reader was in preparation.

Several other staff from **the NSPCC Training and Consultancy, the NSPCC Library and Information Service, and the NSPCC Child Protection Research Department** gave support and practical assistance throughout.

Last, but most definitely not least, we thank **the people who acted as critical readers**, ensuring that the editors were aware of the best practice and research, of multi-agency issues and perspectives, and of the needs of practitioners in the many statutory and voluntary agencies that work to support and safeguard children.

Any limitations and failings in the Reader, however, are our responsibility. We hope that all those who contributed will feel that we made good use of their help.

Introduction

... it is important to emphasise that we all share responsibility for safeguarding and promoting the welfare of children and young people. All members of the community can help to safeguard and promote the welfare of children and young people if they are mindful of their needs, or willing and able to act if they have concerns about a child's welfare.

HM Government, 2006, Paragraph 2.2

Ensuring that safeguarding and promoting the welfare of children is everyone's responsibility is a primary aim of government policy. Relevant training is, therefore, one of the key features of a framework to be used by agencies for making effective arrangements to safeguard and promote children's welfare under both section 11 of the Children Act 2004 (HM Government, 2006) and sections 175 and 157 of the Education Act 2002. In order to respond appropriately to concerns about a child's welfare, it is necessary for staff to have an understanding of their new roles and responsibilities as well as those of other professionals and organisations. Both sets of guidance accompanying the above legislation (HM Government, 2006; Department for Education and Skills, 2006) encourage agencies and schools respectively to enable their staff to participate in inter-agency as well as single agency training.

Furthermore, 'It is the responsibility of the LSCB to ensure that single agency and inter-agency training on safeguarding and promoting welfare is provided in order to meet local needs. This covers both the training provided by single agencies to their own staff, and inter-agency training where staff from more than one agency train together' (HM Government, 2006, Paragraph 3.22).

Chapter 4 of *Working Together* provides guidance on the training and development of staff and volunteers to help them safeguard and promote the welfare of children effectively. It describes three types of practitioner groups to whom training on safeguarding and promoting the welfare of children should be targeted:

Safeguarding Children   Edited by Hedy Cleaver, Pat Cawson, Sarah Gorin and Steve Walker
Copyright © 2009 by John Wiley & Sons, Ltd

(i) those in **regular contact** with children and young people and with adults who are parent/s or carers;

(ii) those who **work regularly** with children and young people, and with adults who are carers, who may be asked to contribute to assessments of children in need; and

(iii) those with a **particular responsibility** for safeguarding children, such as designated or named health and education professionals, police, social workers and other professionals undertaking section 47 enquiries or working with complex cases including fabricated or induced illness.

HM Government, 2006, Paragraph 4.19

Training and development is also relevant to managers of staff who are in contact or work with children and families. This means

(i) operational managers; and

(ii) those with strategic and managerial responsibility for commissioning and delivering services for children and families.

HM Government, 2006, Paragraph 4.20

Training should be available at a number of levels to address the learning needs of both managers and practitioners. The following table provides suggested learning outcomes for these target groups. This table can also be found at www.everychildmatters.gov.uk/workingtogether.

The training resource *Safeguarding Children – A Shared Responsibility* to which this book relates was commissioned by the government to support the implementation of its guidance on managing individual cases. This guidance is set out in Chapter 5 of *Working Together* (HM Government, 2006). It provides advice on what should happen if somebody has concerns about the welfare of a child (including those living away from home) and in particular concerns that a child may be suffering, or may be at risk of suffering, significant harm.

This book was commissioned to support the effective use of the training resources. It provides an up-to-date knowledge base for use by practitioners during each of the stages of assessment, planning, intervention and review which underpin work with children and families, as well as in specific situations in which children may be living when maltreatment is suspected or identified.

Being child centred is a fundamental principle of work with children and families. A key theme of this book is, therefore, seeing the child, listening and taking account of his or her wishes and feelings when making decisions about future action. Ascertaining children's wishes and feelings and considering them before determining what services to provide or what action to take is a statutory requirement for children's social care (sections 17 and 47 of the

Children Act 1989 as amended by section 53 of the Children Act 2004). It should also be considered part of the responsibilities of all those working with children (HM Government, 2006).

Victoria Climbié arrived in the United Kingdom in April 1999. She was known to 12 different agencies, but despite this she died 10 months later as a result of horrific injuries and neglect inflicted by her carer and carer's partner. During this time no professional had spoken to Victoria in her own language, French, and nor had they recognised that she was being badly maltreated. This book and associated training resources are intended to assist everyone to fulfil their responsibilities to safeguard and promote the welfare of all our children in the future.

Jenny Gray
Professional Adviser
Safeguarding Children Policy Team
Department for Children, Schools and Families

REFERENCES

Department for Education and Skills (2006) *Safeguarding Children and Safer Recruitment in Education*, Department for Education and Skills, London, http://www.teachernet.gov.uk/publications.

HM Government (2006) *Working Together to Safeguard Children: A Guide to Inter-Agency Working to Safeguard and Promote the Welfare of Children*, The Stationery Office, London, http://www.everychildmatters.gov.uk/socialcare/safeguarding/workingtogether.

SUGGESTED LEARNING OUTCOMES FOR TARGET GROUPS

Those with a particular responsibility for safeguarding children

Those who work regularly with children, young people and adults who are parents/carers

Those in contact with children, young people and adults who are parents/carers

Practitioners: key outcomes

Introduction to working together to safeguard children	Working together to identify, assess, plan, intervene and review	Working together on complex cases to identify, assess, plan, intervene and review
Understand what is meant by safeguarding and promoting the welfare of children and the different ways in which children and young people can be harmed. Be aware of the statutory duty to safeguard and promote the welfare of children in accordance with the Children Act 2004. Be familiar with *What to do if...* national guidance and local procedures and appreciate own role and	Understand the safeguarding roles of parents and carers and recognise factors that can impact on parenting capacity. Have confidence to challenge own and other's practice. Understand boundaries of personal competence and responsibility, know when to involve others and where to get advice and support. Be able to communicate effectively and develop	Be able to work with other practitioners, children and families on complex tasks or particular areas of practice that have specific knowledge or skill requirements. For example, joint enquiries under section 47 of the Children Act 1989. Have the confidence to challenge decisions in complex situations by looking beyond immediate role and asking questions. Be able to assess the relevance and status of

responsibilities and those of others in safeguarding and promoting the welfare of children
Be able to make judgements about how to act to safeguard and promote the welfare of a child in line with *What to do if...*
Be aware of the LSCB and its remit.
Understand statutory requirements governing consent, confidentiality and information-sharing.
Understand the necessity for information-sharing and accurate recording within the context of safeguarding and promoting the welfare of a particular.
Provide appropriate, succinct information to enable other practitioners to deliver support to the child and family.
Know the boundaries of personal competence and responsibility, when to involve others and where to seek advice and support.
Understand when they are required to consult with a manager/designated person.
Be able to identify concerns about possible maltreatment arising from completion of a Common Assessment Framework
Know when and how to respond to immediate safety issues in relation to a particular child and other children within the household
Be aware of the impact of aggression, anger and violence from carers on practice and know how to manage this
Know what to do when there is an insufficient response from other organisations and agencies, while maintaining a focus on safeguarding and promoting the welfare of the child

working relationships with other practitioners and professionals, children and families to safeguard and promote the welfare of children.
Understand the role of other practitioners and agencies in supporting and advising families and safeguarding and promoting the welfare of children and the impact of own interviewing style, decisions and actions on others.
Work together with others as outlined in the *What to do if ...guidance*.
Have a sound understanding of the principles and processes for effective collaboration and be able to forge and sustain relationships with other practitioners and families to safeguard and promote the welfare of children.
Know who to share information with, when and how to record information related to assessment, planning, intervention and review.
Appreciate the effect of cultural and religious beliefs on practice when working together to safeguard and promote the welfare of children.
Have the skills to work with others to address issues of aggression and /or non-compliance by service users that may impinge on practitioners' ability to safeguard and promote the welfare and know when and how to seek support/advice.
Understand the role of assessment, planning and review in effective service provision and the change process.
Understand when they are required to consult with a manager or designated person.
Be able to write clear evidence based and outcome focused reports.

information and to pass it on when appropriate.
Be able to establish and maintain working partnerships of trust and mutual respect whilst recognising ways in which group process can influence and distort decision-making.
Understand and be able to make an effective contribution through report writing and verbal communication to multi-disciplinary case planning and review meetings.
Know how to manage conflict and disagreement between professionals when working together on complex cases.
Have the skills to work with others to address issues of aggression and /or non-compliance that may impinge on practitioners' ability to safeguard and promote the welfare of a child in complex cases.
Have an understanding of factors at an inter-personal, intra-personal and systemic level which influence the possibility of change.

Those with a particular responsibility for safeguarding children

Those who work regularly with children, young people and adults who are parents/carers

Those in contact with children, young people and adults who are parents/carers

Operational managers who supervise practitioners and volunteers: key outcomes

Introduction to working together to safeguard children	Working together to identify, assess, plan, intervene and review	Working together on complex cases to identify, assess, plan, intervene and review
Be aware of the statutory duty to safeguard and promote the welfare of children and recognise the roles and responsibilities of staff as outlined in *What to do if....* Be able to make judgements about ways in which practitioners should act to safeguard and promote the welfare of a child in line with *What to do if....* Be aware of the LSCB and its remit. Be aware of LSCB Inter-agency policies, procedures and protocols. Understand statutory requirements governing	Understand parents and carers safeguarding role and recognise factors that can impact on parenting capacity. Be able to develop an accurate assessment of a practitioner's competence with regard to safeguarding and promoting children's welfare and address areas for development. Be able to recognise the boundaries of staff and own competence and responsibility, know when to involve others and where to get advice and support.	Be aware of the specific knowledge and skill requirements necessary for working on complex cases. For example, joint enquiries under section 47 of the Children Act 1989. Ensure that practitioners have the appropriate knowledge and skills and are managed and supported. Know what to do when there is an insufficient response from other organisations and agencies, while maintaining a focus on safeguarding and promoting the welfare of the child.

consent, confidentiality and information-sharing. Understand the necessity for information-sharing and accurate recording within the context of safeguarding and promoting the welfare of children and have the knowledge and skills to advise practitioners. Understand the role and influence of the front line manager, including in facilitating multi-disciplinary communication and conflict resolution. Understand and be able to address the impact of practitioner anxiety on performance. Be able to offer advice, guidance and support in line with national and local guidance to practitioners who have concerns about safeguarding and promoting the welfare of a child. Be aware of the impact of aggression, anger and violence from carers on practice and ensure practitioners are supported when working in these situations. Understand the emotional impact of working together to safeguard children and promote the welfare of children and support practitioners appropriately. Have the knowledge and skills to identify how practitioners can get stuck, lose focus and be drawn into poor performance and respond accordingly.	Have a sound understanding of the principles and processes for effective collaboration and be able to communicate, forge and sustain relationships with other managers and address any issues encountered by practitioners working with others to safeguard and promote the welfare of children. Understand the role of other practitioners and agencies in supporting and advising families to safeguard and promote the welfare of children and advise staff accordingly. Be able to supervise staff who are working together with others on the processes outlined in this guidance and in *What to do if ...* guidance. Know who to share information with and when and how to record information and be able to advise practitioners accordingly. Understand and be able to address issues of practitioner-anxiety, and of aggression and non-compliance from carers when working together to safeguard and promote the welfare of a child. Appreciate and be able to address to address with practitioners the effect of cultural and religious beliefs on practice when working together to safeguard and promote the welfare of children.	Be able to assess the relevance and status of information and ensure staff manage this information appropriately. Be able to assess ways in which practitioners are working together on complex cases and ways in which group process can influence and distort decision-making. Know how to deal with professional disagreement. Be able to help practitioners sustain purposeful and respectful relationships with service users over time and under stressful conditions. Be able to recognise when the relationship between practitioner and service user is in danger of breaking down and take appropriate action. Know how to manage aggression and non-compliance in complex cases.

Those with a particular responsibility for safeguarding children

Those who work regularly with children, young people and adults who are parents/carers

Those in contact with children, young people and adults who are parents/carers

Those who have strategic responsibility for commissioning and providing services to children, young people and adults who are parents/carers including members of the LSCB: key outcomes

Managers within agencies	New members of LSCBs	Members of LSCBs: ongoing development
Be aware of the statutory duty to safeguard and promote the welfare of children and identify a lead senior manager who is accountable for the agency fulfilling this duty.	Be aware of the statutory duty to safeguard and promote the welfare of children and recognise the roles and responsibilities of staff as outlined in this guidance and in *What to do if....*	Understand how recent policy, practice and research developments, serious case reviews and the findings of the local screening teams should inform the work of the LSCB.
Recognise the roles and responsibilities of practitioners as outlined in this guidance and in *What to do if...*	Understand the statutory requirements of the LSCB under sections 13–16 of the Children Act 2004 and the LSCB regulations.	Recognise the factors that are promoting and inhibiting the effective functioning of the LSCB and be able to address these in order to improve performance.
Understand the development and support needs of staff, enabling them to effectively work together with others to safeguard and promote the welfare of children.	Be aware of the key purposes, functions and tasks of the LSCB and be able to follow procedures as outlined in guidance.	Work together to assess the developmental needs of the LSCB.
Understand the need for management plans for recruitment, training, support and supervision of all staff undertaking safeguarding duties.	Understand the individual and joint roles and responsibilities of members of the LSCB.	Be able to ensure effective communication between the local LSCB, the local children's workforce and local community.
Recognise the systems that should be in place within an organisation and between organisations in order to comply with statutory duties to	Know how to ensure own agency is able to demonstrate their duties to safeguard and promote the welfare of children in their strategic and operational plans.	Be able to identify ways of learning from service user experience and taking account of the views of children and young people.
	Ensure that own agency job descriptions reflect	

cooperate to safeguard and promote the welfare of children . Understand statutory requirements governing consent, confidentiality and information-sharing and the implications for developing and maintaining intra and inter-agency systems and protocols. Recognise the management information required to ensure that the agency is discharging its duty to safeguard and promote the welfare of children. Be aware of the Local Safeguarding Board and its remit. Know what actions n eed to be taken to ensure the agency is demonstrating its safeguarding duties in both strategic and operational plans.	the responsibilities of LSCB membership. Understand the mandate and organisational support required to ensure meaningful representation. Know how to obtain necessary professional/ expert advice to fulfil role. Understand the role of the Children's Service Authority, the Director of Children's Services, the lead elected member and the LSCB chair.

I Themes and Principles of Safeguarding

1 Putting Children and Their Rights at the Heart of the Safeguarding Process

CAROLYNE WILLOW

This chapter looks at the safeguarding process from the child's viewpoint: what a good childhood means; who children trust to help them be and feel safe; and how adults can get better at listening to and supporting children. It explains the rights of all children under the Convention on the Rights of the Child 1989 and the Human Rights Act 1998, and it describes the additional rights of disabled children and other vulnerable groups. It demonstrates that listening to children and taking them and their lives seriously is the linchpin of safeguarding and promoting children's welfare.

CORE KNOWLEDGE

- Children want and have the right to be listened to, respected and involved.
- All children can communicate and all adults can become good listeners.
- All children have the right to be free from all forms of violence and abuse.
- Children can be silenced through fear and intimidation, as well as through negative beliefs and attitudes.
- Children want adults to be happy and approachable, and reliable and useful.
- Not enough children know about or trust the statutory child care system.
- Children need information communicated in an appropriate way at all stages of the safeguarding process.
- Children are harmed by not being seen and heard – some even die.

CHILDREN ARE PEOPLE NOW

When Roger Morgan, the Children's Rights Director of the Commission for Social Care Inspection, consulted children and young people about the *Every*

Safeguarding Children   Edited by Hedy Cleaver, Pat Cawson, Sarah Gorin and Steve Walker
Copyright © 2009 by John Wiley & Sons, Ltd

Child Matters Green Paper (Cm 5860, 2003), discussions sometimes moved to children's general social status. He reported:

> One group felt angered that children are often not listened to in their own right [because] children are treated as less important than adults. One child summed this up powerfully – 'they think we're there to become adults – you're only a child because you can't be born as an adult.'
>
> Morgan, 2003, p. 16

It could be argued that children have a greater need than adults to be validated and heard, given their vulnerability, low social status and dependence on adults. The United Nations recognised this when it drafted the Convention on the Rights of the Child: Article 12 grants all children the right to express and have their views given due weight. It is the first human rights treaty to give a group of people – in this case under 18-year-olds – the right to participate in decisions affecting them.

For further information on children's rights and perceptions of childhood, see United Nations (1989) and Alderson (2000).

THE INVISIBLE CHILD

Despite statutory guidance putting children at the centre of professional practice (Department of Health *et al.*, 2000; Chief Inspector of Social Services *et al.*, 2002; HM Government 2006a, 2006b, 2006c), individual children are frequently sidelined. Finding out children's wishes and feelings, and seeking to understand children's own perceptions of *their* needs and *their* life, is still too often viewed among professionals as a 'good practice' rather than as a 'must do'.

The approach taken by all services in responding to concerns about the welfare of 8-year-old Victoria Climbié powerfully demonstrates how children can be invisible in the safeguarding process (Cm 5730, 2003).

Three nurses had expressed concerns that Victoria may have been deliberately harmed. There were worries that Victoria may have been hit with a belt, that she may have been deliberately scalded or bitten, and there were concerns that she may have been burned with a cigarette. Despite these serious professional anxieties, the social worker's first home visit did not involve *any* direct communication with Victoria (an interpreter was never used by social services, despite Victoria's first language being French):

> The [social worker's first of] two visits to Somerset Gardens took place ... shortly after Victoria was discharged from the North Middlesex Hospital. She found her to be smartly dressed and well cared for. Victoria spent most of the visit playing with a doll – one of a number of toys seen by [the social worker]. Although [the social worker] did not talk to Victoria during the course of this visit, she formed the impression that Victoria was happy ...
>
> Cm 5730, 2003, Paragraph 3.51

Two months later, in October 1999, the social worker made a second home visit. Lord Laming observed:

Victoria seems to have been all but ignored during this visit as she sat on the floor playing with a doll. The fact that she was still not attending school was raised during the conversation, but no questions seem to have been asked about how Victoria was spending her days.

Cm 5730, 2003, Paragraph 3.60

The following month, Victoria's aunt alleged that her niece had been sexually abused; the aunt later withdrew the allegation. Victoria was not given any opportunity to talk to a social worker or a police officer. Within 12 weeks, Victoria was admitted to casualty with severe hypothermia and multi-system failure. She had injuries 'too numerous' to record and medical staff were unable to straighten her legs. She died the next day.

The cataclysmic failures in Victoria Climbié's case should not tarnish the hundreds of thousands of practitioners and volunteers who every day make positive interventions in children's lives. However, Lord Laming's inquiry and its aftermath unearthed some fundamental problems in the system. One of these is the low priority given – by the system overall and by individual practitioners – to ascertaining the child's wishes and feelings. Social workers increasingly report that they do not have the time or capacity to build meaningful relationships with children and young people.

In February 2003, the government issued NHS organisations and local councils with a self-audit checklist to assess the implementation of the urgent recommendations of the Victoria Climbié Inquiry Report (those that were to be implemented within 3 to 6 months). All four recommendations relating to the child's voice were included in this audit. In October 2003, the Commission for Health Improvement, Her Majesty's Inspectorate of Constabulary and the Social Services Inspectorate reported on progress. In relation to the child's voice, the three inspectorates concluded:

Communication with children is not always a priority. Access to interpreting services for children whose first language is not English varies. Some councils do not include children's views and wishes in assessments as a matter of course.

Commission for Health Improvement et al., 2003, p. 5

In April 2004, newspapers reacted with horror to the report of the serious case review into the fatal shooting in September 2003 of 7-year-old Toni-Ann Byfield. Toni-Ann was a looked-after child, the responsibility of Birmingham social services. Her immigration status was not resolved when her foster carers went on holiday. Social services therefore agreed that she could visit her father in London, staying overnight with a woman identified as her father's aunt because her father did not have suitable accommodation. Toni-Ann spent less than 5 weeks with her father: they were both shot fatally in September 2003. The summary report from the serious case review undertaken by

Birmingham Area Child Protection Committee to learn the lessons from her death noted:

> The overriding impression ... is that the primary focus of professional work was on the assessment of [Toni-Ann's father's] parental capacity and the practicalities of the arrangements for him to undertake his parental role and that inadequate attention was paid to the full and necessary assessment of Toni-Ann's needs. In respect of both [the social worker and the children's guardian] it is difficult to see how, given the very limited number of occasions made available when they were actually in a position to have a direct and private conversation with Toni-Ann, they could make a full and sensitive assessment of her needs and wishes.
>
> Birmingham Area Child Protection Committee, 2004, pp. 5–6

There are stark similarities between the lives and deaths of Toni-Ann By-field and Victoria Climbié. Both of these young children were born outside the United Kingdom and were subject to informal kinship care arrangements that were brought to the attention of public authorities. There were concerns about each child's welfare, leading to contact with a range of professionals. Both children were extremely vulnerable and dependent upon professionals to see, hear and protect them. In this, they were let down gravely.

CHILDREN ARE EASY TO HURT

> Children need to be protected – they need to feel safe. We want to feel comfortable and safe and not worried or scared.
>
> Children's Rights Alliance for England, 2004, p. 16

Children are physically small, emotionally dependent and they cannot easily articulate their suffering or get out of bad situations. The level and extent of adult abuse and mistreatment of children are, to say the least, disturbing. A research commissioned by the Department of Health showed that from a sample of 99 families, 52% of babies under 1 were smacked/hit by a parent at least once a week (Nobes and Smith, 1997). Up to two children each week are killed by a parent or carer (Creighton and Tissier, 2003). Behind these homicide statistics are gruelling accounts of torture and human degradation. Stories of children being deprived of food, dry clothes and bedding, and toys and other forms of pleasure – and of not being loved or praised – sit underneath the headlines. Then there is the everyday impact on children of low status and disabling attitudes and environments – described by two leading advocates for disabled children's rights as 'small a' abuse:

> Sally has cerebral palsy and has high physical dependency needs and no speech. She has good cognitive and language abilities and she uses a communication board. She attends further education and was staying in residential provision but felt she was being 'driven mad' by carers who failed to inform her what they were

going to do or ask her what she wished for – even as to the simplest things such as how she liked her tea. She felt forced into leaving the college.

Marchant and Page, 2003, p. 60

For further information on safeguarding and disabled children, see National Working Group on Child Protection and Disability (2003).

SEEKING HELP FROM ADULTS

We know that significant numbers of children require high levels of support from adults outside their family, to keep them safe and well. Yet, these children's tremendous need for protection is not matched by a demand from them to be protected.

In 2004–2005, there were 23 per 10 000 children on local child protection registers (Department for Education and Skills, 2006). Research on the prevalence of child abuse carried out by the NSPCC suggests that the number of children severely physically abused by adults in the family is at least 20 times this number. About 1 in every 100 children is sexually assaulted in the family; many more are neglected and denied what they need to flourish (Cawson *et al.*, 2000). As Cooper, Hetherington and Katz (2003, p. 19) explain:

> Only a small proportion of the children who are abused are ever reported to statutory child protection agencies. Those referrals by children themselves form an even smaller number.

When a 10-year-old boy was asked to whom he would talk about negative experiences or worries, he replied:

> Nobody. I just sit on my bed and talk to myself. Grown-ups don't take you seriously. They just say 'good, good, good' 'cos they're not really that bothered. And I don't really trust my friends; they'd never keep a secret.
>
> Butler and Williamson, 1994, p. 71

A girl the same age reported:

> I know it sounds a bit silly, but I talk to my dog.
>
> Butler and Williamson, 1994, p. 72

Featherstone and Evans (2004) carried out a literature review of the research relating to 'maltreated' children seeking help. They summarised:

- The NSPCC prevalence study (Cawson *et al.*, 2000; Cawson, 2002) found that only a quarter of people who were sexually abused as children had told anyone at the time of the abuse; 31% had still not told anyone by the time of their adulthood.
- From an analysis of the 1121 letters to the National Commission of Inquiry into the Prevention of Child Abuse, Wattam and Woodward (1996) found

that only 32% of people had told someone of their abuse as a child; for 13% of people writing to the Commission, it was the first time they had ever told anyone of the abuse.

- NSPCC research in the mid-1990s (Creighton and Russell, 1995) asked adults who had been sexually abused as children to identify when and how the abuse had stopped. For 6% of the respondents, the abuse never stopped or continued until after the age of 16.

For further information on children seeking help, see Featherstone and Evans (2004).

WHAT MAKES CHILDREN INVISIBLE?

The reasons why children do not seek help from adults are complicated and varied. They might not know that what is happening to them is unacceptable – especially pertinent for younger children, or for children living away from home:

> One young person told us about being locked out of her foster home when her foster parents were out. She had resorted to wandering the streets or travelling on buses to fill in the time. Sadly, she had not been aware that she should question this treatment or make it known to her social worker.
>
> Social Services Inspectorate, 1998, Paragraph 4.31

Children might choose to blank out their abuse and focus on the positive aspects of their lives; or they might be too afraid of the consequences of disclosing. Dominant attitudes and beliefs about children, and about different groups of children, can make their suffering go unnoticed. Children can also be made invisible if the needs of their parents or carer dominate the household.

SWITCHING OFF

Even if they have a sense that they are being abused or badly treated, children might switch off this part of their life, and concentrate on other more positive aspects. As Schofield and Thoburn (1996, pp. 13–14) report:

> Children often resort to defence mechanisms, such as denial, in order to cope with their feelings. They can become effectively unable to think about what has happened to them.

LESSER OF TWO EVILS

Older children, especially, can make what appear to be rational judgements about the costs and benefits of disclosure. In calculating what they will potentially lose, children not only consider their own lives, but they also think about

the impact of disclosure on the 'abuser' and on the rest of
their father, uncle or mother be sent to prison? Will their sist
be 'taken away' and put into care? Will their family be ostr:
particular concern for children from close-knit communities
that everyone will hear about the abuse or neglect that they h:

SHAME AND EXPOSURE

Exposure is much more likely for children from minority ethnic communities,
especially if they are poor and – like white working-class children – live in close
proximity to others. Children from minority ethnic communities may feel that
the cost is too high of exposing their whole family to shame and criticism, and
to the loss of support from within their community. Gorin (2004, pp. 51–52)
reports on a study carried out by Mullender *et al.* (2002), which found that
Muslim children and young people of South Asian descent were affected by
the concept of 'family honour'. This could stop them and their mothers from
taking action against domestic violence:

> He wanted to keep us under his control – that is why he terrorised us. Mum stayed
> so long because of us and because of Izzat, you know. 'What will people say?' She
> hid it from her family – wouldn't tell them how bad things were for such a long
> time.

Concern about 'institutionalised racism', and the belief, however mistaken,
that adults in positions of power will not treat them sensitively, can silence
black children.

Featherstone and Evans (2004, p. 35) explore the reasons for sexual abuse
still being seen predominantly as a female issue. Using the work of Baginsky
(2001), they report that boys in particular can feel too ashamed to disclose
abuse or maltreatment, because their experiences challenge dominant perceptions that boys are tough and strong. Boys who have been sexually assaulted
by other males can be afraid to tell because they assume that they will be seen
as gay; such is the power of homophobia.

TOO SCARED TO ACT

Children can be too terrified to take action. In 2003, the Children's Rights
Alliance for England and the NSPCC ran a consultation weekend for 13 children and young people with experience of child protection. A 13-year-old boy
reported:

> I've had to give advice to somebody ... My little sister, she was 7 or 8 years old.
> She was getting sexually abused by that person I told you about earlier ... I kept
> telling her to tell my mum ... she didn't tell my mum till we left [name of step-
> father] and went to live back with my real dad. I knew that if I told someone
> I would get battered by [step-father] ... He'd broke my little brother's rib. The

only person I could really talk to was my social worker but I hated her ... she always wanted me to go into care, all the time. My sister kept crying every time she came to talk to me.

Children's Rights Alliance for England, 2004, p. 13

When asked why he had not felt able to tell his mum, the boy replied:

Because [step-father] would have beaten us all up. Because he made up that he used to do karate and stuff so that none of us would get on the wrong side of him.

DOMINANT ATTITUDES

Adult perceptions of children are a major consideration. Children might not expect to be believed. Here children's status and dominant conceptions of different groups of children are important, just as they have been seen to be a major influence on women reporting violence. The summary report from Sir William Utting's Children's Safeguards Review (1997, p. 1) cautioned:

Bear in mind that the abuse of children in institutions is part of the wider issue of the abuse of children generally. The bottom line is drawn by the values and attitudes to children which characterise the society in which we live.

Children who are deemed troublesome and untrustworthy – those in custody or in trouble with the law, for example – might calculate that any disclosure of abuse will be dismissed as malevolent or as negative attention-seeking. On the other hand, the abuse of disabled children or the cruel treatment of babies and very young children can go undetected because it challenges the dominant perception that the most weak and vulnerable in our society are cared for. Put simply, adults can find this kind of abuse too much to bear, so we do not allow ourselves to see it.

Four-year-old John Smith was killed by his pre-adoptive parents in Brighton and Hove in December 2000. John died with 54 bruises on his body and three adult bite marks. Social workers had visited his home on 20 separate occasions; they believed his foster parents when they said that his injuries were self-inflicted. When John was admitted to hospital in a terminal condition, his pre-adoptive carers and their support social worker told hospital staff that he was a disturbed child who self-harmed.

Six-year-old Lauren Wright died in May 2000 after her stepmother struck her so hard in the stomach that her digestive system collapsed. There were 60 bruises on her body, including marks on the back of her legs, which were probably made by a stick.

> Jurors at Norwich Crown Court were told that the stepmother had been seen punching Lauren to the ground while walking in the street, that Lauren had been made to stand in front of a fire for more than an hour and 'half a pot' of pepper had been put into a sandwich for her. Lauren was still attending school in the weeks before she died. She weighed less than two stone and her hair was falling out. Her stepmother – who was a playground assistant at the school – managed to convince concerned teachers that Lauren's injuries were a result of her clumsiness.

Alyson Leslie (2001, Paragraph 1.46), the author of the Part 8 review (see Glossary: Serious case review) into the circumstances surrounding John Smith's death, reported:

Social workers exist because there are aspects of our society the rest of us do not want to deal with. They are our eyes, our ears and our judgement when it comes to the care of our society's vulnerable children. They are there to ensure such children have access to safe, nurturing, fulfilling environments where they can achieve their full potential. To do their job effectively, social workers must, on our behalf, ask awkward questions and always be thinking the unthinkable.

Ideas about what is normal, either for adults or for children, also come into play. Adults who lack knowledge or experience of children's needs and rights can rely uncritically on second-hand beliefs, passed down from generation to generation. Classic examples are 'parents have the right to discipline their children as they see fit' and 'children should respect their elders'.

> The social worker noted 'a sense of formality' in Victoria Climbié's relationship with her aunt and Carl Manning, characterised by Victoria standing to attention in her aunt's presence. This was perceived by the social worker to be a normal feature of child/adult relationships within African-Caribbean families.

FOCUS ON PARENTS

The child's needs and concerns are too easily eclipsed when a parent has chronic needs of his or her own (Cleaver, Unell and Aldgate, 1999). Parents with a history of substance misuse or mental health problems often struggle to give priority to the child's needs. In these situations, the parents' needs can easily become all consuming for professionals, with little time or energy left over for the smaller and less-demanding family members.

The Advisory Council on the Misuse of Drugs carried out a 2-year inquiry into the needs of babies and children of problem drug users. It reported in 2003:

> Whilst there has been huge concern about drug misuse in the UK for many years, the children of problem drug users have largely remained hidden from view. The harm done to them is usually unseen: a virus in the blood, a bruise under the shirt, resentment and grief, a fragmented education.
>
> Advisory Council on the Misuse of Drugs, 2003, p. 90

For further information on children's perspectives of seeking help, see Butler and Williamson (1994), Maurice (1998) and Gorin (2004).

SAFEGUARDING FROM THE CHILD'S PERSPECTIVE

Safeguarding is the responsibility of all those working, or in contact, with children. The Children Act 1989 places a duty on local authorities to safeguard and promote the welfare of children in need in their area. Section 175 of the Education Act 2002 places a duty on local authorities and on school and college governing bodies to make arrangements to safeguard and promote the welfare of children. The Children Act 2004 places a duty on key persons and organisations to make arrangements to ensure that their functions are carried out with regard to the need to safeguard and promote the welfare of children. Those covered by this new duty in the Children Act 2004 include children's services authorities together with district councils, police, probation, NHS bodies, Connexions, youth offending teams, governors/directors of prisons and young offender institutions, the British Transport Police and those on contract. So, for professionals working in statutory agencies or under a contract to these agencies, the defining tasks in safeguarding children are to protect children from maltreatment and prevent impairment of their health or development (Department of Health *et al.*, 2000; HM Government, 2005).

WHAT DO CHILDREN WANT FROM THEIR CHILDHOODS?

In 2001, the government's Children and Young People's Unit consulted children and young people on its draft children's strategy. This was the first time that children and young people in England had been asked *en masse* to contribute to a national vision of what makes a good childhood. It was the first time they had been invited to suggest how the state should intervene to ensure that children and young people can fulfil their potential (Children and Young People's Unit, 2001).

When asked which aspects of the government's vision for a good childhood they most agreed with, the two most popular answers among those aged

12 years and under were 'more activities' and 'more parks'. More than half of disabled children and children with special educational needs rated activities as the most important aspect of the government's vision. For older respondents, 'health' and 'families' were named the most important parts of this vision. A 12-year-old girl explained (Children and Young People's Unit, 2003):

> If a family doesn't work as a unit then children in that family would have problems . . . and would be an outcast of society.

Ten-year-old Georgie advised:

> If I could change something I would make sure that every child had a loving family to care for them and give them lots of support.

Within the 'families' heading, a 13-year-old highlighted the importance of financial security:

> Child Support [is the most important] – I do not live with my mum and dad, only with my nan. And we only get £20 a week; that is not even enough to feed and clothe me.

When children and young people were asked how the government could find out if their plans for children were working, younger children most often suggested 'surveys'; older respondents rated 'meet the children' highest, closely followed by surveys. Checking whether children are happy was a common suggestion. An 11-year-old girl recommended:

> By checking that children are getting their happiness.

HOW TO BE A GOOD ADULT

We can see, therefore, that the principal tasks of adults living and working with children include minimising risks of harm and at the same time helping children to be happy and fulfilled. This is a broad spectrum that takes in the different responsibilities of the child's parents, relatives and adult friends and neighbours, as well as professionals. Despite the variety of roles, when children are asked what they want from the adults in their lives, there are more similarities than differences. Certain personal characteristics seem to be uniformly rated by children. A happy disposition and an 'even temper' are critical, as is the ability to listen and really take on the child's views.

A consultation with 25 disabled children and young people aged between 7 and 19 years, undertaken for Sir William Utting's review of safeguards for children living away from home (Utting, 1997, p. 84), revealed a strong preference for staff who

- have a good sense of humour;
- have a good attitude towards children;

- try to understand children;
- do not shout at children;
- have been closely vetted.

The theme of children and young people being put off by grumpy and ill-tempered adults continued in the Children's Rights Alliance for England/NSPCC consultation. A 13-year-old girl explained (Children's Rights Alliance for England, 2004, p. 24):

> I don't like it when foster dad shouts advice at me. My foster mother puts things into nice terms.

Youth workers were rated highly by a 17-year-old male:

> Youth workers are more like friends. They are not always telling you 'this is your best interests; do it this way'. They are not in your face all the time.

In a different context, a child involved with statutory agencies said why she valued her independent advocate (Children's Rights Alliance for England, 2004, p. 75):

> [When I first met my advocate] she had a nice smile and was all nice and happy, not like social workers.

Jones (2003, p. 71) lists the core skills required for effective communication with children. These include listening, being able to convey genuine interest, empathic concern, understanding, emotional warmth, respect for the child, and the capacity to self-reflect and to manage emotions. He stresses the importance of these skills in seeking to communicate with children who have suffered adverse experiences:

> ... good communication skills on the part of the professional are desperately needed by children who have been victimised, in order to allow them to impart any information or express their concerns. Equally, the potential consequences of poorly developed professional skills are serious for such children, as they can lead to erroneous accounts and distortions of children's memories. The consequences can be serious, psychologically, emotionally and legally.

Butler and Williamson's (1994, p. 33) seminal account of children's views of trauma and social work eloquently summarises what children want:

> When asked about the characteristics of adults in whom they might place their trust, it was somewhat embarrassing but also rather flattering that a number of younger children said to the researcher, 'someone like you'. [They wanted] someone who smiled a lot, had a sense of humour, maintained a lot of eye contact, did not interrupt, and appeared engaged and interested in what they were saying.

But personal attributes are not enough; children and young people want to see hard evidence of professionals actively working on their behalf. A 15-year-old boy in Butler and Williamson's study (1994, p. 95) reported:

> I don't want any support from social workers. They're a load of shit. All they do is remind you of what you're like. They're not worth it. What can they do for you, except talk to you? All it is is talking – nothing to do with what's really going on. Just gets you into more trouble – other people contact them to moan about you. They're all talk and no action.

The Blueprint Project was set up by the Voice for the Child in Care with support from the National Children's Bureau to identify the vital ingredients for a child-centred approach to children in public care. Concerning relationships with professionals, children and young people involved in the project made the following key recommendations (Voice for the Child in Care and National Children's Bureau, 2004, p. 49):

- be on time, do not cancel unless you absolutely have to;
- invest time in getting to know children;
- be honest;
- do what you say you will do – keep promises;
- show interest in the positives as well as the problems;
- be responsive to what children and young people say;
- believe in their capabilities.

The TOTAL RESPECT training pack for ensuring children's rights and participation in care gives advice for professionals wishing to communicate effectively with young children (Dalrymple *et al.*, 2000, p. 37):

- Never be too busy to listen. Children often have important things to say at inconvenient moments.
- Give the child all your attention.
- Sit on an equal level – on the floor if necessary.
- Respect what the child is saying.
- Do not patronise young children by acting surprised when they make intelligent comments, or by expecting them to amuse or entertain you.
- Do not try to guess what will be said next.
- Pay attention to both what is being said and how it is being said.
- Do not interrupt – wait until the child has paused before you ask a question.
- If you disagree, do not dismiss the child or get angry.
- If the child is talking for a long time, and you need to remember exactly what he or she has said, make notes when there is a pause or when the child has finished speaking.

All of this advice adds up to seeing and respecting each child and getting to know him or her and the family. It means getting behind the professional labels, good and bad, to find the people. As Gorin (2004, p. 72) reports:

> Children do not talk about 'domestic violence', 'parental substance misuse', 'parental ill health' or 'abuse'. Indeed these are not necessarily terms that they understand or can identify with. Similarly, they do not think of themselves as being 'a young carer' or 'a child of a parent with substance misuse problems'. They think about themselves as individuals with different roles and responsibilities within and outside their family. Their accounts reflect the complexity of family situations and their own subjective experience.

While direct communication and relationships are seen as critical, children also recommend that adults stand back and notice changes in a child's behaviour. Children and young people taking part in the CRAE/NSPCC consultation weekend gave the following tips on recognising children who may be at risk of harm (Children's Rights Alliance for England 2004, p. 9):

> They become very shy, keeping themselves to themselves. They're on edge all the time.

> If you change how you act e.g. you cry when you don't normally.

> Like where the mum and dad are not being a mum and dad to their children. They're just letting children do what they want ... They're not making sure children are fed and watered [and] not making rational decisions – like my mother.

> Notice whether parents come to pick children up from school. If [they] didn't come there's something wrong – go and see if [the] child is all right. Keep a close eye on them.

This advice is reflected in the professional literature. In relation to professional assessments of children in need, Adcock (2000, p. 82) notes:

> It is very helpful to observe the adults and children together as soon as possible in order to assess the quality of their relationship and the child's attachment to each parent. The child's appearance and manner should be noted. Sometimes the worker may immediately note a developmental delay or be concerned about a child who seems very sad or very wary. The parents' or carer's ability to anticipate and respond to the child's needs and to show care and affection, the tone of the voice when speaking to or about the child and the way in which the child is described are very relevant.

A SAFEGUARDING SYSTEM FIT FOR CHILDREN

Whenever a child dies at the hands of its parents or carers and it is revealed that education, health or social services had previously been aware of the child's vulnerability, the same question is posed – when will we ever learn? Since 1945, there have been 70 public inquiries into severe child abuse (House of Commons Health Committee, 2003). The most recent was Lord Laming's inquiry into the torture and eventual manslaughter of 8-year-old Victoria Climbié.

One of the most remarkable omissions from all of these inquiries is the lack of any exploration from children's perspective of what needs to be done to make the system better at protecting them. Only adults are considered to be experts in safeguarding children. It was more than a century ago when the first Act of Parliament was passed protecting children from abuse; it was modelled on legislation that had existed for 66 years to protect animals. But we have yet to see a child being invited to give expert advice at a public inquiry concerning child abuse. There have been no studies or projects focusing solely on children's ideas for the design of a safeguarding children system fit for them.

Eleven-year-olds were interviewed for a radio programme on whether the Children Act 2004 should give children equal protection from being hit as adults. The children were asked what they would do if their friend came to school with bruises on the body. Their instant remarks all focused on their friend's feelings: 'try to cheer him up', 'tell some jokes', 'I would show her she's got friends'.

How much weight do adults give to children's *feelings* when they are seeking to safeguard and promote their welfare?

Under the Children Act 2004 children's wishes and feelings have to be taken into account when assessing children under section 17 and carrying out enquiries under section 47 of the Children Act 1989.

Piecemeal research with children has been brought together providing key headlines of what children want and need from statutory agencies. Schofield and Thoburn (1996, p. 52–54) summarise the key lessons from research:

- Children need a dependable relationship with a trusted and skilled helper.
- Children and young people need comprehensive information at all stages in the process. (Information is especially important to make a reality of the child's right to consent to medical or psychiatric assessments ordered by the court – see also Brandon, Schofield and Trinder, 1998, Chapter 5.)
- The early stages of investigation and offering support are critical for establishing a relationship with the child and ensuring that he or she is an active participant.
- To take part in child protection conferences successfully, children need the following: preparation before meetings from workers or advocates who are positive about their contribution; support during the meeting, skilful chairing of the meeting and a respectful approach by conference members; an immediate opportunity after the meeting to discuss their feelings about it and the decisions made.

Independent advocates can play a vital role in ensuring that children have appropriate information and support to communicate their views in formal settings such as child protection conferences and court proceedings (Department for Education and Skills, 2004).

Sonny is 7 years old. His name was placed on the child protection register 10 months ago. His mum had forcibly pushed him into his bedroom, and he had tripped over a toy on the floor and fallen hard onto the wall. One of the bones in his hand was fractured and he had a bloody nose. This is not the first time Sonny's mum has lost her temper, though previously her attacks on Sonny were all verbal. Since social services' involvement, Sonny's mum has been attending parenting classes and having individual anger management sessions with a counsellor. They are going well.

The social worker is visiting Sonny and his mum to discuss the forthcoming child protection review conference. He sees Sonny by himself and has brought along a children's storybook about the process. They look through Sonny's football sticker album first, as they had on the previous visit. Then the social worker asks Sonny if there is anything he wants to talk about today.

As soon as the social worker finishes his sentence, Sonny says he wants to come off the 'stupid list'. The social worker checks that Sonny is talking about the child protection register[*] – he is. He asks why he thinks it is stupid. Sonny replies that his granny and grandad want to take him to Spain for a week's holiday but they can't because he's on the register. He says he heard them talking to his mum and they were saying Sonny would not be able to leave the country while he is on the register.

The social worker explains the purpose of the register and thanks Sonny for sharing his worries. He says that everyone – including Sonny's mum and grandparents – are working together to try to keep Sonny safe and happy. He says the holiday sounds like a great idea and he will discuss it with Sonny's mum.

[*]From April 2008 local authorities are required to have replaced the child protection register with individual child protection plans.

POSITIVE ACTION

- Do not assume the child is too young to be part of the process.
- Make time for the child.
- Do not rush into your own agenda – check what is on the child's mind.
- Take seriously the child's worries or questions.
- Stress that everyone wants the child to be safe and happy.

For further information on children's participation in decision making, see Schofield and Thoburn (1996).

CONFIDENTIALITY AND CONSENT

A duty of confidence may be owed to a child or young person in their own right.

Children over the age of 16 are assumed in law to be competent to consent to medical advice or treatment, without the involvement of their parents (Family Law Reform Act 1969, s 8(1)). A child under 16, who has the capacity to make their own decisions, may give (or refuse) consent. The child has to show that he or she understands both the proceedings and the implications of his or her wishes (Gillick v West Norfolk and Wisbech Health Authority [1986] AC 112).

Children and young people have the same common law right to confidentiality as adults – providing that those aged under 16 are judged by professionals to understand their choices and the potential outcomes of sharing information. This follows from the Gillick case and is known in practice as Fraser competence.

Judgements have to be made on a child's capacity to consent on each particular issue. The same child may be able to give consent on a straightforward matter, but may not have the capacity in relation to a complex decision. It is important to remember, though, that children and young people faced with complicated decisions – for example, relating to a medical procedure or a change in the family – often have had years of experience of the difficult issues at stake. A lack of capacity should not be assumed, but neither should they feel compelled to make decisions that they do not understand fully, or do not want to make.

If a child under 16 does not have the capacity to understand and make his or her own decisions, a person with parental responsibility can consent on his or her behalf (HM Government 2006c, Appendix 3, Paragraph 4.19). If action is taken without a child's consent, he or she should be informed of the action and why it is being taken. Good practice is always to keep the child fully informed.

There is an overwhelming and consistent call from children for confidential spaces where they can, at their own pace and in their own time, discuss difficult experiences, including abuse, with trusted adults.

The fact that ChildLine each day attracts about 30 000 direct calls from children of all ages shows the importance of adults being there, but not taking over. The propensity of adults to take away any sense of control is certainly one of the major reasons cited by children for seeking help from peers rather than from grown-ups. But even when complete confidentiality cannot be offered, there are ways of responding to children that preserve their dignity and keep them firmly at the centre.

Jamelia is 9 years old. She lives in a cramped council flat with her mother and twin siblings, 3-year-old boys. Jamelia is an intelligent child who likes to write poems and stories. She seems to get on well with her mother and brothers, but is especially close to her maternal grandmother with whom she stays each weekend.

Jamelia's teacher notices that she is walking with a slight limp and during the morning break asks if she is all right. Jamelia explains that the lifts in her flats were not working this morning and she tripped while helping one of her brothers down the stairs. Jamelia becomes tearful, and says her mum called her 'stupid' and 'clumsy'. Jamelia tells her teacher that this is not fair – she was feeling sleepy because her mum's new boyfriend had been shouting and throwing things about in the night, and it had been hard for her to sleep. She says her mum has never called her stupid before; she usually describes her as 'my bright little princess'.

The teacher suggests that they sit together at lunchtime and have a longer chat about how things are at home. She says she likes Jamelia and her mum and brothers and would like to help them if they are having difficulties. She explains that she will probably need to contact some other people who can help Jamelia and her family be happy and safe.

At lunchtime, Jamelia tells her teacher that she thinks her mum's boyfriend was thrown out by his previous girlfriend because of his violent temper. Jamelia says that she is frightened of the boyfriend and that she thinks her mum and brothers are scared too. The teacher asks Jamelia's permission to pass on this information to the person in the school whose special job is to keep children safe. She says that she thinks Jamelia's mum and grandmother will understand why some help is needed for the family.

POSITIVE ACTION

- Be alert to a change in the child's behaviour.
- Ask the child to explain the change.
- Show concern.
- Be honest about sharing concerns with others.
- Go at the child's pace; try not to panic.
- Build on the child's own support networks.

What if Jamelia had told the teacher she should not tell anyone about her worries? What could the teacher do or say to reassure Jamelia that passing on concerns would not lead to her or her mum getting into trouble? What could the teacher do or say to help Jamelia understand what might happen next? What risks and benefits might there be to waiting until Jamelia is happy for information to be passed on?

Wattam (1998) points out that children understand the rules of secrets and confidentiality and know that sometimes adults have the power to break the rules. For this reason, children may try to keep control of information and to restrict disclosure. Negotiating confidentiality and disclosure must be undertaken with an understanding of the child's perspective, and in a way that empowers children.

In Jamelia's case, the teacher would have to decide whether Jamelia's account was serious enough to justify an immediate referral to social services, regardless of Jamelia's wishes, or whether it would be better to take a little longer to build up the trust that would enable Jamelia to accept the actions that are suggested.

Alderson's (1993, p.166) groundbreaking research on children's consent to surgery shows the benefits of making time, wherever possible, for children to work through their fears:

> One senior house officer described a 12-year-old with a slipped vertebra: 'He was well prepared and it really needed doing, but at the last moment he couldn't face it. The ward staff phoned theatre, and there was no problem, immediate agreement to cancel. He stayed in for a week, and then agreed and it went ahead. Choices are being made, and discussions are going on all the time, when some children keep coming back to clinics for years. It is very important to allow them breathing space and thinking time and to discuss it calmly ...'.

For further information on children's competence and seeking informed consent, see Alderson (1993).

CHILDREN'S RIGHTS AND SAFEGUARDING

The United Nations adopted in 1989 an international human rights treaty especially for children – the Convention on the Rights of the Child. The United Kingdom ratified the Convention in December 1991, thus taking on legal obligations to fully implement it. The international treaty monitoring body – the Committee on the Rights of the Child – has issued guidelines for implementing the Convention, stressing four guiding principles:

- Article 2 – all children have all the rights in the Convention without discrimination.
- Article 3 – in any matter concerning the child, the child's best interests shall be a paramount consideration.
- Article 6 – the child's right to survival and development.
- Article 12 – the child's right to have his or her views given due weight in all matters affecting him or her.

The Convention grants all children a comprehensive set of social, economic and cultural, and civil and political rights. The 'family environment', whose defining features are 'happiness, love and understanding', is seen as critical to the child's 'full and harmonious development'. Article 19 grants all children protection from all forms of violence, abuse and neglect, while Article 37 protects children from cruel, inhuman or degrading treatment or punishment. In Article 23, disabled children get the right to 'a full and decent life', characterised by dignity, self-reliance and active participation in the community. They also have the right to 'special care'. Children separated from their parents are entitled to 'special protection', while refugees and young asylum seekers are given the right to 'appropriate protection and humanitarian assistance'.

The European Convention on Human Rights (ECHR) (Council of Europe, 1950/1998) gives children (as well as adults) a set of rights that can be legally tested and protected. However, when Convention rights are breached, children cannot seek a remedy directly through the courts. In 1998, the United Kingdom incorporated the ECHR into domestic law, through the Human Rights Act. This Act came into force in October 2000 and means that UK citizens can seek a legal remedy for breaches of their rights in domestic courts, as well as through the European Court of Human Rights in Strasbourg. There have been several UK cases in recent years concerning safeguarding children (Willow, 2004).

ECHR rights that are particularly relevant to safeguarding children are:

- Article 3 – the right to protection from cruel, inhumane or degrading treatment or punishment.
- Article 8 – the right to respect for private and family life.
- Article 6 – the right to a fair trial.
- Article 13 – the right to an effective remedy when rights have been infringed.

A commitment to children's human rights is much more than accepting that a small number of children will need to challenge their treatment through the courts – to stop something harmful from happening or, more positively, to get the services and support they need to fully develop.

Adopting a children's rights perspective is about seeing and valuing children as individual people. It is about making the most of that distinctive period in life, childhood, which brings immeasurable and unrepeated opportunities to assist another human being. There is no other time in life when the impact of help or harm is so great, affecting the here and now as well as the future. In 1998, Voice for the Child in Care published a self-help book for young people. In it a 37-year-old man reflects on his harrowing childhood, recalling the impact of living with an alcoholic and violent father, his mother's suicide when he was 4 years old and sexual abuse in his children's home. His advice, though aimed at children and young people, powerfully communicates how adults can be a positive force for change in children's lives (Maurice, 1998, pp. 95–96):

> The most important message that I have to give is that there is the possibility that you can again taste happiness. You need to come across a person in the world in whom you can find some solace, someone who actually listens to you, whoever it may be, a teacher at school, a friend, whatever ... the hardest thing in the world is to hope and to trust; to overcome the feeling that everyone and everything is just an utter pointless waste. If you can link in with someone and begin to talk about your experiences, then you can gain the strength to move on from them. Get out there into the world, link up with what is positive and what is good. Even if you fail every exam, even if it all amounts to not very much on paper, the mere process of having gone out there and involved yourself in what is the real world changes things.

EVERYTHING MUST CHANGE

In recent years, the need to consult children about the development of policy and services that concern them has become accepted in government practice. There are consultation exercises to which children are encouraged to respond, children's and young people's pages on government web sites and summaries of documents written specifically for children. A Children's Rights Director has been appointed in the Commission for Social Care Inspection, and there are now Children's Commissioners in England, Wales, Northern Ireland and Scotland.

The same degree of openness and consultation is not always present in individual practitioner behaviour. Masson and Oakley (1999) found that children were often not fully informed of their rights in public law proceedings, or told that they could attend the court hearing with the judge's permission. The Joint Chief Inspectors' report notes that few children are attending child protection conferences (Chief Inspector of Social Services *et al.*, 2002).

The government has promised that support to children, including those who require safeguarding, will be transformed. The *Every Child Matters* Green Paper stresses listening to and involving children in the design, development and evaluation of services (Cm 5860, 2003, p. 78):

> The creation of an organisation defined by its client group rather than professional functions offers an important opportunity to involve children and young people in decision-making.

The focus is not just on children influencing general decision making; it is about them having a voice and an influence on decisions that affect them as individuals. In a GMTV interview on the day the Children Bill was published, the then Minister for Children, Young People and Families, Margaret Hodge, said of Victoria Climbié: 'Nobody talked to her, nobody asked her how she felt, nobody asked her what she wanted. That must never happen again' (HL Deb, 2003–2004).

Recognising children as individual people and as holders of rights disturbs deep-rooted beliefs about the nature and purpose of childhood. Putting into practice children's rights, especially their right to be heard and taken seriously, requires a shift from acting on *images* of children, of which there are many – cute and amusing, unfortunate and needy, empty vessels to be filled with adult wisdom, and dangerous and out of control – to seeing children as having the full range of human characteristics that adults have. It means knowing and respecting each child as a whole person and doing our level best to ensure that children get what they are entitled to.

REFERENCES

Adcock, M. (2000) The core assessment: how to synthesise information and make judgements, in *The Child's World: Assessing Children in Need* (ed. J. Horwath), Jessica Kingsley, London.

Advisory Council on the Misuse of Drugs (2003) *Hidden Harm: Responding to the Needs of Children of Problem Drug Users*, Home Office, London, http://www.drugs.homeoffice.gov.uk/publication-search/acmd/hidden-harm (accessed 30 August 2008).

Alderson, P. (1993) *Children's Consent to Surgery*, Open University Press, Buckingham.

Alderson, P. (2000) *Young Children's Rights: Exploring Beliefs, Principles and Practice*, Save the Children and Jessica Kingsley, London.

Baginsky, M. (2001) A summary of findings from the UK, in *Counselling and Support Services for Young People Aged 12–16 Who Have Experienced Sexual Abuse* (ed. M. Baginsky), NSPCC, London.

Birmingham Area Child Protection Committee (2004) *Chapter 8 Case Review: Toni-Ann Byfield*, www.birmingham.gov.uk, http://www.birmingham.gov.uk/Media/TAB%20summary%20report.doc? (accessed 30 August 2008)

Brandon, M., Schofield, G. and Trinder, L. (1998) *Social Work with Children*, Macmillan, Basingstoke.

Butler, I. and Williamson, H. (1994) *Children Speak: Children, Trauma and Social Work*, Longman, Essex.

Cawson, P. (2002) *Child Maltreatment in the Family: The Experience of a National Sample of Children*, NSPCC, London.

Cawson, P., Wattam, C., Brooker, S. and Kelly, G. (2000) *Child Maltreatment in the United Kingdom: A Study of the Prevalence of Child Abuse and Neglect*, NSPCC, London.

Chief Inspector of Social Services, Director for Health Improvement, Commission for Health Improvement, Her Majesty's Chief Inspector of Constabulary, Her Majesty's Chief Inspector of the Crown Prosecution Service, Her Majesty's Chief Inspector of the Magistrates' Courts Service, Her Majesty's Chief Inspector of Schools, Her Majesty's Chief Inspector of Prisons and Her Majesty's Chief

Inspector of Probation (2002) *Safeguarding Children: A Joint Chief Inspectors' Report on Arrangements to Safeguard Children*, Department of Health, London, http://www.dh.gov.uk/en/Publicationsandstatistics/Lettersandcirculars/Chiefinspectorletters/DH_4004286 (accessed 30 August 2008).

Children Act 1989, Chapter 41, HMSO, London, http://www.hmso.gov.uk/acts/acts1989/Ukpga_19890041_en_1.htm (accessed 30 August 2008).

Children Act 2004, Chapter 31, HMSO, London, http://www.hmso.gov.uk/acts/acts2004/20040031.htm (accessed 30 August 2008).

Children and Young People's Unit (2001) *Learning to Listen: Core Principles for the Involvement of Children and Young People*, Children and Young People's Unit, Annesley, Nottinghamshire, http://www.everychildmatters.gov.uk/_files/1F85704C1D67D71E30186FEBCEDED6D6.pdf (accessed 30 August 2008).

Children and Young People's Unit (2003) *Young People's Consultation Report*, Children and Young People's Unit, Annesley, Nottinghamshire.

Children's Rights Alliance for England (2004) *Let Them Have Their Childhood Again*, Children's Rights Alliance for England, London, http://www.crae.org.uk (accessed 23 September 2008).

Cleaver, H., Unell, I. and Aldgate, J. (1999) *Children's Needs – Parenting Capacity: The Impact of Parental Mental Illness, Problem Alcohol and Drug Use, and Domestic Violence on Children's Development*, Department of Health, London.

Cm 5730 (2003) *The Victoria Climbié Inquiry: Report of an Inquiry by Lord Laming*, The Stationery Office, London, http://www.victoria-climbie-inquiry.org.uk/finreport/finreport.htm (accessed 30 August 2008).

Cm 5860 (2003) *Every Child Matters*, The Stationery Office, London, http://www.everychildmatters.gov.uk/_content/documents/EveryChildMatters.pdf (accessed 30 August 2008).

Commission for Health Improvement, Her Majesty's Chief Inspector of Constabulary and The Social Services Inspectorate (2003) *The Victoria Climbié Inquiry Report: Key Findings From the Self-Audits of NHS Organisations, Social Services Departments and Police Forces*, Commission for Health Improvement, London, http://www.healthcarecommission.org.uk/_db/_documents/04010951.pdf (accessed 30 August 2008).

Cooper, A., Hetherington, R. and Katz, I. (2003) *The Risk Factor: Making the Child Protection System Work for Children*, Demos, London, http://www.demos.co.uk/publications/riskfactor (accessed 30 August 2008).

Council of Europe (1950/1998) *Convention for the Protection of Human Rights and Fundamental Freedoms*, Council of Europe Publications, Strasbourg, http://conventions.coe.int/Treaty/en/Treaties/Html/005.htm (accessed 30 August 2008).

Creighton, S. and Russell, N. (1995) *Voices from Childhood*, NSPCC, London.

Creighton, S. and Tissier, G. (2003) *Child Killings in England and Wales*, NSPCC, London, http://www.nspcc.org.uk/inform/research/briefings/childkillingsinenglandandwales_wda48218.html (accessed 30 August 2008).

Dalrymple, J., Willow, C., Plowden, V. and Gledhill, K. (2000) *Total Respect: Ensuring Children's Rights and Participation in Care. Course Handbook*, Children's Rights Officers and Advocates (CROA) and Department of Health, London, http://www.dcsf.gov.uk/qualityprotects/pdfs/issue10_21_32.pdf (accessed 30 August 2008).

Department for Education and Skills (2004) *Get it Sorted: Providing Effective Advocacy Services for Children and Young People Making a Complaint Under the Children Act 1989*, Department for Education and Skills, London, http://publications.teachernet.gov.uk/eOrderingDownload/GIS04.pdf (accessed 30 August 2008).

Department for Education and Skills (2006) *Referrals, Assessments, and Children and Young People on Child Protection Registers, England – Year Ending 31 March 2005*, The Stationery Office, London, http://www.dcsf.gov.uk/rsgateway/DB/SFR/s000614/index.shtml (accessed 30 August 2008).

Department of Health, Department for Education and Employment and Home Office (2000) *Framework for the Assessment of Children in Need and Their Families*, The Stationery Office, London, http://www.dh.gov.uk/en/Publicationsandstatistics/Publications/PublicationsPolicyAndGuidance/DH_4003256 (accessed 30 August 2008).

Education Act 2002, Chapter 32, HMSO, London, http://www.hmso.gov.uk/acts/acts2002/20020032.htm (accessed 30 August 2008).

Family Law Reform Act 1969, Chapter 46, HMSO, London.

Featherstone, B. and Evans, H. (2004) *Children Experiencing Maltreatment: Who do They Turn to?* NSPCC, London.

Gillick v. West Norfolk and Wisbech Health Authority (1986) AC 112.

Gorin, S. (2004) *Understanding What Children Say: Children's Experiences of Domestic Violence, Parental Substance Misuse and Parental Health Problems*, National Children's Bureau, London.

HL Deb (2003–2004) Vol. 661, Monday 24 May 2004, Col 1053, http://www.publications.parliament.uk/pa/ld200304/ldhansrd/vo040524/text/40524-03.htm (accessed 30 August 2008).

HM Government (2005) *Statutory Guidance on Making Arrangements to Safeguard and Promote the Welfare of Children under s11 of the Children Act*, Department for Education and Skills, London, http://www.everychildmatters.gov.uk/socialcare/safeguarding (accessed 30 August 2008).

HM Government (2006a) *Working Together to Safeguard Children: A Guide to Inter-Agency Working to Safeguard and Promote the Welfare of Children*, The Stationery Office, London, http://www.everychildmatters.gov.uk/socialcare/safeguarding (accessed 30 August 2008).

HM Government (2006b) *Common Assessment Framework for Children and Young People: Practitioners' Guide*, Department for Education and Skills, London, http://www.everychildmatters.gov.uk/deliveringservices/caf/ (accessed 30 August 2008).

HM Government (2006c) *What To Do If You're Worried A Child Is Being Abused*, Department for Education and Skills, London, http://www.everychildmatters.gov.uk/socialcare/safeguarding (accessed 30 August 2008).

House of Commons Health Committee (2003) The Victoria Climbié Inquiry Report. 6th report. Session 2002–03. HC 570.

Human Rights Act 1998, Chapter 42, HMSO, London, http://www.hmso.gov.uk/acts/acts1998/19980042.htm (accessed 30 August 2008).

Jones, D. (2003) *Communicating with Vulnerable Children: A Guide for Practitioners*, Gaskell, London.

Leslie, A. (2001) *Report of the Part 8 Review for Brighton and Hove ACPC of the Care and Protection of JAS (Aged 4) Who Died on 24 December 1999*, Brighton and Hove ACPC, Brighton.

Marchant, R. and Page, M. (2003) Child protection practice with disabled children, in *'It Doesn't Happen to Disabled Children': Child Protection and Disabled Children*, NSPCC, London.

Masson, J. and Oakley, M. W. (1999) *Out of Hearing: Representing Children*. Care Proceedings. John Wiley & Sons, Ltd, Chichester.

Maurice (1998) Abuse was normal, in *Sometimes You've Got to Shout to Be Heard: Stories From Young People in Care About Getting Heard and Using Advocates* (ed. T. Growney), Voice for the Child in Care, London.

Morgan, R. (2003) *Children's Views From Care and Residential Education on Proposals in the Green Paper 'Every Child Matters'. Report of the Children's Rights Director*, National Care Standards Commission, London, http://www.csci.org .uk/about_csci/publications/views_every_child_matters.aspx (accessed 30 August 2008).

Mullender, A., Hague, G., Umme, I. *et al.* (2002) *Children's Perspectives on Domestic Violence*, Sage, London.

National Working Group on Child Protection and Disability (2003) *'It Doesn't Happen to Disabled Children': Child Protection and Disabled Children*, NSPCC, London.

Nobes, G. and Smith, M. (1997) Physical punishment of children in two-parent families. *Clinical Child Psychology and Psychiatry*, **2** (2), 271–81.

Schofield, G. and Thoburn, J. (1996) *Child Protection: The Voice of the Child in Decision-Making*, Institute for Public Policy Research, London.

Social Services Inspectorate (1998) *Someone Else's Children: Inspections of Planning and Decision-Making for Children Looked After and the Safety of Children Looked After*, Social Services Inspectorate, London.

United Nations (1989) *Convention on the Rights of the Child* (adopted by the General Assembly of the United Nations 20 November 1989), UNICEF, Geneva, http://www.unicef.org/crc/ (accessed 30 August 2008).

Utting, W. (1997) *People Like Us: The Report of the Review of the Safeguards for Children Living Away from Home*, Department of Health and Welsh Office, HMSO, London.

Voice for the Child in Care and National Children's Bureau (2004) *Start with the Child, Stay with the Child: A Blueprint for a Child-Centred Approach to Children and Young People in Public Care*, Voice for the Child in Care, London, http://www.voiceyp.org/ngen_public/default.asp?id=44 (accessed 30 August 2008).

Wattam, C. (1998) Confidentiality, in *Child Sexual Abuse: Responding to the Experiences of Children* (eds N. Parton and C. Wattam), John Wiley & Sons, Ltd, Chichester.

Wattam, C. and Woodward, C. (1996) 'And do I abuse my children? No!', in *Childhood Matters: Report of the National Commission of Inquiry into the Prevention of Child Abuse: Volume 2: Background Papers*, The Stationery Office, London.

Willow, C. (2004) Children's rights as a force for change, in *Human Rights in the Community: Rights as Agents for Change* (ed. C. Harvey), Hart, Oxford.

2 Working Effectively with Parents

RUTH GARDNER
HEDY CLEAVER

This chapter provides an overview of what is known about the importance of working effectively with parents where there are concerns about a child's safety or welfare. The first section looks at parenthood, the legal concept of parental responsibility and what is meant by parenting. The next section explores why, when there are concerns that a child is being abused, it is important to work with parents. The third section focuses on the challenge of working with parents in different settings. Finally, the possible barriers to involving parents are highlighted, and the principles that should underpin this work are set out. In this chapter, the term 'parents' includes caregivers: adults who are in a parental role, even if they do not hold parental responsibility for the child.

CORE KNOWLEDGE

- The concept of parental responsibility is defined in the Children Act 1989. In most cases, the child's birth parents will have parental responsibility.
- 'Parenting' refers to the day-to-day activities that are undertaken as part of bringing up a child.
- Where there are concerns about a child's safety or welfare, both the law and best practice require that work with parents be fair, open and accountable while maintaining a focus on the child and ensuring that the child is not placed at increased risk of harm.
- Involving parents and working effectively with them is associated with better outcomes for children.
- Working with parents is not an end in itself; the objective should always be to safeguard and promote the welfare of the child, and improve outcomes for the child.
- Whatever the setting, an open approach to parents when raising concerns about a child can reassure parents and enable working relationships to be maintained.

Safeguarding Children   Edited by Hedy Cleaver, Pat Cawson, Sarah Gorin and Steve Walker
Copyright © 2009 by John Wiley & Sons, Ltd

• Practitioners should be honest and explicit with parents about their roles, responsibilities, powers and expectations, and about what is and is not negotiable.

PARENTS' ROLES, RIGHTS AND RESPONSIBILITIES

WHAT DO WE MEAN BY PARENTHOOD AND PARENTAL RESPONSIBILITY?

It might be assumed that most people know what parenthood is and who has parental responsibility, but it is not always as obvious as it may seem. Parenthood includes biological and genetic components, but it also has legal and social aspects (Henricson, 2003). If they are married to each other, a child's genetic parents, with whom they share DNA, obtain legal parental responsibility automatically. In most cases, the legal parents are also the genetic parents, but this is not always so in, for example, the case of adoption, or sperm or egg donation:

> In England and Wales, parental responsibility 'means all the rights, duties powers, responsibility and authority which by law a parent has in relation to the child and his property'.
>
> Children Act 1989, s 3(1)

Until recently, unmarried fathers did not automatically have parental responsibility for their children. However (for registrations after 1 December 2003), fathers may acquire parental responsibility by registering the child's birth, by agreement with the mother or by court order. While many genetic fathers do not hold or seek legal parental responsibility, as parents they are entitled to the right to respect for their family life with their children as set out in the European Convention of Human Rights (Council of Europe, 1950, Article 8).

Adults who may or may not be related to the child can acquire responsibility via an Adoption Order or a Residence Order. Under the Adoption and Children Act 2004, a Special Guardianship Order can give parental responsibility to someone who is not the child's parent and will also enable a step-parent to acquire parental responsibility by agreement with the child's parents.

Day-to-day carers (e.g. a partner, grandparent or friend) carry a degree of delegated parental responsibility, as do all those who work with children (e.g. foster carers, childminders, volunteers) in addition to their contractual and professional duties. In some cultures, child-rearing practices result in a greater reliance on relatives and friends in the upbringing of children. Any or all these people may be crucial to a child's safe and healthy development, whether or not the child actually lives with them, and so be entitled to be included, directly or otherwise, in planning for that child's future.

The Children Act 1989 recognises the wider network of people in contact with the child:

A person who

(a) does not have parental responsibility for a particular child; but
(b) has care of that child,

may (subject to the provisions of the Act) do what is reasonable in all the circumstances of the case for the purpose of safeguarding or promoting the child's welfare.

Children Act 1989, s 3(5)

For further information, see the Children Act (1989), Department of Health (1991a), Ryan (2000) and Henricson (2003).

WHAT IS MEANT BY PARENTING?

A clear understanding of what we mean by parenting is essential when working with parents to safeguard children and promote their welfare. The fundamental objective of parenting is to enable children to become autonomous individuals capable of participating fully in the culture in which they live. Parenting refers to

the activities and behaviours of parents which are necessary to achieve the objective of enabling children to become autonomous. These activities and behaviours change as the child develops. Thus, parenting as an activity is firmly yoked to child outcomes.

Jones, 2001, p. 256

The principles of parenting are similar for parents in all communities. Every child, regardless of his or her ethnic background and culture, needs parents to respond to his or her fundamental needs by keeping him or her safe and providing him or her with basic care, emotional warmth, stimulation, guidance and boundaries and stability (Department of Health, Department for Education and Employment and Home Office, 2000).

For further information on what is meant by parenting, see Quinton (2004).

DIVERSITY AND CULTURE IN PARENTING

Although research shows that parents in all communities share common values and aspirations for their children (Barn, Ladino and Rogers, 2005), not all parents bring their children up in the same way. The way in which parents bring up their children may differ within and between cultures and ethnic groups, but generalisations and assumptions about cultural norms may leave children at risk of significant harm. The Victoria Climbié Inquiry Report (Cm

5730, 2003, Chapter 16) – and many others before it (Department of Health, 1991b) – argues against generalisations about parenting:

> Cultural norms can vary considerably between communities and even families. The concept of Afro-Caribbean behaviour referred to in Victoria's case illustrates the problem. The range of cultures and behavioural patterns it includes is so wide that it would be meaningless to make generalisations, and potentially damaging to an effective assessment of the needs of the child. The wisest course is to be humble when considering the extent of one's own knowledge about different 'cultures' and to take advice whenever it is available.
>
> Cm 5730, 2003, p. 345, 16.5

Although it is important to take account of social and cultural differences or backgrounds, this should not result in an exclusive focus on 'culture' when carrying out an assessment of children's needs:

> Racial and stereotyping of black and ethnic minority families can lead to inappropriate interventions in families as well as a failure to protect these children from abuse.
>
> Dutt and Phillips, 2000, p. 56

Research on professional practice found evidence of racism affecting the assessment of risk of significant harm (Birchall and Hallett, 1995). The clear message from research and inquiries is that false assumptions about ethnic groups can have an adverse and, at times, dangerous impact on practitioners' work to safeguard and promote the welfare of children.

For further information, see Butt and Box (1998), Dutt and Phillips (2000), Social Services Inspectorate (2000), Cm 5730 (2003) and Keay (2003).

WHY IS IT IMPORTANT TO WORK WITH PARENTS AND FAMILY MEMBERS?

There is much evidence that the key to successfully protecting children from harm and promoting their welfare is a positive working partnership between the family and practitioners (Department of Health, 1995a; Butt and Box, 1998; Tunstill and Aldgate, 2000).

Working in partnership with parents when there are concerns about a child's welfare is associated with better outcomes for children and less distress for both parents and children because

- cooperation between the child's parents and the practitioners reassures the child;
- parents hold key information about their children that should inform practitioners' decisions;
- parents are more likely to commit to a plan they have helped to create;

- acknowledging parental strengths enables parents to learn and change the behaviours that negatively affect their children;
- involving parents can help reverse feelings of social exclusion.

There is growing evidence from research and evaluation that involving parents and caregivers in decisions and plans about their children can increase parents' self-esteem, motivation and skills in promoting their children's welfare. A recent research review concludes:

> Engagement is the first requirement of an effective service for parents and parenting. In this respect family centres have won the argument for their style of delivering many services to families. This is the central idea behind Sure Start and related initiatives.
>
> Quinton, 2004, p. 172

Eileen attended an NSPCC family support project to help her deal with problems in caring for her children and with her feelings of stress and depression linked with her own childhood abuse. She said:

> ... the people who work here have dealt with adults and children in awkward situations and – they understand problems with kids and partners. My mother said 'Why are you going there? They will keep an eye on your kids?' It's not like that – it is to keep the family together. I wish it had been here when I was little. I have become a volunteer and worked with the crèche and workshops here.
>
> Gardner, 2003, p. 98

The importance of working with parents to ensure good outcomes for children is also emphasised in Standard 2 of the *National Service Framework for Children, Young People and Maternity Services*. It specifies that parents and caregivers should be

> enabled to receive the information, services and support which will help them to care for their children and equip them with the skills they need to ensure that their children have optimum life chances and are healthy and safe.
>
> Department of Health and Department for Education and Skills, 2004a, p. 6

The Family Rights Group provides advice sheets for families, and the NSPCC has publications in a number of languages, including a booklet on child protection procedures.

For further reading on the importance of working with parents, see Social Services Inspectorate (1995), Thoburn, Lewis and Shemmings (1995), ATD Fourth World (1996), HM Government (2006a), Wheal (2000), Department of Health and Department for Education and Skills (2004b, 2004d), Family Rights Group (www.frg.org.uk) Advice Line 0800 731 1696, and NSPCC (www.nspcc.org.uk) National Child Protection Helpline 0808 800 5000 (calls are free).

WORKING WITH PARENTS IN COMMUNITY SETTINGS

Many different agencies, practitioners and volunteers are involved in working with parents in community settings. They may be working with parents to help support parenting and prevent problems from occurring; they may be working with families when a child is 'in need', to help safeguard a child or when a child is being looked after by a local authority. Families may need support for a range of reasons. For example, they may lack informal sources of support, parents may be experiencing problems and finding it hard to cope, a child may be ill, disabled or presenting emotional or behavioural difficulties, or there may be problems in the wider family and environment that are causing stress to the family. Families may face a range of disadvantages including poverty, unemployment, poor housing or homelessness, racism, social isolation and exclusion.

For more information on support from the wider family and community, see Chapter 3.

In community settings, especially in less formal settings such as family centres, it is often tempting to do without agreed procedures or records of meetings and discussions. At any time, and unexpectedly, a parent may talk about concerns either about his or her own child, or someone else's; or a child may do the same. Not to record these matters and agree the record may lead to misreporting and a perceived lack of fairness and openness at a later date, for instance if the conversation was seen as confidential by one party but not by the other.

To introduce procedures for the first time at a time of stress for the family is unhelpful. It is much more effective to prepare all families who start to use a service with clear, well-understood procedures for dealing with child welfare concerns, confidentiality, recording and complaints, and to include these matters systematically in induction both for service users and for staff and volunteers.

Research on family support projects showed that children and parents approved of clear procedures, and told one another about them, encouraging parents to seek help. If an injury to a child was reported, parents knew that staff would offer support in the process of investigation and that they would still be kept informed (Gardner, 2003).

WORKING WITH PARENTS IN STATUTORY SETTINGS

The following section focuses on practitioners in key statutory organisations that may find themselves working with parents and those working under contract to these organisations.

In carrying out their normal functions, practitioners in the following organisations should always have regard to safeguarding and promoting the welfare of the children with whom they work or are in contact with through their work (Children Act 2004, s 11):

- local authorities, including district councils;
- Connexions;
- the National Health Service;
- the police;
- British Transport Police;
- the probation service;
- youth offending teams;
- prisons;
- secure training centres.

CHILDREN'S SOCIAL CARE

Once a referral of a child considered to be in need has been accepted by children's social care, the child should be seen and parents involved in the assessment as soon as possible. Any difficulty in communicating with parents is magnified by delay; parents who are involved belatedly in an assessment are likely to start off the working relationship feeling excluded.

The degree of care taken to involve parents from this early stage is likely to be reflected in the quality of collaboration between parents and practitioners later on. Parents should be told who is going to be asked for information about the child and family, and for what purpose. Their consent should be obtained unless this would place the child at risk of significant harm. They should also be kept informed about the availability of relevant resources. Assessment without any subsequent services is a major source of frustration:

> ... when we were told after many assessments that no respite was on offer [my husband] asked 'what would you do if we left Chris on the doorstep one day?' The response 'you would be prosecuted for abandonment'. Yet if by doing so, we demonstrated that we couldn't cope, we would get support more readily.
>
> Evans, 2004, p. 43

SECTION 47 ENQUIRIES

The importance of social work practitioners involving and working with parents continues to apply when an enquiry under section 47 of the Children Act 1989 substantiates that the child is at continuing risk of significant harm. Following such a decision, a child protection conference should be convened. This will assess all the relevant information and plan how best to safeguard the child and promote his or her welfare (HM Government 2006d, Paragraphs 44–45).

The evidence indicates that involving parents, if this activity is well prepared, is highly constructive in most cases (Cleaver and Freeman, 1995; Cleaver, Walker and Meadows, 2004):

> The information recorded on the outcome of the s47 enquiries should be consistent with the information set out in the Outcome of the s47 Enquiries Record (Department of Health, 2002) and parents and children of sufficient age and appropriate level of understanding (together with professionals and agencies who have been significantly involved) should receive a copy of this record, in particular in advance of any initial child conference that is convened. This information should be conveyed in an appropriate format for younger children and those people whose preferred language is not English.
> HM Government, 2006a, Paragraph 5.72

The government's guidance on safeguarding children emphasises the importance of treating families sensitively and with respect during section 47 enquiries and subsequent procedures, bearing in mind just how difficult an experience these may present to the family (HM Government, 2006a, Paragraphs 5.69 and 5.70).

LOOKED AFTER CHILDREN

Situations arise in which parents' circumstances may be so difficult or their own needs so dominant that they are unable to care for their children or, in some instances, to prioritise their children's needs or ensure their safety. As a result, some children need to be looked after by the local authority.

When parents and practitioners agree that the child needs to be looked after, this can be done by voluntary arrangement under section 20 of the Children Act 1989. In these circumstances, the local authority does not acquire parental responsibility and parents remain the key decision makers in relation to their child.

When children are looked after because of a care order made under section 31 of the Children Act 1989, the local authority shares parental responsibility with parents and can in some circumstances override their wishes in relation to the child:

> A local authority may limit parents' exercise of that responsibility when a child is looked after by a local authority as a result of a court order, but only if it is necessary to do so to safeguard and promote the child's welfare.
> Department of Health, 1991a, p. 4, 2.10

Although working in partnership with parents will be more difficult when a care order has been made by a court, wherever possible parents should be consulted and notified about decisions that affect their child (Department of Health, 1991a).

If a child is looked after by the local authority, it is accepted that in all but exceptional cases, where there is a risk of significant harm, children benefit from maintaining contact with their birth family, even though this can be stressful and time consuming for all involved. Contact is more likely when parents have been consulted and involved in the arrangements and plans for their child (Cleaver, 2000). Contact is important because research suggests that it increases the likelihood of children being able to return successfully to the family and is beneficial for children's identity and self-esteem (Bullock, Gooch and Little, 1998; Cleaver, 2000).

For further information, see Masson, Harrison and Pavlovic (1997), Bullock, Gooch and Little (1998), Masson, Harrison and Pavlovic (1999), Cleaver (2000), National Working Group on Child Protection and Disability (2003) and Thoburn, Chand and Procter (2004).

For discussion of safeguarding children living away from home, see Chapter 4.

SCHOOL AND EARLY YEARS

Schools have a primary responsibility to children to meet their educational needs, and effective partnership with parents is key to achieving that aim. Research has indicated that parents' support in their children's learning is crucial to educational outcomes. In addition, section 175 of the Education Act 2002 requires local education authorities and the governing bodies of maintained schools and further education institutions to make arrangements to ensure that their functions are carried out with a view to safeguarding and promoting the welfare of children. Stevens (2000) gives a good example of the benefits of teachers keeping in close touch with the parents and the home situation:

> ... in a recent case pupil X started to come to school regularly out of uniform. Fortunately ... the parents had contacted the school to say that mother was going into hospital ... This very simple case illustrates clearly how knowledge of the home situation totally changed the action required. Instead of being spoken to and punished ... he was offered support and understanding while his mother recovered.
>
> Stevens, 2000, p. 180

The Education Act 2002 enables schools to set up and run child care facilities and to provide out-of-school child care based around well-planned activities suitable for the age of the children and young people involved. The government's 10-year strategy for child care (Her Majesty's Treasury et al., 2004) is working towards providing parents with access to reliable, affordable child care that wraps around the school day and school year.

Because children and young people will spend the greater part of their day at school, teachers and early years practitioners will often be the first people outside the family to realise when there are difficulties affecting children's safety or welfare. The point at which they should discuss their concerns with parents, or should consider a referral to specialist services, can be particularly difficult to gauge.

Baginsky (2000) analysed responses from 420 schools on the issues they wanted help with in relation to child protection. She found that 'just under two thirds of schools reported some degree of uncertainty about when to contact social services in relation to a child protection concern and for half of these it was a major concern' (p. 29).

Almost all of the schools (92%) gave as one of their reasons for anxiety 'how to maintain relationships with parents when the schools were involved in child protection cases and two thirds of respondents were very worried about this' (p. 32). Some said that when they were able to work with a social worker skilled in dealing with sensitive situations, this was a great help:

> Relationships can be very sensitive and need to be handled with care. However, an openness of opinion which demonstrates how you care for the child is often the best way forward.
>
> Head teacher quoted in Baginsky (2000, p. 33)

HEALTH BODIES

The Child Health Promotion Programme, which has been incorporated into the Core Standards of *The National Service Framework for Children, Young People and Maternity Services* (Department of Health and Department for Education and Skills, 2004a), is designed to ensure that provisions are in place to support health practitioners working with children to identify signs of physical or mental ill health or developmental difficulties and make appropriate referrals. It makes clear that all those providing primary care, and staff who work for primary care providers, have a duty wherever possible to promote children's welfare, prevent the impairment of children's health and development, prevent children from being abused or neglected, identify those children who are or may be at risk of suffering significant harm, and follow the local procedures for referral to social services or the police.

Health visitors are central to safeguarding children (Lupton, North and Khan, 2001; Department of Health, 2004) because they provide a universal service of health screening for the under 5-year-olds and have a mandate to visit the home and see babies and young children with the parent. Research indicates that health visitors are generally welcomed, or at least tolerated, in this role and are committed to joint work to safeguard children, attending the majority of child protection conferences on younger children (Cleaver and Freeman, 1995; Thoburn, Wilding and Watson, 2000; Browne *et al.*, 2000; Douglas *et al.*, 2006).

The role of health visitors is wider than just working directly with young children and parents:

> Health visitors [also have responsibility to] work in partnership with other early years staff to raise awareness and understanding of children's health and development needs, and act as a referral contact for them to the primary care team, or other services such as therapy services, if they or the parents are concerned about a child.
>
> Department of Health and Department for Education and Skills, 2004a, p. 40

Support and training for health visitors on working with parents, both in their own right and with other practitioners, are therefore essential.

Other health practitioners, such as general practitioners (GPs), are less involved in child protection work. Lupton, North and Khan (2001) identify a number of reasons for this 'patchy' involvement including concerns about confidentiality, uncertainty about outcome and sheer pressure of work as well as the wish not to jeopardise their relationship with parents. GPs, however, have a crucial role in identifying concerns at an early stage. Moreover, when they raise such concerns with parents they can often encourage and assist them to seek help, because services provided by or through a doctor are not usually considered to be stigmatising.

To help parents, GPs need good networks with colleagues and providers of family resources within the community, so that they can seek advice and refer families on appropriately, including referrals to children's social care if they are concerned about a child's safety and welfare.

Hill (2000) offers a helpful guide for health practitioners working with children and parents, which shows that allowing parents time to voice their concerns increases the efficacy of the meeting. Hill's advice for 'breaking bad news' about a medical diagnosis is equally applicable to safeguarding, particularly where there are medical findings relevant to abuse or neglect:

- It is always important to find out what the parents know and understand already... prevarication should be avoided. The diagnosis should be given concisely.
- Use of medical terminology is important but only if supported by clear explanations.
- It is easier for the parents if the news is given incrementally allowing for questions along the way.

Hill, 2000, p. 150

Health practitioners will also have a key role to play in relation to ensuring the safety and welfare of disabled children (Department of Health and Department for Education and Skills, 2004c). Typically, these children will have multiple contacts with health, education and social care practitioners, and no individual may have a comprehensive picture of the child's needs and circumstances; hence, the importance of health practitioners working collaboratively with other relevant practitioners, as well as with parents, particularly where there are specific concerns about the child's welfare. Collaborative working, the adoption of a Common Assessment Framework (HM Government 2006b, 2006c) and the Integrated Children's System (Department of Health, 2002) should ensure that children are not subjected to unnecessary assessments, and information given to children and families is coordinated and timely. Such an approach has benefits for the practitioners and families because inconsistencies and misunderstandings between practitioners are ironed out before being passed on to the family.

For further information about working with parents in education or health, see Williamson (2000), Lupton, North and Khan (2001), Cm 5860 (2003), Evans (2004), Department of Health and Department for Education and Skills (2004d), Department of Health (2004) and www.everychildmatters.gov.uk/socialcare/ics.

POLICE SERVICE

The main roles of the police are to uphold the law, prevent crime and disorder and protect the citizen. Children, like all citizens, have the right to the full protection offered by the criminal law. The police have a duty and responsibility to investigate all criminal offences and as Lord Laming pointed out in his report into the circumstances leading to the death of Victoria Climbié (2003) 'the investigation of crimes against children is as important as the investigation of any other serious crime and any suggestions that child protection policing is of lower status than any other form of policing should be eradicated.' Offences committed against children can be particularly sensitive and will often require the police to work with other organisations, such as children's social care, in the conduct of any investigation.

HM Government, 2006a, Paragraph 2.97

There are many different reasons why police may be the first practitioners to identify children at risk of significant harm, and as a result need to speak to parents or carers. All forces have child abuse investigation units (CAIUs) that work jointly with children's social care in combating child abuse; the child abuse investigation units generally take primary responsibility for investigating child abuse cases.

However, safeguarding children is not solely the role of the CAIU officers; it is a fundamental part of the duties of all police officers. For example, patrol officers attending to domestic violence incidents should be aware of the effects of such violence on children within the household and take action when necessary. Police officers using their emergency powers to enter premises may need to act quickly to safeguard the children. Police officers working in specialised services such as transport or the 'vice squad' may also identify children at risk of significant harm in the course of their work. The police may become involved with parents to ensure good outcomes for children in a number of different circumstances (Masson, Winn Oakley and McGovern, 2001) including when they

- are called to an incident of domestic violence where children are present in the home, or where the violent conflict is between parents and teenagers;
- return runaway children or children found in dangerous situations to the care of their parents or ensure their safety through the use of police protection powers under section 46 of the Children Act 1989;
- deal with anti-social and offending behaviour by children and as a result have contact with parents;
- identify situations in which they think the child is not being adequately safeguarded in the family home or when parents are not able on their own to provide the care and control necessary to keep children safe outside the home.

Government guidance is clear that police officers who become involved with a child about whom they have child welfare concerns should make a referral to social services and agree on a plan of action (HM Government, 2006d).

Research suggests a wide variation in how police respond to families where children may be at risk of significant harm (Masson, Winn Oakley and McGovern, 2001). Police officers may become involved in negotiating short-term care for children with parents, other family members and neighbours when parents are not thought able to cope safely with their child, are arrested, or are unwilling to have a child returned to their care after episodes of offending or running away.

Such negotiations which do not involve children's social care can be a risky option, as officers on the beat are not always in a position to know or check whether the care is a safe alternative (Masson, Winn Oakley and McGovern, 2001). Masson, Winn Oakley and McGovern (2001) conclude from their study that non-statutory action to provide alternative care for children is appropriate only when it is fully consensual and when the parents are able to give valid consent – not, for example, if parents are absent or incapacitated. This is particularly relevant in the cases when parents appear to have serious psychiatric problems, or to be under the influence of drugs or alcohol.

Responding to reports of domestic violence means that a police officer is often the first professional to become aware of the situation; ensuring that the safety of children living in the household is part of their duties – indeed the children may have called the police for help (McGee, 2000).

The impact of domestic violence on children should not be underestimated. A national survey of young people found that 26% had at some time seen physical violence between their parents, and for 5% it was 'constant' or 'frequent' (Cawson et al., 2000). Women experience more frequent and more serious violence than men, and risk of violence is highest for women who are pregnant, have young children and do not work outside the home (Rowsell, 2003). There is now considerable evidence that domestic violence makes it likely that children will also experience physical abuse and that the effects of living with and witnessing parental violence results in children suffering or being likely to suffer significant harm.

The Home Office commissioned a series of reviews of evidence of 'what works', which highlighted the importance of the police role in working with incidents of domestic violence (Mullender and Hague, 2000). Women with children were often afraid to seek help from the police for fear of an unsympathetic child protection response; fear of losing children has been identified as one of the main motives for women staying in a violent relationship. This fear is more acutely felt when the abused woman is from a minority community. In these circumstances, women may see the police as threatening, particularly if the woman is of refugee status, or they have little faith in their ability to explain their situation (Hyton, 1997).

Hanmer and Griffiths (2000) identify police tactics that appear effective in offering immediate protection to mothers and their children following an incident of domestic violence:

- A focus on repeat victimisation, to target resources most effectively. In some innovatory schemes a database of callouts is maintained.
- Training all police officers to deal with domestic violence rather than relying solely on specialist domestic violence teams.
- Having standardised definitions of what constitutes domestic violence and repeat victimisation.
- Following up calls within 24 hours to ensure that the family are safe.
- Locating the perpetrator of violence if that person is not in the house.
- Making it clear to perpetrators that their behaviour is an offence that will be responded to and monitored.
- The use of pendant alarms for vulnerable women, especially repeat victims.
- Monitoring of police response and activities.

Good liaison between all community and specialist police teams and the child protection team is essential. In McGee's (2000) study, children and mothers who lived with domestic violence described how frightening it was when the police called to an incident simply spoke to the violent father and then went away leaving the mother and children unprotected. Several of the children and their mothers had become victims of the revenge violence this generated. On the other hand, when there was an effective police response, children and mothers identified police as the most helpful service they experienced.

In most situations, where the police need to work with parents to ensure the best outcomes for their children, parents are likely to feel that their competence as parents is being questioned. An approach that further undermines their confidence could make it less, rather than more, likely that they will give safe care to their children in future. Masson, Winn Oakley and McGovern (2001) give examples of great sensitivity on behalf of police officers dealing with some of these situations, but also emphasise the need for increased preparation and training of police officers, as well as better support for the police from social services.

For further reading, see the Home Office web site section on domestic violence: www.homeoffice.gov.uk/crime/domesticviolence/index.html. This links to all the briefing papers reviewing evidence on domestic violence. Also see Cleaver, Unell and Aldgate (1999) and Hester, Pearson and Harwin (2000).

YOUTH JUSTICE SERVICES

The statutory duty of the youth justice system is to prevent offending. Youth offending teams (YOTs) have a vital role in both preventing offending in the first place and responding to young people who have offended (Home Office, Department for Constitutional Affairs and the Youth Justice Board, 2004). YOTs must also cooperate with the local authority to improve the well-being of children in their area and safeguard and promote their welfare (Children Act 2004, s 10 and s 11 respectively).

Inclusive approaches to working with parents when children and young people have developed anti-social or offending behaviour face the immediate obstacle that there is a culture of blaming parents for their children's behaviour (Haines and Drakeford, 1998). Yet, troublesome children are among the most vulnerable groups of children in need, and among those most likely to experience abuse both within the family and outside it. Anti-social and offending behaviour is a common response to family difficulties, domestic violence and childhood abuse.

Moreover, studies of young offenders also found this group experience high levels of mental illness, self-harm, suicide attempts and substance abuse (Hagell, 2002). These are often linked with family pressures and parenting problems.

Problems in managing children's behaviour, and difficulties in accessing help with them, are among the main motivations for parents seeking help from practitioners (see, e.g., Gardner, 2003). Parents at the end of their tether over children's behaviour can resort to progressively harsher disciplinary tactics that place children at risk of harm. A recent report by the Audit Commission told 'James's Story', which it describes as

'not untypical' of young offenders at the 'heavy end'. It is 'a catalogue of errors and missed opportunities to provide help at times when it could have made a real difference'.

Audit Commission, 2004, p. 92, Paragraph 190

James's behaviour began to be problematic at home at the age of five. His mother told his school that she had problems managing him, but received no help. At age six it was clear that he had some difficulties with learning and school attendance. He was assessed but no extra help was provided. However some two years later … he was moved to a special school. Although it was apparent at the time that he was behaving oddly and was being neglected at home, no other action was taken.

Audit Commission, 2004, p. 92, Paragraph 191

Between the ages of 10 and 15, the Audit Commission report says that James had numerous cautions and court appearances for offences, including an arson attack on his school and some assaults. He rarely attended school and had several exclusions. There were assessments by several agencies, none of which led to any services being provided for James or his family. When he was put on an ISSP (Intensive supervision and surveillance programme) at age 13

only then did it become fully apparent that the family had multiple problems and a family assessment was made.

No social worker was allocated however. An allegation of abuse made by James led to a strategy meeting but there was no follow-up. By age 15, James was serving his second custodial sentence.

The Audit Commission, 2004, Appendix 6, pp. 115–117

James's story of repeated assessments with no service being provided is all too familiar in accounts of work with children in need, whether offenders or not. His early childhood predates the current structure of services and the introduction of multi-agency, multi-disciplinary YOTs.

The National Standards for Youth Justice Services (Youth Justice Board, 2004) include a requirement for a preventive strategy that addresses any difficulties between young people and their parents (Standard 1). Parenting orders introduced through the Crime and Disorder Act 1998 are intended to give an opportunity for constructive support to parents and can include parenting programmes.

For guidance on parenting contracts and orders, see Home Office *et al.* (2004).

POSSIBLE BARRIERS TO WORKING WITH PARENTS

When practitioners raise concerns about children's safety and welfare, most parents feel threatened and violated, depressed and worthless. Parents' main

fear is that they will lose their children, and many react very defensively towards practitioners (Cleaver and Freeman, 1995):

> I was frightened, you know, because I imagined them taking me kids off me for
> the way I was and things like that. Because I thought 'Well, if I'm not well and this
> is the way I am the social services are going to take me kids off me for the way
> I am'. So instead of bringing help in I was pushing them away because I was too
> frightened of it...
>
> > Pauline, 36, suffering from depression, quoted in Aldridge and Becker, 2003,
> > p. 49

The way parents react to practitioners, concerned about their children, is
affected by their past experience, their present situation and expectations of
what will happen (Cleaver and Freeman, 1995). For example, research shows
that two-thirds of families referred to social services for child protection concerns have had some prior contact with children's social services (Farmer and
Owen, 1995).

The experiences of some parents may result in their feeling so resentful
of interference and so determined to keep 'the authorities' at bay that they
threaten or use violence against practitioners who attempt to intervene and
carry out their statutory duties. When this happens, practitioners may be reluctant to pursue their enquiries and allow themselves to be forced out of the
picture by a parent's continued refusal to cooperate (Department of Health,
1991b; Cleaver, Wattam and Cawson, 1998). If feeling intimidated, practitioners may also fear expressing to colleagues and other agencies their views about,
and experience of, parents (Chief Inspector of Social Services et al., 2002).

Practitioners must be guided by the following principle:

> The child should be seen ... and kept in focus throughout work with the child and
> family.
>
> > HM Government, 2006a, Paragraph 5.4

May-Chahal and Coleman (2003) point out the

> contradictions inherent in any situation where the children are assumed to be 'safe
> enough' in households where adults are deemed to pose a serious risk to staff.
>
> > p. 131

It is crucial for the child's safety that staff discuss their fears with their managers and that agencies offer adequate support to practitioners in contact with
violent families. Staff must be able to rely on backup from colleagues or the
police when necessary.

Lack of knowledge about minority communities can also be a barrier to understanding what is happening to the children. Communication can be eased
when parents have the opportunity to communicate in the language of their
choice. For example, although a family recently arrived in the United Kingdom
may have a sufficient grasp of the English language for everyday exchanges,
the opportunity to discuss sensitive and complex issues in their own language

may result in clearer and more accurate communication. This is particularly relevant for children and families who are asylum seekers. These families may have had frightening experiences of government agencies in their home countries which leave them afraid of becoming involved with statutory services.

Finally, the life experiences of many parents with learning disabilities cause them to feel particularly powerless. When practitioners ask about their parenting or discuss issues about their children, these parents tend to agree with everything that is said to them in an effort to please. This hampers practitioners' ability to assess children's needs and judge the extent to which parents will be able to follow through plans to ensure children's safety and welfare. Practitioners should set aside additional time and consider calling upon colleagues who have the expertise of working with adults with learning disabilities.

For further information on supporting parents, see Cleaver, Unell and Aldgate (1999), Ghate and Hazel (2002), May-Chahal and Coleman (2003) and Quinton (2004).

For further information on working with parents with learning disabilities, see Cotson *et al.* (2001), Cleaver and Nicholson (2007), Cm 5086 (2003), Morris (2003) and James (2004).

PRINCIPLES FOR WORKING WITH PARENTS

Fifteen essential principles for working in partnership
- Treat all family members as you would wish to be treated, with dignity and respect.
- Ensure that family members know that the child's safety and welfare must be given first priority.
- Take care not to infringe privacy.
- Be clear with yourself and with family members about your power to intervene.
- Be aware of the effects on family members of the power you have as a professional.
- Respect confidentiality.
- Listen to the concerns of the children and their families.
- Learn about and consider children within their family relationships and communities.
- Consider the strengths and potential of family members.
- Ensure that children, families and other carers know their responsibilities and rights.
- Use plain, jargon-free language appropriate to the age and culture of each person.
- Be open and honest about your concerns and responsibilities.

- Allow children and families time to take in and understand concerns and processes.
- Take care to distinguish between personal feelings, values, prejudices and beliefs, and professional roles and responsibilities.
- If a mistake or misinterpretation has been made, or you are unable to keep to an agreement, provide an explanation.

Department of Health, 1995b, p. 14, Paragraph 2.20

The above principles for working with parents in the context of safeguarding and promoting the welfare of children were set out in *The Challenge of Partnership* (Social Services Inspectorate, 1995) and are integral to *Working Together to Safeguard Children* (HM Government, 2006a). These principles can be generalised to apply to all practitioners and agencies working with children and families.

Further principles that apply at all stages of working with parents were added in the court judgement (Re, 2002):

- Notify parents as soon as possible of any problem or potential criticism, of what they are expected to do differently and how they can achieve that.
- Keep clear, accurate and factual notes of any concerns and relevant follow-up conversations, actions and meetings.
- Give parents access to key documents and meetings or have very clear reasons as to why this is not possible.

These principles of working with parents reflect best practice and should apply irrespective of what brings children and their parents in contact with practitioners.

CONCLUSION

All practitioners, regardless of the context in which they work, must always have regard to safeguarding and promoting the welfare of the children with whom they are working. Doing this successfully is dependent on engaging with parents. Working with parents when there are concerns about a child is essential because the majority want the best for their children, have greater knowledge about the background and current events that have given rise to the concern, and have important insights into how problems can best be resolved.

Parents, however, rarely instigate discussions with practitioners about their child's safety or welfare, or welcome practitioners who approach them with such concerns. This reluctance to engage with children's social care practitioners when there are concerns about children is because many parents fear discussions will spiral out of their control and result in them losing their children. To overcome these fears, practitioners should provide clear explanations about their concerns, be open and honest, and treat parents with respect. When practitioners take such an approach, parents feel less alienated and more in control, and as a result are more likely to work with practitioners to safeguard and promote the welfare of their children.

REFERENCES

Adoption and Children Act 2002 (Commencement No. 7) Order 2004, http://www. legislation.hmso.gov.uk/si/si2004/20043203.htm (accessed 3 September 2008).

Aldridge, J. and Becker, S. (2003) *Children Caring for Parents with Mental Illness: Perspectives of Young Carers, Parents and Professionals*, Policy Press, Bristol.

ATD Fourth World (1996) *Talk With Us, Not At Us: How to Develop Partnerships Between Families in Poverty and Professionals*, Fourth World, Paris, www.atd-uk. org (accessed 3 September 2008).

Audit Commission (2004) *Youth Justice 2004: A Review of the Reformed Youth Justice System*, Audit Commission, London, http://www.audit-commission.gov.uk/reports/NATIONAL-REPORT.asp?CategoryID=&ProdID=7C75C6C3-DFAE-472d-A820-262DD49580BF (accessed 3 September 2008).

Baginsky, M. (2000) *Child Protection and Education*, NSPCC, London.

Barn, R., Ladino, C. and Rogers, B. (2005) *Parenting in Multi-Racial Britain*, Joseph Rowntree Foundation, York.

Birchall, E. and Hallett, C. (1995) *Working Together in Child Protection*, HMSO, London.

Browne, K., Hamilton, C., Heggarty, J. and Blissett, J. (2000) Identifying need and protecting children through community nurse home visits. *Representing Children*, **13** (2), 111–23.

Bullock, R., Gooch, D. and Little, M. (1998) *Children Going Home: The Re-Unification of Families* (*Dartington Social Research Series*), Ashgate, Aldershot.

Butt, J. and Box, L. (1998) *Family Centred: A Study of the Use of Family Centres by Black Families*, Race Equality Unit, London.

Cawson, P., Wattam, C., Brooker, S. and Kelly, G. (2000) *Child Maltreatment in the United Kingdom: A Study of the Prevalence of Child Abuse and Neglect*, NSPCC, London.

Chief Inspector of Social Services, Director for Health Improvement, Commission for Health Improvement, Her Majesty's Chief Inspector of Constabulary, Her Majesty's Chief Inspector of the Crown Prosecution Service, Her Majesty's Chief Inspector of the Magistrates' Courts Service, Her Majesty's Chief Inspector of Schools, Her Majesty's Chief Inspector of Prisons and Her Majesty's Chief Inspector of Probation (2002) *Safeguarding Children: A Joint Chief Inspectors' Report on Arrangements to Safeguard Children*, Department of Health, London, http://www.hmica.gov.uk/files/safeguarding_children_report.pdf (accessed 3 September 2008).

Children Act 1989, Chapter 41, HMSO, London, http://www.hmso.gov.uk/acts/acts1989/Ukpga_19890041_en_1.htm (accessed 3 September 2008).

Children Act 2004, Chapter 31, HMSO, London, http://www.hmso.gov.uk/acts/acts2004/20040031.htm (accessed 3 September 2008).

Cleaver, H. (2000) *Fostering Family Contact. Studies in Evaluating the Children Act 1989*, The Stationery Office, London.

Cleaver, H. and Freeman, P. (1995) *Parental Perspectives in Cases of Suspected Child Abuse*, HMSO, London.

Cleaver, H. and Nicholson, D. (2007) *Children Living with Learning Disabled Parents*, Jessica Kingsley, London.

Cleaver, H., Unell, I. and Aldgate, J. (1999) *Children's Needs – Parenting Capacity: The Impact of Parental Mental Illness, Problem Alcohol and Drug Use, and Domestic Violence on Children's Development*, The Stationery Office, London.

Cleaver, H., Walker, S. and Meadows, P. (2004) *Assessing Children's Needs and Circumstances: The Impact of the Assessment Framework*, Jessica Kingsley, London.

Cleaver, H., Wattam, C. and Cawson, P. (1998) *Assessing Risk in Child Protection*, NSPCC, London.

Cm 5086 (2003) *Valuing People: A New Strategy for Learning Disability for the 21st Century*, The Stationery Office, London, http://www.archive.official-documents. co.uk/document/cm50/5086/5086.htm; http://www.dh.gov.uk/PolicyAndGuidance/ HealthAndSocialCareTopics/LearningDisabilities/LearningDisabilityPublications/ fs/en?CONTENT_ID=4032080&chk=w%2Bvo48 (accessed 3 September 2008).

Cm 5730 (2003) *The Victoria Climbié Inquiry. Report of an Inquiry by Lord Laming*, The Stationery Office, London, http://www.victoria-climbie-inquiry.org.uk/ finreport/finreport.htm (accessed 3 September 2008).

Cm 5860 (2003) *Every Child Matters*, The Stationery Office, London, http://www. everychildmatters.gov.uk/_content/documents/EveryChildMatters.pdf (accessed 3 September 2008).

Cotson, D., Friend, J., Hollins, S. and James, H. (2001) Implementing the framework for the assessment of children in need and their families when the parent has a learning disability, in *The Child's World: Assessing Children in Need* (ed. J. Horwath), Jessica Kingsley, London.

Council of Europe (1950) *European Convention for the Protection of Human Rights and Fundamental Freedoms*, Council of Europe, Rome, http://conventions.coe.int/ treaty/Commun/QueVoulezVous.asp?NT=005&CL=ENG (accessed 3 September 2008).

Crime and Disorder Act 1998, Chapter 37, HMSO, London, http://www.legislation. hmso.gov.uk/acts/acts1998/19980037.htm (accessed 3 September 2008).

Department of Health (1991a) *The Children Act 1989: Guidance and Regulations. Volume 3: Family Placement*, HMSO, London.

Department of Health (1991b) *Child Abuse: A Study of Inquiry Reports 1980–1989*, HMSO, London.

Department of Health (1995a) *Child Protection: Messages from Research*, HMSO, London.

Department of Health (1995b) *The Challenge of Partnership in Child Protection: Practice Guide*, HMSO, London.

Department of Health (2002) *The Integrated Children's System: Working with Children in Need and Their Families* (consultation document), Department of Health, London, http://www.everychildmatters.gov.uk/socialcare/ics/ (accessed 3 September 2008).

Department of Health (2004) *The Chief Nursing Officer's Review of the Nursing, Midwifery and Health Visiting Contribution to Vulnerable Children and Young People*, Department of Health, London, http://www.dh.gov.uk/PublicationsAnd Statistics/Publications/PublicationsPolicyAndGuidance/PublicationsPolicyAnd GuidanceArticle/fs/en?CONTENT_ID=4086949&chk=4jYqAb (accessed 3 September 2008).

Department of Health and Department for Education and Skills (2004a) *The National Service Framework for Children, Young People and Maternity Services: Core Standards*, Department of Health, London, http://www.dh.gov.uk/Publications AndStatistics/Publications/PublicationsPolicyAndGuidance/PublicationsPolicyAnd GuidanceArticle/fs/en?CONTENT_ID=4089099&chk=VBBAQJ (accessed 3 September 2008).

Department of Health and Department for Education and Skills (2004b) *The National Service Framework for Children, Young People and Maternity Services: Key Issues for Primary Care*, Department of Health, London, http://www.dh.gov.uk/Publica tionsAndStatistics/Publications/PublicationsPolicyAndGuidance/PublicationsPolicy AndGuidanceArticle/fs/en?CONTENT_ID=4089113&chk=OK6NXz (accessed 3 September 2008).

Department of Health and Department for Education and Skills (2004c) *National Service Framework for Children, Young People and Maternity Services: Standard 8: Disabled Children and Young People and Those with Complex Health Needs*, Department of Health, London, http://www.dh.gov.uk/en/Publicationsandstatistics/ Publications/PublicationsPolicyAndGuidance/DH_4089112 (accessed 3 September 2008).

Department of Health and Department for Education and Skills (2004d) *National Service Framework for Children, Young People and Maternity Services: for Parents*, Department of Health, London, http://www.dh.gov.uk/en/Publications andstatistics/Publications/PublicationsPolicyAndGuidance/DH_4089121 (accessed 3 September 2008).

Department of Health, Department for Education and Employment, and Home Office (2000) *Framework for the Assessment of Children in Need and Their Families*, The Stationery Office, London, http://www.dh.gov.uk/en/Publicationsand statistics/Publications/PublicationsPolicyAndGuidance/DH_4003256; http://www. dh.gov.uk/assetRoot/04/01/44/30/04014430.pdf (accessed 3 September 2008).

Douglas, J., Browne, K., Hamilton-Giachritsis, C. and Hegarty, J. (2006) *A Community Health Approach to the Assessment of Infants and Their Parents*, John Wiley & Sons, Ltd, Chichester.

Dutt, R. and Phillips, M. (Department of Health) (2000) Assessing black children in need and their families, in *Assessing Children in Need and their Families: Practice Guidance*, The Stationery Office, London, http://www.dh.gov.uk/assetRoot/ 04/07/93/83/04079383.pdf (accessed 3 September 2008).

Education Act 2002, Chapter 32, HMSO, London, http://www.hmso.gov.uk/acts/acts 2002/20020032.htm (accessed 3 September 2008).

Evans, K. (2004) One family's fight. *Community Care* (1522), 42–43.

Farmer, E. and Owen, M. (1995) *Child Protection Practice: Private Risks and Public Remedies*, HMSO, London.

Gardner, R. (2003) *Supporting Families: Child Protection in the Community*, John Wiley & Sons, Ltd, Chichester.

Ghate, D. and Hazel, N. (2002) *Parenting in Poor Environments: Stress, Support and Coping*, Jessica Kingsley, London.

Hagell, A. (2002) *The Mental Health of Young Offenders*, The Mental Health Foundation, London.

Haines, K. and Drakeford, M. (1998) *Young People and Youth Justice*, Macmillan, London.

Hanmer, J. and Griffiths, S. (2000) *Reducing Domestic Violence ... What Works? Policing Domestic Violence*, Home Office, London, http://www.homeoffice.gov.uk/rds/prgpdfs/poldv.pdf (accessed 3 September 2008).

Henricson, C. (2003) *Government and Parenting: Is There a Case for a Policy Review and a Parents' Code?* National Family and Parenting Institute, London.

HM Government (2006a) *Working Together to Safeguard Children: A Guide to Inter-Agency Working to Safeguard and Promote the Welfare of Children*, The Stationery Office, London, http://www.everychildmatters.gov.uk/socialcare/safeguarding/workingtogether/ (accessed 3 September 2008).

HM Government (2006b) *Common Assessment Framework for Children and Young People: Managers' Guide*, Department for Education and Skills, London, http://www.everychildmatters.gov.uk/resources-and-practice/IG00063/ (accessed 3 September 2008).

HM Government (2006c) *Common Assessment Framework for Children and Young People: Practitioners' Guide*, Department for Education and Skills, London, http://www.everychildmatters.gov.uk/resources-and-practice/IG00063/ (accessed 3 September 2008).

HM Government (2006d) *What To Do If You're Worried A Child Is Being Abused*, Department for Education and Skills, London, http://www.everychildmatters.gov.uk/socialcare/safeguarding (accessed 3 September 2008).

Her Majesty's Treasury, Department for Education and Skills, Department for Work and Pensions and DTI (2004) *Choice for Parents, the Best Start for Children: A Ten Year Strategy for Child Care*, The Stationery Office, London, http://www.everychildmatters.gov.uk/earlyyears/tenyearstrategy/ (accessed 3 September 2008).

Hester, M., Pearson, C. and Harwin, N. (2000) *Making an Impact: Children and Domestic Violence. A Reader*, Jessica Kingsley, London.

Hill, C. (2000) A paediatrician's perspective, in *Working with Parents: Learning from Other People's Experiences* (ed. A. Wheal), Russell House, Lyme Regis.

Home Office, Department for Constitutional Affairs and the Youth Justice Board (2004) *Parenting Contracts and Orders Guidance*, Home Office, London, http://www.crimereduction.homeoffice.gov.uk/youth/youth51.htm (accessed 3 September 2008).

Hyton, C. (1997) *Black Families' Survival Strategies: Ways of Coping*, Joseph Rowntree Foundation, York.

James, H. (2004) Promoting effective working with parents with learning disabilities. *Child Abuse Review*, **13** (1), 31–41.

Jones, D. (2001) The assessment of parental capacity, in *The Child's World* (ed. J. Horwath), Jessica Kingsley, London.

Keay, L. (2003) *Child Protection and Its Impact for Black Families Living in the UK*, Report of workshop based on handout by Ashok Chand, 6 November, Research in Practice, Dartington.

Lupton, C., North, N. and Khan, P. (2001) *Working Together or Pulling Apart? Child Protection and the NHS*, Policy Press, Bristol.

Masson, J., Harrison, C. and Pavlovic, A. (1997) *Working with Children and 'Lost' Parents: Putting Partnership into Practice*, York Publishing Services Ltd, York.

Masson, J., Harrison, C. and Pavlovic, A. (1999) *Lost and Found: Making and Remaking Working Partnerships with Parents of Children in the Care System*, Ashgate, Aldershot.

Masson, J., Winn Oakley, M. and McGovern, D. (2001) *Working in the Dark: The Use of Police Protection*, University of Warwick, Warwick.

May-Chahal, C. and Coleman, S. (2003) *Safeguarding Children and Young People*, Routledge in association with Community Care, London.

McGee, C. (2000) *Childhood Experiences of Domestic Violence*, Jessica Kingsley, London.

Morris, J. (2003) *The Right Support: Report on the Task Force on Supporting Disabled Adults in Their Parenting Role*, Joseph Rowntree Foundation, York.

Mullender, A. and Hague, G. (2000) *Reducing Domestic Violence . . . What Works? Women Survivors' Views*, Home Office, London, http://www.homeoffice.gov.uk/rds/prgpdfs/womsurv.pdf (accessed 3 September 2008).

National Working Group on Child Protection and Disability (2003) *'It Doesn't Happen to Disabled Children': Child Protection and Disabled Children*, NSPCC, London, http://www.nspcc.org.uk/inform/research/findings/itdoesnthappentodisabledchildren_wda48257.html (accessed 3 September 2008).

Quinton, D. (2004) *Supporting Parents: Messages from Research*, Jessica Kingsley, London.

Re, L. (Care Assessment: Fair Trial) (2002) EWHC 1379 (Fam) 2 Family Law Review 730, Family Division.

Rowsell, C. (2003) Domestic violence and children: making a difference in a meaningful way for women and children, in *Assessment in Child Care: Using and Developing Frameworks for Practice* (eds M. Calder and S. Hackett), Russell House, Lyme Regis.

Ryan, M. (2000) *Working with Fathers*, Radcliffe Medical Press, Oxon.

Social Services Inspectorate (1995) *The Challenge of Partnership in Child Protection: Practice Guide*, HMSO, London.

Social Services Inspectorate (2000) *Excellence Not Excuses: Inspection of Services for Ethnic Minority Children and Families*, Department of Health, London, http://www.dh.gov.uk/en/Publicationsandstatistics/Publications/PublicationsInspectionReports/DH_4009334 (accessed 3 September 2008).

Stevens, J. (2000) A teacher's perspective, in *Working with Parents: Learning from Other People's Experiences* (ed. A. Wheal) Russell House, Lyme Regis.

Thoburn, J., Chand, A. and Procter, J. (2004) *Child Welfare Services for Minority Ethnic Families: The Research Review*, Jessica Kingsley, London.

Thoburn, J., Lewis, A. and Shemmings, D. (1995) *Paternalism or Partnership? Family Involvement in the Child Protection Process*, HMSO, London.

Thoburn, J., Wilding, J. and Watson, J. (2000) *Family Support in Cases of Emotional Maltreatment and Neglect*, The Stationery Office, London.

Tunstill, J. and Aldgate, J. (2000) *Services for Children in Need: From Policy to Practice*, The Stationery Office, London.

Wheal, A. (ed.) (2000) *Working with Parents: Learning from Other People's Experiences*, Russell House, Lyme Regis.

Williamson, E. (2000) *Domestic Violence and Health: The Response of the Medical Profession*, Policy Press, Bristol.

Youth Justice Board (2004) *National Standards for Youth Justice Services*, Youth Justice Board for England and Wales, London, http://www.yjb.gov.uk/publications/scripts/prodView.asp?idproduct=155&eP (accessed 3 September 2008).

3 The Wider Family and Community

ANNA GUPTA
MEGAN MCNEILL-MCKINNELL

All of our lives are influenced by our relationships with our family and friends, the neighbourhood in which we live, as well as wider society. Some of these will have a positive effect on our lives; other influences will be negative and stressful. *The Framework for the Assessment of Children in Need and their Families* (Department of Health, Department for Education and Skills and Home Office, 2000) is based on the ecological model of human development, which recognises that the needs of the child cannot be met without considering the immediate and extended family, as well as the neighbourhood and society in which the child lives (Bronfenbrenner, 1979).

In this chapter, we consider the wider family, community and environmental factors in assessments and interventions with children in need, including those at risk of significant harm, highlighting protective as well as adverse factors.

CORE KNOWLEDGE

- Assessments should be based on an ecological approach, which considers the child within his or her immediate and extended family networks, the community in which he or she lives and wider societal influences.
- The involvement of relatives and close family friends should be considered when working with children in need. This involvement ranges from decisions about providing support for children and their parents to alternative placements for children unable to live with their parents for short or long periods of time.
- Poverty, social isolation, racism, poor housing, unemployment and living in deprived areas have a negative impact on both children's development and parenting capacity, and are central to many of the difficulties faced by children in need and their families. The aim of interventions should be to minimise the effects of adverse factors and develop strengths in a child's family

Safeguarding Children   Edited by Hedy Cleaver, Pat Cawson, Sarah Gorin and Steve Walker
Copyright © 2009 by John Wiley & Sons, Ltd

and wider environment, thereby seeking to promote the welfare of children and safeguard them from harm.

- Resilience-led practice provides a sound basis for intervention, which aims to promote self-esteem, a secure base and sense of belonging for children in need. Children and parents can benefit from relationships with professionals, which are based on mutual respect and uphold their dignity and enhance self-esteem.
- Workers should have an awareness of their own values and belief systems, and how prejudice and discrimination can influence their own and their agency's practices to the detriment of children and their families.

WIDER FAMILY NETWORKS

> You can take the child out of the family, but you cannot take the family out of the child.
>
> Gilligan, 1995, p. 60

The involvement of family members in a child's life is something that most people take for granted. Maintaining and strengthening supportive relationships with wider family networks is an important principle when working with children in need, including those at risk of significant harm. Most children have attachment relationships of greater and lesser emotional significance involving siblings, grandparents, aunts and uncles, cousins, family friends and neighbours (Trinke and Bartholomew, 1997). One of the most consistent findings in research on resilience is the protective influence of supportive and enduring relationships with a caring and committed adult outside of their immediate family (Rutter, 1990). Grandparents and other relatives may provide very important 'arenas of comfort' when home circumstances are difficult, and wider family relationships can contribute to a child's sense of belonging (Gilligan, 2000).

Every family is situated within a cultural and socio-economic environment that will influence how each member views the family and their role within it. Finding out who is important to the child and to the parents is the starting point for including family members in the safeguarding process (Department of Health, Department for Education and Skills and Home Office, 2000). Careful thought must be given at each stage of the process as to who should be included from the wider family. This is particularly important when working with families from minority ethnic backgrounds, whose cultural and familial values may put particular emphasis on wider family and kinship responsibility (Dwivedi, 2002).

CONSULTATION AND DECISION MAKING

There are different ways in which the wider family can be involved in making decisions and providing help to children and families involved with statutory and voluntary services. Wider family and friendship networks can provide useful information about a child and his or her needs, as they will generally have intimate and in-depth knowledge of the specific child. Schools, health services and voluntary agencies may hold information about wider family members who could be consulted, and staff from these sectors may have established a rapport and could encourage relatives to become involved. Wider family members, friends or neighbours may refer a child to social services because they have concerns. In their study on the implementation of the *Framework for the Assessment of Children in Need and their Families*, Cleaver, Walker and Meadows (2004) found that cases referred by non-professionals were less likely to progress to an assessment, and they advised that these referrals should be given equal weighting to referrals from professionals. The nature of wider family involvement must take account of the wishes and feelings of children and parents. However, careful and sensitive consultation with members of the wider family, mindful of confidentiality and data protection issues, is usually possible. At the analysis stage of an assessment, the professional(s) must undertake the difficult task of weighing up conflicting formation and views (Department of Health, Department for Education and Skills and Home Office, 2000).

One method of engaging the wider family in decision-making processes about children in need is the use of a family group conference (FGC). An FGC is a forum for empowering and facilitating families to make their own decisions and plans for meeting the needs of the children. FGCs can be used in a range of cases, including child protection, family support and youth justice. In their review of the research, Lupton and Nixon (1999) concluded that on the whole professionals and family members alike consider that the process is considerably more enabling of effective family participation, including children and young people, than traditional decision-making processes. The benefits of this process for the child will often depend on the commitment of professionals, as well as family members, to providing the support outlined in the agreed plan (Marsh and Crow, 1998).

SUPPORT

> Child-focused family support is about supporting children's social, psychological and educational development. It is about supporting their belonging to family, school and neighbourhood.
>
> Gilligan, 2000, p. 13

The child's wider family can be a key component of a family support package that also includes statutory and voluntary sector services. Support can take many forms, and can be categorised as emotional support, information and advice, and practical help (Jack, 2000). Relatives and friends may be a source of emotional support for children and parents, and this ought to be considered when planning for their involvement in high-anxiety meetings such as child protection conferences, looked after children reviews and court hearings. In some cases, relatives and friends become skilled supporters, helping parents and children express their views and know their rights. In this way, the emotional support overlaps with an information and advice role, and could lead to the relative acting as an advocate. Training and support for relative advocates is sometimes available in the voluntary sector, and should ideally be endorsed by children's social care (Lindley and Richards, 2002).

In their study of parental stresses, support and coping, Ghate and Hazel (2002) found a significant variation in the amount and type of help received by parents. Yet, in terms of coping with parenting, it seemed that feeling supported was more important than the amount of help provided. Informal support provided by family and friends can be problematic, and the authors found that parents wanted support that left them in control and not expected to 'return the favour'. In a review of research studies on supporting parents, Quinton (2004) found that parents of disabled children were less likely to be able to receive normal day-to-day support, like babysitting or taking children out, from their families and friends. A study on the experiences of disabled parents (Olsen and Clarke, 2003) found that some services made assumptions about the capacity of the informal network to take on the burden of caring without adequately assessing whether this was possible. Practical support from relatives does not always come free of charge, but it can offer the best solution for all family members. Financial incentives can assist in the mobilising of support from family and friends who may themselves be stretched practically and emotionally (Quinton, 2004).

Support for parents is discussed in more detail in Chapter 2.

Ahmed live with his parents and siblings. The family is Muslim and speaks Arabic. Ahmed has a severe physical impairment and requires assistance with all daily activities and personal care. Ahmed's school made a referral to children's social care, with the consent of Ahmed and his parents, because Ahmed's hygiene was poor and his mother appeared exhausted.

The social worker interviewed the family with an interpreter. Domiciliary care and respite were offered but the family refused. They did not want a stranger in the home, and also stated that any carer must be Muslim.

The social worker discussed the situation with his manager. They agreed to ask the family if any relatives could help with Ahmed's care and offer respite. Children's social care would assess and train the family member and, jointly with the Primary Care Trust, pay them as a carer. One of Ahmed's aunts was suggested as a carer and a package of support begun. After a few months, Ahmed's personal care significantly improved, and his mother reported that she was less tired. Ahmed said he likes his aunt as she is fun and much younger than his parents.

PLACEMENT

Where children cannot live with their parents, a principle underpinning the Children Act 1989 is that they should be placed with wider family or friends as long as this is consistent with their welfare (Department of Health, 1991). A number of research studies have found that kinship care placements are more stable than non-relative foster care, and that generally the outcomes are favourable for young people. Child placements with relatives and friends can offer greater continuity and coherence in relationships and a sense of belonging than other non-family placements (Flynn, 2000; Broad, Hayes and Rushforth, 2001; Harwin *et al.*, 2001). Kinship care placements are usually valued by children and young people and by their relative carers:

> I love to know that I belong to somebody, I'm loved by people and it's good to know that I've got somewhere to come after school that I can call home.
> Young person living with relatives, in Broad, Hayes and Rushforth, 2001, p. 4

A placement with relatives can be a private arrangement by parents, or it can be supported by children's social care. A placement with wider family might only be temporary, for example while a parent is in hospital, but it can also be a permanent substitute placement for children who cannot be cared for by their parents. As in all cases, individual assessment of the child and family circumstances is necessary to ensure that a kinship care placement is the best option. Effective emotional, practical and financial support services are crucial to the success of many placements with family and friends, particularly for grandparents living on pensions with no capacity to increase their incomes and who have to cope emotionally with parenthood and the ageing process (Richards, 2001). A kinship care placement arranged and supported by children's social care entitles the caring relative to support and training, and to financial assistance at the same level as foster carers (RL and others v Manchester CC, 2001; Family Rights Group, 2003).

Rebecca was a new mother with a 1-month-old baby. She had separated from the baby's father. Rebecca had a long history of mental illness with occasional hospital stays, sometimes lasting 2 months or more. The baby was accommodated in foster care until Rebecca and the baby could begin an assessment at a mother and baby unit.

Following the assessment, children's social care remained concerned about the risk of Rebecca having further hospital admissions. Rebecca discussed the situation with her community mental health team, social worker and her wider family. They came up with the following plan:

- Rebecca's grandmother, who had arrived recently from overseas, would move in and live with Rebecca for 2 years (possibly longer) and would be assessed by children's social care as a joint carer for the baby.

- When her grandmother's visa expired, Rebecca's brother and sister would support Rebecca and care for the baby should Rebecca have any further hospital admissions.

Children's social care supported the plan, and agreed to fund Rebecca's grandmother as a kinship carer.

For discussion of safeguarding in private foster care and of children living away from home, see Chapter 4.

For further discussion of planning and decision making for children's long-term safety and welfare, see Chapter 9.

COMMUNITY AND ENVIRONMENTAL INFLUENCES

CHILDREN'S DEVELOPMENT

Any assessment and intervention with children must consider the impact of community and environmental influences on children's development and parenting capacity, and strive to promote strengths whilst reducing the impact of adversity. Different practitioners will be able to provide information about a child and his or her family's strengths and difficulties, as well offering services aimed at safeguarding and promoting the child's welfare.

There is clear evidence that chronic poverty, social isolation, racism and the problems associated with living in disadvantaged areas, such as high crime, poor housing, child care, transport and education services, and limited employment opportunities, are at the root of the difficulties faced by many children in need and their families (Jack and Gill, 2003). These adverse environmental factors can impact on children's development in varied and complex ways. These are some examples:

- Children from poorer families are more likely to be excluded from school, leave school early and have fewer or no qualifications (Bradshaw, 2001).
- Harassment and bullying blights the school experience for many children. A ChildLine study (1996) found that black and minority ethnic children in Britain experienced high levels of racial harassment, which affected many children's self-esteem and confidence.
- Having generally positive peer relationships, and specifically a close friendship, is a protective factor associated with the promotion of resilience (Cleaver, Unell and Aldgate, 1999; Daniel and Wassell, 2002). A school or community environment that does not facilitate the fullest participation for children with disabilities can restrict their ability to develop positive peer relationships and self-esteem.

- Communities where children feel threatened, frightened and unvalued can have a negative impact on children's development by directly affecting their physical development and mental health (Jack and Gill, 2003).

An understanding of the concept of resilience is particularly useful when working with vulnerable children; the aim of intervention being to promote protective factors that help children develop resilience whilst working to minimise the adverse stress factors that can impair children's health and development. Resilience is a concept which crosses cultural boundaries and can be understood as 'normal development under difficult conditions' (Fonagy *et al.,* 1994, p. 231). Resilience factors operate on the dimensions of the individual, the family and the external environment. In their review of the research, Newman and Blackburn (2003, p. 5) concluded that 'resilience-promoting factors remain fairly consistent, with supportive families, positive peer relationships, external networks and the opportunity to develop self-esteem and efficacy through valued social roles being of particular importance.'

The resilience literature offers a framework for considering interventions, which can minimise or cushion children from the negative factors in their life. There is evidence to suggest that just as multiple adversities can harm children's development, there is a cumulative, positive effect of protective factors. Some protective factors will be about the individual child's characteristics, for example good intellectual functioning, and some as a result of family functioning, such as secure attachment relationships. Other protective factors relate to the context of their lives outside of the family (Werner, 1990; Gilligan, 2001). Child welfare practitioners have a crucial role to play and need to recognise themselves as a potential source of support. A committed mentor or other person outside of the family is particularly important for a child with difficult home circumstances. However,

> Caregivers, teachers and social workers should remember that the detail of what they do counts. The rituals, the smiles, the interest in little things, the daily routines, the talents they nurture, the interests they stimulate, the hobbies they encourage, the friendships they support, the sibling ties they preserve make a difference. All of these little things may foster in a child the vital senses of belonging, of mattering, of 'counting'. All of these little things we do, these details, may prove decisive turning points in a young person's developmental pathway.
>
> Gilligan, 2000, p. 18

These ideas are relevant for children of all ages, and some examples of ways community resources can be protective factors include

- family centres which work directly with children, as well as support vulnerable parents (Tunstill, Hughes and Aldgate, 2006);
- creating inclusive environments in schools, including well planned and resourced, school-based social work services (Pritchard and Williams, 2001);
- encouraging positive school experiences and achievements by seeking to identify children's strengths even if they are not directly related to a formal curriculum (Newman and Blackburn, 2003);

- participation in a range of extra-curricular activities that promote self-esteem, including open access youth clubs and subsidised holidays (Holman, 2000);
- provision of opportunities to develop both problem-solving abilities and pro-social activities, for example mentoring schemes and voluntary activities for teenagers (Newman and Blackburn, 2003).

PARENTING CAPACITY

When assessing children's needs, consideration should also be given to how adverse environmental factors can impact on a parent's functioning. Numerous research studies about families involved with child protection services have indicated that many, across the range of ethnic groups, share the common experiences of a low income, housing difficulties and social isolation. Apart from a small proportion of exceptions, all these parents want what is best for their children (Department of Health, 1995, 2001).

Poverty and other forms of social exclusion can affect parents' ability to care for their children in various ways. For example, Ghate and Hazel's (2002) study indicates that parents in poor environments are three times more likely to experience depression; long-term physical health problems also affect the lives of poor people more than other groups in society. A Joseph Rowntree funded study found that about 33% of British children go without at least one of the things they need, like three meals a day, toys, out-of-school activities or adequate clothing. Eighteen per cent of children go without two or more items or activities defined as necessities by the majority of the population (Gordon, 2000). 'Social capital', that is, the wide range of community-level interactions, both informal and formal, is important in fostering a collective sense of trust and mutual respect, thereby creating environments conducive to promoting children's development. Social capital, however, can be seriously undermined by poverty, inequalities, divisions and exclusion, which can militate against open and reciprocal interactions on which social cohesion thrives (Jack and Jordon, 1999). Living in a disadvantaged area contributes additional stresses to parenting, independent of individual and family factors:

Parenting in poor environments is a more 'risky' business than parenting elsewhere, and it gets riskier the poorer the area.

Ghate and Hazel, 2002, p. 101

A group of parents living in poverty, and who have had experience of social services, identified the following ways in which poverty can affect family life:

- low self-esteem – if you are struggling you feel worthless and think others have a low opinion of you and your children;
- depression – a reaction to stress and feelings of hopelessness;
- isolation – less access to a social life;

- being compared with others – 'other families survive on the same money, it must be your problem';
- being judged on what you have or how your home looks;
- living in fear – of your children being removed;
- fear of getting deeper into poverty and debt;
- no respite from problems – no holidays;
- lack of choice of schools, neighbourhood – no escape;
- not meeting normal expectations as defined by wider society;
- not being cared about – being blamed;
- never being 'good enough' in some professionals' eyes;
- concern about children being denied life chances or opportunities from an early stage;
- your children not having what other children at school have, and getting angry with you for this;
- no treats for yourself and your children.

A conclusion from this group was that 'poverty is not just about lack of money, but also about dignity and self-respect for parents and children'.

Some of the ways that families suggested social workers and other child welfare practitioners could make a difference included

- demonstrating an understanding that neglect can be created by society as well as individuals;
- recognising that people do not want handouts – they want to help themselves;
- respecting people enough to explain things;
- listening to what families think would help them;
- recognising other sources of powerlessness or oppression, for example, racism and disability;
- treating people with courtesy and respect – being honest and open, offering a human touch – 'don't be a robot' just carrying out procedures or form filling;
- not offering people in poverty a poor service because you think they are not in a position to challenge you;
- recognising and developing people's strengths and aspirations – what they have done to survive and what they want for the future (ATD Fourth World, 2005).

SHAPING COMMUNITY SERVICES TO MEET FAMILIES' NEEDS

Many parents living in poor environments will be relatively well supported by family and friends. However, some groups – such as some minority ethnic families, those with current problems and the poorest families – may have more restricted social networks. Many receive support from semi-formal and formal services, but others are missing out. Lack of knowledge about services is one reason. In Ghate and Hazel's (2002) study, 13% of respondents were unaware of the universal health visiting service. In their study on family support for South Asian communities, Qureshi, Berridge and Wenman (2000) found a low level of family support services being provided for South Asian families. One woman explains a reason for this:

> There is nothing different about Asians, we love our children same as other people do, we want the best for them. But we also know that some people have problems with their children, all communities have similar things happen, but the only difference I can see is that some of us [Asian community] don't know where to turn for help.
>
> Qureshi, Berridge and Wenman, 2000, p. 3

Practitioners' assumptions about a family, including assumptions about their informal support networks, their knowledge of local services, and the things they would find helpful, can seriously affect the usefulness and accessibility of community resources (Chahal, 2004). This applies both to resources for people with specific situations, such as disability or lone parenthood, and to general resources for the whole community such as educational, recreational and play facilities. Penn and Gough (2002) describe the way in which practitioners' lack of understanding about family resources and lack of knowledge about local services other than those offered by their own agency or department have an impact on families. Local services that could have offered parents support to relieve stress, promote children's development, enrich children and parents' quality of life, and overcome economic disadvantage were not used, either because parents were unaware of the services' existence or because families were given no help to overcome obstacles to access them. The obstacles were often practical or economic such as the availability of affordable transport, the need for help with claiming financial entitlements or obtaining equipment.

Quinton's (2004) review of the research on supporting parents emphasises the importance of recognising that central to effective support, whether informal, semi-formal or formal, is a good relationship based on respect and partnership. Effective support should also be seen as a process, with services starting well and being aware of and responsive to changing needs. Quinton's review (2004, p. 131) includes a section on parenting and support in the context of disability.

Messages from the studies on disability include

- parents with disabled children require their own physical and mental health needs to be addressed;
- disabled parents should have their needs as parents recognised;
- services should be especially careful about providing emotional support;
- provision of short breaks should be flexible and appropriate;
- support should include paying attention to material disadvantage and employment opportunities.

In Chapter 2, there is further discussion of what families in general find are effective community support services. Here is a summary of the messages from recent studies:

- **Services that are accessible and responsive to community needs** – this is a particular issue for families of black and ethnic minority origin (Thoburn, Chand and Procter, 2005).
- **Services that are informative** – for example, on child development, managing problem behaviour, education or school resources.
- **Services that allow parents to feel in control** – making parents feel listened to and respected, and acknowledging that they are also experts in their own lives and in 'therapeutic alliances'.
- **Practical, useful services to meet parents' self-defined needs** – attention paid to parents' perceptions of what would be supportive for them, and raise their self-esteem and sense of self-efficacy.
- **Timely services** – for example, extending opening hours, reducing waiting lists, and being available in times of crisis.
- **A diverse range of services** – many families have multiple problems and therefore require well-coordinated, multi-agency provision.
- **Services that build on the existing strengths of parents and their communities** – services which value potential and strengthen community and social cohesion and integration.

                    Gilligan, 2000; Ghate and Hazel, 2002; Jack and Gill, 2003

WORKERS' VALUES AND BELIEF SYSTEMS

PREJUDICE AND DISCRIMINATION

Adults working with children should be aware of how prejudice and discrimination can influence their own and their agency's practices. A commitment to challenging discrimination and oppression is essential in order to safeguard and promote the welfare of all children. Research studies and inquiries into child deaths have identified how racism can affect practice in complex and contradictory ways to the detriment of the child's needs and rights, for example a lack of effective protective and support services, as well as harsher, more punitive responses. For example, the *Inquiry into the Death of Victoria Climbié* (Cm 5730, 2003) identified how a negative stereotype of African families led to the failure to identify a clearly physically and emotionally abusive relationship. Conversely, a study of families involved in court proceedings found that, in comparison to white families, a range of black and other minority ethnic families tended to become involved in care proceedings at an earlier stage and had less prior involvement with social services, a less troubled profile, and the children were more likely to be removed through emergency action (Hunt, Macleod and Thomas, 1999; Brophy, Jhutti-Johal and Owen, 2003).

POVERTY

Even though most families involved with social care are living in poverty, studies show that professionals' attitudes towards poverty and poor people are characterised by ambivalence, confusion and lack of awareness (Jack and Gill, 2003). The group of families living in poverty mentioned above developed the term 'povertyism' and gave the following examples:

- a lack of knowledge, understanding and appreciation of the impact of poverty on children and families – a poverty-blind approach. Poverty is seen as the norm;
- prejudices and preconceived ideas – 'you are irresponsible and need vouchers not cash'; 'if you were in care, you must be a bad person';
- poverty as a risk factor – being blamed for being in poverty and having difficulties – 'it must be your fault because other people cope on benefits';
- a system that can make people feel they don't matter, their perspectives and needs are not recognised, for example, having to wait three weeks when in a crisis; not listening to what families feel would help and support them.

DISABLED CHILDREN AND THEIR FAMILIES

Any assessment of the needs of disabled children and their families should be based on the social model of disability, which recognises disabling barriers within society, including attitudes and values which focus on weaknesses rather than strengths (Marchant and Jones, 2000). Kennedy and Wonnacott (2003, p. 191) suggest examples of how assessments can identify discrimination and oppression that could be experienced by disabled children, such as

- negative attitudes of professionals towards the disabled child;
- stereotyping of disabled children;
- greater vulnerability to abuse and lesser access to the child protection and criminal justice systems;
- exclusive education systems or low expectations;
- bullying within mainstream schooling;
- poor and fragmented service provision.

CONCLUSION

In this chapter, we have considered the influence of wider family, community and environmental factors on children's development and parents' ability to meet these needs. All professionals working with children should strive to provide services, which both safeguard children and promote strengths and protective factors within their family and wider environment. Positive interventions can occur on different levels, including organisational structures, access to supportive community resources and interpersonal relationships, which respect and value individual children and their families.

REFERENCES

ATD Fourth World (2005) *Getting the Right Trainers – Enabling Service Users to Train Social Work Students and Practitioners About the Realities of Family Poverty in the UK*, http://www.atd-uk.org/publications/Pub.htm#key (accessed 4 September 2008).

Bradshaw, J. (2001) *Poverty: The Outcomes for Children*, Family Policy Studies Centre, London.

Broad, B., Hayes, R. and Rushforth, C. (2001) *Kith and Kin: Kinship Care for Vulnerable Young People*, NCB and Joseph Rowntree Foundation, London.

Bronfenbrenner, U. (1979) *The Ecology of Human Development: Experiments by Nature and Design*, Harvard University Press, Cambridge, MA.

Brophy, J., Jhutti-Johal, J. and Owen, C. (2003) *Significant Harm: Child Protection Litigation in a Multi-Cultural Setting*, Department for Constitutional Affairs, London.

Chahal, K. (2004) *Experiencing Ethnicity: Discrimination and Service Provision*. Foundations 914, September 2004, Joseph Rowntree Foundation, York, http://www.jrf.org.uk/knowledge/findings/foundations/914.asp (accessed 4 September 2008).

ChildLine (1996) *Children at Crisis Point: A Study by ChildLine*, ChildLine, London.

Cleaver, H., Unell, I. and Aldgate, J. (1999) *Children's Needs – Parenting Capacity: The Impact of Parental Mental Illness, Problem Alcohol and Drug Use, and Domestic Violence on Children's Development*, The Stationery Office, London.

Cleaver, H., Walker, S. with Meadows, P. (2004) *Assessing Children's Needs and Circumstances: The Impact of the Assessment Framework*, Jessica Kingsley, London.

Cm 5730 (2003) *The Victoria Climbié Inquiry: Report of an Inquiry by Lord Laming*, The Stationery Office, London, http://www.victoria-climbie-inquiry.org.uk/index.htm (accessed 4 September 2008).

Daniel, B. and Wassell, S. (2002) *The School Years: Assessing and Promoting Resilience in Vulnerable Children 2*, Jessica Kingsley, London.

Department of Health (1991) *The Children Act 1989: Principles and Practice in Regulations and Guidance*, HMSO, London.

Department of Health (1995) *Child Protection Messages from Research*, HMSO, London.

Department of Health (2001) *The Children Act Now: Messages from Research*, The Stationery Office, London.

Department of Health, Department for Education and Skills and Home Office (2000) *Framework for the Assessment of Children in Need and Their Families*, The Stationery Office, London, http://www.dh.gov.uk/PublicationsAndStatistics/Publications/PublicationsPolicyAndGuidance/PublicationsPolicyAndGuidance Article/fs/en?CONTENT_ID=4003256&chk=Fss1ka (accessed 4 September 2008).

Dwivedi, K.N. (ed.) (2002) *Meeting the Needs of Ethnic Minority Children – Including Refugee, Black and Mixed Parentage Children: A Handbook for Professionals*, 2nd edn, Jessica Kingsley, London.

Family Rights Group (2003) *Together – The Family Group Conference Network Newsletter*, FRG, London.

Flynn, R. (2000) *Kinship Foster Care* (*NCB Highlight 179*), NCB, London.

Fonagy, P., Steele, M., Steele, H. *et al.* (1994) The theory and practice of resilience. *Journal of Child Psychology and Psychiatry*, **35** (2), 231–57.

Ghate, D. and Hazel, N. (2002) *Parenting in Poor Environments: Stress, Support and Coping*, Jessica Kingsley, London.

Gilligan, R. (1995) Family support in child welfare: realising the promise of the Child Care Act 1991, in *On Behalf of the Child: Professional Perspectives on the Child Care Act 1991* (eds H. Ferguson and P. Kenny), A and A Farmar, Dublin.

Gilligan, R. (2000) Family support: issues and prospects, in *Family Support: Direction from Diversity* (eds D. Canavan, P. Dolan and J. Pinkerton), Jessica Kingsley, London.

Gilligan, R. (2001) *Promoting Resilience: A Resource Guide on Working with Children in the Care System*, British Association for Adoption and Fostering, London.

Gordon, D. (2000) *Poverty and Social Exclusion in Britain*, Joseph Rowntree Foundation, York.

Harwin, J., Owen, M., Locke, R. and Forrester, D. (2001) *Making Care Orders Work: A Study of Care Plans and Their Implementation*, The Stationery Office, London.

Holman, B. (2000) *Kids at the Door Revisited*, Russell House, Dorset.

Hunt, J., MacLeod, A. and Thomas, C. (1999) *The Last Resort: Child Protection, the Courts and the 1989 Children Act*, The Stationery Office, London.

Jack, G. (2000) Ecological influences on parenting and child development. *British Journal of Social Work*, **30** (6), 703–20.

Jack, G. and Gill, O. (2003) *The Missing Side of the Triangle: Assessing the Importance of Family and Environmental Factors in the Lives of Children*, Barnardo's, Ilford, Essex.

Jack, G. and Jordon, B. (1999) Social capital and child welfare. *Children and Society*, **13**, 242–56.

Kennedy, M. and Wonnacott, J. (2003) Disabled children and the assessment framework, in *Assessment in Child Care: Using and Developing Frameworks for Practice* (eds M. Calder and S. Hackett), Russell House, Dorset.

Lindley, B. and Richards, M. (2002) *Protocol on Advice and Advocacy for Parents (Child Protection)*, Centre for Family Research, University of Cambridge.

Lupton, C. and Nixon, P. (1999) *Empowering Practice? A Critical Appraisal of the Family Group Conference Approach*, Policy Press, Bristol.

Marchant, R. and Jones, M. (Department of Health) (2000) Assessing the needs of disabled children and their families, in *Assessing Children in Need and Their Families: Practice Guidance*, The Stationery Office, London, http://www.dh.gov.uk/PublicationsAndStatistics/Publications/PublicationsPolicyAndGuidance/PublicationsPolicyAndGuidanceArticle/fs/en?CONTENT_ID=4006576&chk=M3Qrpp (accessed 4 September 2008).

Marsh, P. and Crow, G. (1998) *Family Group Conferences in Child Welfare*, Blackwell Science, Oxford.

Newman, T. and Blackburn, S. (2003) *Transitions in the Lives of Children and Young People: Resilience Factors* (*Interchange 78*), Scottish Executive, Education Department, Edinburgh.

Olsen, R. and Clarke, H. (2003) *Parenting and Disability: Disabled Parents' Experiences of Raising Children*, Policy Press, Bristol.

Penn, H. and Gough, D. (2002) The price of a loaf of bread. *Children and Society*, **16** (1), 17–32.

Pritchard, C. and Williams, R. (2001) A three-year comparative longitudinal study of a school-based social work family service to reduce truancy, delinquency and school exclusions. *Journal of Social Welfare and Family Law*, **23** (1), 23–43.

Quinton, D. (2004) *Supporting Parents: Messages from Research*, Jessica Kingsley, London.

Qureshi, T., Berridge, D. and Wenman, H. (2000) *Where to Turn? Family Support for South Asian Communities – A Case Study*, National Children's Bureau, London.

R (L and others) v. Manchester City Council and R (R and another) v. Manchester City Council, EWHC Admin 707, Family Law Review, January 2002.

Richards, A. (2001) *Second Time Around: A Survey of Grandparents Raising Their Grandchildren*, Family Rights Group, London.

Rutter, M. (1990) Psychosocial resilience and protective mechanisms, in *Risk and Protective Factors in the Development of Psychopathology* (eds J. Rolf, A. Masten, D. Cichetti, K. Nuechterlein and S. Weintraub), Cambridge University Press, Cambridge.

Thoburn, J., Chand, A. and Procter, J. (2005) *Child Welfare Services for Minority Ethnic Families: The Research Reviewed*, Jessica Kingsley, London.

Trinke, S. and Bartholomew, K. (1997) Attachment hierarchies in young adults. *Journal of Social and Personal Relationships*, **14** (5), 603–25.

Tunstill, J., Hughes, M. and Aldgate, J. (2006) *Family Support at the Centre: Family Centres, Services and Networks*, Jessica Kingsley, London.

Werner, E. (1990) Protective factors and individual resilience, in *Handbook of Early Childhood Intervention* (eds S. Meisels and J. Shonkoff), Cambridge University Press, Cambridge.

4 Children Living Away from Home

PAT CAWSON

This chapter is about safeguarding and promoting the welfare of children living away from their families: in foster care, residential care, at boarding school, in custody, in hospital and when children are missing and 'living rough' or exploited through trafficking or prostitution. Threats to children's safety and welfare that can result from the behaviour of other children, from self-harm, or from poor practice and misconduct by staff are discussed. What is known about effective practice in countering bullying, aggression and sexually harmful behaviour between children and in dealing with allegations or concerns about staff behaviour is presented. Finally, the safeguarding of 'missing' children who are not engaged with any of the systems for supporting children and families, or who are in the power of exploitative adults, is considered.

CORE KNOWLEDGE

- Children away from home are not inevitably more vulnerable to harm than other children. Vulnerability depends on the quality of the alternative care given.
- Quality of care in institutional or foster placements depends on the lead given by management and the standards maintained by staff. It is not an inevitable consequence of the type of placement.
- Safeguarding issues more often arise if children have experience of previous abuse or bullying; they cannot access help due to age, language, or disabilities that affect their mobility or communication; they display challenging behaviour, when adults may view them as untrustworthy and disbelieve them.
- Public inquiries provide lessons about the conditions that enable abusive staff or regimes to continue. While it is important not to be complacent about the standards of care from practitioners, recent evidence suggests that the most common risk of harm to children away from home is from other children. It is often easier to identify and deal with unacceptable staff behaviour than to confront abusive behaviour between children.

Safeguarding Children   Edited by Hedy Cleaver, Pat Cawson, Sarah Gorin and Steve Walker
Copyright © 2009 by John Wiley & Sons, Ltd

- Safeguarding children away from home is easier if they have contact with a trusted adult who knows what signs of distress to look out for and what to do about them. This is as important in fostering as in residential care.
- The children least protected live in an underworld of homeless 'street children', runaways, under-age prostitution, or child trafficking. In these children's lives, abuse, neglect and exploitation are normal daily experiences.

Because of the very different histories and functions of the various services for children cared for away from home, each has its own particular issues to address. Nevertheless, the issues that arise over practice in safeguarding children are often very similar, and research findings on what endangers or troubles children are also remarkably similar for all sectors. The issues are: safeguarding children from harm by peers, or from insensitive or abusive treatment by practitioners; safeguarding from harm by exploitative people visiting the service or in the locality; and ensuring that children living away from home have access to community services when needed.

Most of this chapter will be relevant to all foster care and residential (including custodial) settings. Some will also apply to children in non-residential group care, in day schools, childminding, nurseries, sports or youth work settings or to short absences from home at camps and holiday schemes. The primary focus of the chapter, however, is on children in the care of un-related adults for extended stays or considerable portions of their childhood, usually living with groups of unrelated young people.

A DIVERSE GROUP

The Children's Safeguards Review for England and Wales estimated that more than 200,000 children were away from their families for periods of 4 weeks or more in a typical year (Utting, 1997). More than half were in boarding schools. Being away from home for more than a few weeks is still, however, an unusual situation for a child. A recent survey of the childhood experiences of young people in the United Kingdom showed that 4% of the child population had spent some time at boarding school, 1% had spent part of their childhood in foster care and 1% had been in residential care (Cawson et al., 2000).

Children living away from home include the most economically and educationally privileged children in the population and the most socially excluded. Children may be in respite care for part of the week, or in boarding schools, returning home at weekends and during school holidays. Others may have little or no face-to-face contact with their families for years, because of the parents' difficulties, or because they attend boarding school and their parents live or work on the other side of the world. Most children looked after by local authorities are away from home for 1 year or less (Department for Education and

Skills, 2005a) but children in special schools or boarding schools may be away from home for most of the year from starting school until adulthood. All populations away from home include children of loving parents in close contact, and children who may have experienced years of abuse, neglect or disinterest from parents.

There have been major scandals of abuse in residential homes and schools, some high profile cases of abuse and homicide by foster carers and of abusive regimes in custody. As a result many new measures have been put in place to safeguard children. It is, however, very important not to become complacent. There are still safeguarding issues about which practitioners must be vigilant. Most practitioners, nevertheless, aim to give good care to children in their charge, even if they do not get it right all of the time.

RECENT DEVELOPMENTS IN SETTING AND MONITORING CARE STANDARDS

We have recently seen major change in the standards required for residential placements and in the arrangements for regulating and inspecting schools, foster homes, care homes, youth custody, hospitals and nursing homes of all kinds. A series of public inquiries and reviews, and research into the care of looked-after children have given a solid foundation for setting new standards for the social care sector (Utting, 1997; Kent, 1997; Department of Health, 1998; Waterhouse, 2000; National Assembly for Wales, 2002).

Major reports and guidance since 2000 covering issues on safeguarding children away from home

New inspection standards for boarding schools, special schools, children's homes fostering services and residential further education (FE) colleges can be found at www.ofsted.gov.uk.

A revised code of practice from the Department for Education and Skills for working with Special Educational Needs can be found at www.teachernet.gov.uk/docbank/index.cfm?id=3724.

Guidance from the government for practitioners on *What To Do If You're Worried A Child Is Being Abused* (HM Government, 2006a) can be found at www.everychildmatters.gov.uk/socialcare/safeguarding.

A review by the Department of Health and the Department for Education and Skills on the care of disabled children living away from home can be found at www.teachernet.gov.uk/docbank/index.cfm?id=6462.

A joint report on safeguarding children by the Chief Inspectors of all children's services can be found at www.dh.gov.uk/assetRoot/04/06/08/33/04060833.pdf.

Guidance from the Department of Education and Skills on *Safeguarding Children in Education* which addresses issues in boarding schools can be found at www.publications.teachernet.gov.uk/eOrderingDownload/DfES-0027-2004.pdf.

National Standards for Youth Justice can be found at www.yjb.gov.uk/Publications.

Two recent reports from the Joseph Rowntree Foundation summarise the progress made since the publication of the *Children's Safeguards Review*. Stuart and Baines (2004a) review policy and legislative changes across all settings where children live away from home. They also examine safeguards for two especially vulnerable groups: disabled children and children in prison, and review current knowledge about abusers (Stuart and Baines, 2004b).

For further reading on standards, see Department of Health (2002e), Association of Directors of Social Services *et al.* (2003) and Williams (2003).

For information on the prevalence of abuse in out of home care, see Sinclair and Gibbs (1998), Hobbs, Hobbs and Wynne (1999) and Paul and Cawson (2002).

The Care Standards Act 2000 sets out standards for all residential settings and for the foster care of children looked after by local authorities (see Department of Health, 2002c, 2002d, 2002e), and Ofsted now has responsibility for enforcing these standards. The Youth Justice Board has developed national standards for youth justice services (Youth Justice Board, 2004a). The Healthcare Commission (formerly the Commission for Health Care Improvement) is addressing the safeguarding of child patients in hospital (Commission for Health Care Improvement, 2004a, 2004b).

PRIVATE FOSTERING

Private fostering, where children are placed directly by parents, or by institutions such as independent schools, including language schools, is regulated under section 67 of the Children Act 1989. Amendments to the Children Act 1989 came into effect in July 2005 (DfES, 2005b, 2005c). National minimum standards will be used to monitor the local authority performance of statutory duties towards privately fostered children. The law requires parents and foster carers to notify local authorities of the placement. Local authorities must satisfy themselves that the foster carers, the premises and the standard of care are suitable. At present, unlike day carers, private foster carers are not registered. The 2004 Children Act includes provision to enable the Secretary of State to introduce registration should experience of the requirements show that this is necessary in order to safeguard private foster children.

Concerns about private fostering have focused on the difficulties in implementing the current law, especially the evidence that most placements are never notified to local authorities and that some local authorities had no effective systems in place to identify and monitor placements (Social Services Inspectorate, 2000; Department of Health, 2001; Clarke, 2002). Even when good local authority practice is found, enforcement can be difficult. Parents and foster carers may be hostile to social work involvement, and children may be moved abruptly if local authorities attempt enforcement (Clarke, 2002; Holman, 2002). New guidance and advice on publicising legal requirements consider the possibility of liaison with services such as schools and nurseries to help identify private foster care placements (Department for Education and Skills, 2005d):

- If you know of a child who is or may be in private foster care, check that children's social care know of the placement.
- Children living in informal care arrangements with neighbours or friends and language school or other students under 18 years placed with families are privately fostered. Local authorities have duties to visit them and ensure their care is satisfactory in accordance with the Children Acts 1989 and 2004.

THE COMPLEXITIES IN SAFEGUARDING LOOKED-AFTER CHILDREN

ASSESSING RISK OF HARM

Practitioners caring for children in residential and foster care settings face similar challenges and dilemmas to those faced by parents. There is a fine balance to be struck between allowing scope to explore, experiment and learn from experience, respecting children's privacy and growing independence, giving essential guidance and control, and safeguarding them from harm. With adolescents in particular this is one of the most testing aspects of care. Corporate parents and professional carers are usually very conscious of their responsibility for the safety of other people's children. Troubled children in social care services can be particularly vulnerable to harm from damaging people in the locality, and targeting of residential services by sex offenders has occurred (Waterhouse, 2000).

It is easy for managers and practitioners to slide into defensive practice in developing safety policies and rules, but this is counterproductive. It can become a means of protecting staff from accusations of negligence or misconduct rather than a true safeguard for children, and causes frustration for both

staff and children. An exasperated boarding school pupil asked the Children's
Rights Director:

> Does a trip to a local Indian restaurant really require a risk assessment?
>
> Morgan, 2004a, p. 34

Avoidance of defensive practice is easier if staff are confident in the guidance and support from managers and if potential difficulties are dealt with by
forethought and realistic risk management.

One helpful example is the guidance issued on overnight stays for looked-
after children visiting friends (Department for Education and Skills and Department of Health, 2004). This was introduced after children complained that
some local authorities required their friends' parents to have Criminal Records
Bureau checks before allowing sleepovers, creating embarrassing and stigmatising differences from children living with their families. The guidance makes
it clear that residential and foster carers are expected to use the levels of care
that would be appropriate in ordinary, responsible parenting when making decisions about children's activities.

> The guiding principle is that looked after children should as far as possible
> be granted the same permission to take part in normal and acceptable age-
> appropriate peer activities, such as staying with friends, as would reasonably be
> granted by parents of their peers. Parents make judgements on whether or not
> there are known risks to staying in a particular household or in staying overnight
> in particular circumstances, and similar judgements should normally be made for
> children in foster and residential care by their responsible carers.
>
> Department for Education and Skills and Department of Health, 2004,
> Paragraph 12

PARTICULAR CHALLENGES FOR STAFF WORKING WITH
LEARNING DISABLED CHILDREN

Paul, Cawson and Paton (2004) found that staff in special schools for children
with severe learning disabilities ignored school policies on showing physical
affection to children when they prohibited any affectionate touch. Staff knew
that the children, many of them very young, in 52-week care and with little
contact with parents, needed physical affection. Ignoring unrealistic practice guidance led staff to encourage affectionate displays, which were acceptable with young children but were also unwisely adopted with physically
mature but emotionally immature adolescents. This gave wrong messages
about acceptable adult behaviour to children and placed staff at risk of actions
being misunderstood. Schools with safe practice acknowledged children's need
for physical affection and taught staff and children safe approaches:

> You have to consider their age. The difficulty is that staff see teenagers as kids, but
> they are adults. You don't go round kissing people willy nilly as it's inappropriate.
> You don't have to repel them either – you could use a reassuring touch such as an

arm around the shoulder. We teach our students appropriate hugs, which mean affection.

Head of Care, school for children with severe learning disabilities,
Paul, Cawson and Paton, 2004, p. 71

The importance of clear practice standards and guidelines will recur as a theme throughout this chapter. Adolescent sexual development and behaviour can raise difficult safeguarding issues, and the boundaries between normal sexual exploration and sexual exploitation or abuse may not always be clear. Children with learning disabilities are especially vulnerable to abuse and exploitation (National Working Group on Child Protection and Disability, 2003; Morris, 2006). Some children may find it harder than others to learn the normal rules for sexual behaviour, and learning disabled children are over-represented in services for young sexual abusers (Hackett, Masson and Phillips, 2003).

It is important that all settings working with children should ensure that staff have training and management support in dealing with children's sexual development (Farmer and Pollock, 1998; Hackett, Masson and Phillips, 2003; Barter *et al.*, 2004). Safe care will make explicit the rules for acceptable sexual behaviour and the reasons for them, and make sure that everyone – children, staff, foster carers, parents and others in contact with the placement – knows and understands them.

Children are safest when in the care of adults who know them well, recognise when changes of mood or behaviour indicate that something is wrong, and make sure that children have full access to their preferred means of communication. If disabled children are dependent on signers, symbol boards or other equipment for communication, these should always be accessible; if a child with speech does not understand or speak English, interpreters using his or her preferred language and adequate language teaching should be arranged:

> Ninety per cent of our communication is not speech – it's body language and facial expression. And when you work with non-verbal students it becomes absolutely imperative . . . I noticed this morning with a student that he's not right – I don't know whether he's ill. He's non-verbal – so I noted it and recorded it on the shift report to say he's not happy, he's not right. Please keep a close eye.
>
> Teacher, school for children with profound and multiple learning disabilities,
quoted in Paul, Cawson and Paton (2004, p. 64)

Ensuring that children and young people are safe means staff or foster carers are listening to them, respecting their wishes and feelings, and being aware of their developmental needs. This includes sensitivity to children's needs linked to their ethnicity, religion and culture, and specific needs of disabled children. All staff contribute to safeguarding a child. Domestic and administrative staff and the escorts who transfer children between placements need to be alert to children's safeguarding needs as well as the care, teaching or custody staff. All staff should be included in training programmes.

For more detailed discussion on communication with children in safeguarding, see Chapter 1.

SAFEGUARDING FROM HARM CAUSED BY OTHER YOUNG PEOPLE

Friendship and companionship of peers in a situation similar to theirs is identified by children living away from home in all settings as one of the main benefits of living in group care. John, who had attended a special boarding school, said that a good thing about being away at boarding school was that

> I made friends and it wasn't like 'oh come over to my house', we were all friends living together and it was just great. It was like having your friends stop over but all term.
>
> Morris, 1998, p. 20

The downside is that peers can also be harmful, and children may have few escapes from peer pressure. Physical, sexual and psychological aggression between children seriously affects their happiness, and sometimes their safety, and is the most common form of attack described by children in both community and residential contexts (Barter *et al.*, 2004; Morgan 2004b). Threats and attacks from other children are one of the main causes of unhappiness for children in children's homes (Gibbs and Sinclair, 2000) and in custody (Kendrick, 1997), though boarding school pupils are less likely to describe it as a problem (Morgan, 2004a).

Bullying drives some children to self-harm or other self-destructive behaviour, and to suicide (Howard League for Penal Reform, 1995; Marr and Field, 2001). Children looked after by the local authority or in custody are particularly vulnerable. Sinclair and Gibbs (1998) found that 4 out of 10 children in the children's homes they studied said that they had considered killing themselves in the last month. Lader, Singleton and Meltzer (2000) reported that 20% of young male prisoners and 30% of young female prisoners have attempted suicide. These young people have many pressures in their lives. Bullying is not likely to be the only problem they face, but is regularly identified as a contributor to despair.

BULLYING AND PEER ABUSE – IS THERE ANY DIFFERENCE?

Unfortunately, some adults still regard bullying as trivial and fail to take it seriously. We are not consistent when using the terms 'bullying' and 'peer abuse', and assume that the difference between the two is obvious and understood by everyone – but it is not obvious that there is any distinction at all. In many texts, physical and psychological attack is described as 'bullying' and sexual attack as 'peer abuse'. This is not helpful in understanding the seriousness of incidents or their effects on the victim. In deciding how best to safeguard children, it is essential to look at individual experiences rather than attaching labels that may falsely minimise or maximise what has happened.

Carl, aged 17, living in a children's home said:

> Since I've been here my bedroom's been trashed three times. I've had shampoo poured all over and under my door and where my carpet is. I've had some of my clothes stolen, money stolen, things out of my room stolen, things like that. And it really winds me up to come back from seeing my family, and I come back and it winds me up seeing my bedroom being trashed, I come in and my bedroom's upside down, my cupboards on my floor, all my clothes are scattered all over the room ... posters ripped up.
>
> Barter *et al.*, 2004, p. 36

Psychological attack is more common than physical attack. Tactics include name calling, verbal insult to victims or their families, spreading lies and rumours about the victim, using threats and gestures to frighten the victim and ignoring or excluding the victim from the children's group. Children in all settings also report physical assault, having property taken or damaged and sexual assault. Children cannot be neatly divided into 'bullies' and 'bullied'; many are both on different occasions. The smallest and youngest members of a group are the most vulnerable. Girls are more likely than boys to experience both verbal sexual insults and sexual assaults (Barter *et al.*, 2004).

Fiona, aged 14 and living in a children's home, said:

> I think getting, having names called to you is worse ... because it hurts you more and it's, like if you had a fight and you cut yourself, the pain goes and it heals, but having, being called whatever is always at the back of your head.
>
> Barter *et al.*, 2004, p. 29

Children and young people in all settings report that psychological attack is more hurtful than physical attack, and has longer lasting effects. Arrival at a new place is described by children in children's homes, boarding schools and young offender institutions as a difficult time when they need staff support, but do not always get it (Hazel *et al.*, 2002; Barter *et al.*, 2004; HM Inspectorate of Prisons for England and Wales, 2004; Morgan 2004a). Staff should have extra vigilance for new arrivals, especially for children away from home for the first time, for children experiencing their first admission to custody and for children with histories of self-harm or of having previously been bullied.

Psychological bullying involving insults to families is recorded in several settings as especially hurtful and, for children with disrupted family relationships, this is likely to be particularly hard to bear. Psychological attacks also set the conditions for physical attack, and insults to families are among the most common triggers for violent incidents between young people in day schools, and in residential and custodial contexts (Frosh, Phoenix and Pattman, 2002; Barter *et al.*, 2004).

Terry, aged 18, recently released from a young offender institution, said:

There was always shouting between pads [cells]. A lot of the fights started from the windows, people winding each other up and they'd come out fighting in the morning.

Howard League for Penal Reform, 2002, p. 8

HOW SERIOUS IS SERIOUS?

Physical attacks by children are rarely life threatening, but some can be very serious and occasionally fatal. High levels of serious assault, with injuries requiring hospital treatment, are reported in young offender institutions (Solomon, 2004). In a study of children's homes, children described incidents of rape, of younger boys being forced by older boys to swim in a local lake at night and of children being tied to hot radiators by an older boy (Barter et al., 2004). A first-year pupil called ChildLine's boarding school helpline about 'an initiation rite involving being put in messy baths and having their heads put down the toilet – all the boys in his year were terrified' (ChildLine, 1997).

Victims often do not tell adults, even those they love and trust, what has happened to them. They may think there is nothing that can be done (Barter et al., 2004). There are powerful pressures in many settings against 'grassing'. But it should be remembered that for some children, being away from home protects them from harm by peers. A young man in custody told his youth offending team practitioner of his relief at being away from the gang he had belonged to before committal:

I don't have to go out burgling, don't have to go out nicking cars and it was like I can be a kid again, I can be a 14 year old again, I can wear my slippers at night, I can have some football posters on the wall and live the life that I should be.

Hazel et al., 2002, p. 25

Parents reported that their children were happier at boarding school because there was much less bullying than they had experienced at day school (Morgan, 2004a).

EFFECTIVE STRATEGIES TO SAFEGUARD FROM HARM BY OTHER YOUNG PEOPLE

Schools and young offender institutions have substantial experience in 'what works' in preventing and counteracting bullying. Detailed requirements have been set at national government level, with a legal duty on head teachers to prevent bullying (School Standards and Framework Act 1998, s 61(a)), and a prison service anti-bullying strategy was developed in 1993 and revised in 1999. The National Minimum Standards for Children's Homes (Department of Health, 2002c) now require homes to have a policy to deal with bullying.

Effective practice in schools, children's homes and young offenders' institutions, described in the research literature, includes the following:

- Immediate attention to the support needs of victims, involving children in identifying what will help them feel safe.
- A policy for dealing with serious assaults by children linked to the child protection procedures and to local police protocols with the Crown Prosecution Service.
- A strong lead from management, with clear standards for acceptable behaviour.
- A 'whole institution' approach in which everyone – children, staff, management and parents – is involved in establishing and owning the anti-bullying strategies and tactics, and in monitoring compliance.
- Focusing on the positives – a strategy based on rewards for good behaviour rather than on punishments.
- Taking verbal insults seriously, even if they appear to be jokes – checking with the person on the receiving end whether they see the joke.
- Building on the strengths and insights of the children. This can include methods such as peer counselling, mediation, mentoring and listener schemes, 'no blame' approaches in which problems can be discussed openly without fear of reprisals, and monitoring of areas of the premises identified by children as unsafe.
- Restorative justice concepts in conflict resolution and as an alternative to conventional punishment for aggressive behaviour or bullying.
- Identifying times when children are especially vulnerable and focusing support on these times, especially at nights and in the first few days after admission, or after visits to or other contact with families.
- Awareness of behavioural indicators that something is wrong, in particular being aware that behaviour such as running away, or refusal to take part in education programmes or activities, may be an indicator of bullying or other harm, rather than seeing it solely as a disciplinary issue.
- Assessment of the vulnerability of children and of the risk that aggressive (including sexually aggressive) children pose to others.

RACIST BULLYING

Racist bullying has been described in many contexts and most racist violence is carried out by young people or young adults (Barter, 1999). Minority ethnic children are particularly vulnerable where there are very few of them in a group or locality (Barter, 1999; Cline *et al.*, 2002), and several studies conclude that South Asian children are especially vulnerable (Barter, 1999; Barter *et al.*, 2004). Strategies to counteract racism by young people are in many respects the same as those described above. The importance of agencies having strong anti-racist policies, making rules for acceptable behaviour clear to children and staff, is crucial to giving staff confidence to anticipate and tackle problems. Anti-racist strategies should include the following:

- Response to incidents from the most senior manager in direct contact with young people – for example the head teacher or officer in charge.
- Training and good preparation for all staff.
- Teaching that draws on children's cultural and ethnic differences in a sensitive manner.
- Direct work with young people known to have racist and xenophobic beliefs.
- Non-toleration of racist verbal insults, which are known to be profoundly distressing to many children and set the context for violence.

Aggression between young people

Here are some useful sources for evidence and practical help. Much information focuses on schools but the issues and practical solutions are adaptable to most situations where trouble occurs between children and young people.

Department for Education and Skills (2003) – this site has a downloadable anti-bullying pack for schools at www.dfes.gov.uk/bullying.

Bullyweb – a web site with research and other information for professionals, and links to many other useful sites and sources of information at www.uclan.ac.uk/facs/science/psychol/bully/bully.htm.

For a summary of children's views on bullying, see Oliver and Candappa (2003).

For ideas on restorative justice approaches to conflict and bullying between young people in custody and in schools, see Curry *et al.* (2004) and Hopkins (2004).

For further information and strategies to challenge racism with children, see Barter (1999), Cline *et al.* (2002) and Lemos (2005).

BEHAVIOUR MANAGEMENT, 'YOUNG ABUSERS' AND SAFEGUARDING CHILDREN

When there are persistent or serious attacks on peers, specialist support and intervention will be required. Children with histories of being abused and of abusing others are often placed together. In foster and residential care, this can lead to previously abused children suffering further abuse, and to abuse of foster carers' own children (Farmer and Pollock, 1998). As adult surveillance may be lower in foster care than in other 'out of home' settings, children may be more vulnerable when problems do arise (ChildLine, 1997; Farmer and

Pollock, 1998). Epps (1999) reports that adolescents referred for assessment following sexual assaults on other children often have long histories of similar behaviour that had not been taken seriously by practitioners. He notes (p. 69) that

> children who continue to abuse because they are inadequately supervised often find themselves moving from one child care placement to another, creating more victims along the way.

Young abusers are children too. They cannot live in solitary confinement or exclusively with adults. No miracle solutions are available, but the following points have been identified as helpful in maintaining a safe placement (Berridge and Brodie, 1998; Farmer and Pollock, 1998; Epps, 1999; Hayden *et al.*, 1999; Hackett, Masson and Phillips, 2003):

- Whether other children in the placement are similar to the young abuser's previous victims is crucial to judgements about whether a placement is safe. An adolescent who habitually targets much younger children, for example may not be a risk to age peers.
- Placement of children who harm others in a setting with children older than themselves may not be a good solution. The young abusers may be vulnerable in this situation, and a placement designed for older children may not have suitable facilities for them.
- Many young abusers have themselves experienced abuse and neglect, which may be linked to their abusive behaviour. This should be addressed through care planning and provision of services.
- Children with histories of harming other children need close supervision and monitoring, with special attention to times and places where previous incidents have occurred.
- Carers should always explain why actions are being taken or rules exist.
- Where children are persistently violent or sexually aggressive it is essential to identify and provide the psychiatric or other specialist help they need.
- Abrupt moves of either the aggressor or the victim should be avoided where possible. As well as disrupting children's stability, this leads to unplanned emergency placements. Children's homes can thereby come to hold substantial numbers of children whose placement was unplanned, adding to the difficulties of maintaining a safe environment.

Decisions on intervening in these situations should be taken in line with guidance from Local Safeguarding Children Boards (LSCBs). These should reflect the seriousness of the harm, the future risk of harm and the procedure most likely to ensure the victim's long-term safety and welfare.

SELF-HARM AND SUICIDAL BEHAVIOUR

Some safeguarding needs arise because children are a risk to themselves. Many looked-after children and children in custody have thought about or attempted suicide and/or self-harm (Sinclair and Gibbs, 1998; Hagell, 2002), as have children admitted to adolescent psychiatric units (Mears *et al.*, 2003b). In other contexts, it is likely to be less common but by no means unknown. Self-harm can take many forms. The most usual are overdosing on medication or other drugs, use of solvents, cutting or otherwise injuring the skin, hair pulling and swallowing toxic or other non-food objects.

Causes for self-harming are not well understood. Some evidence indicates that present or previous abuse by adults and bullying by other young people can be among the triggers. Contact with families – especially where families are in distress, relationships are strained or there are restrictions on contact imposed by a court or by someone holding parental responsibility – is another possible area where staff vigilance may be particularly necessary. Contact with families is crucial for children living away from home. Inspection standards for all care, education and custody sectors now include requirements to support family contact. However, staff should be sensitive to the possibility of children's distress associated with contact.

For further discussion on working with parents of looked-after children, see Chapter 2.

Children away from home are most vulnerable to self-harm and suicide in the first few days after admission, especially children in custody known to have previous histories of self-harm and suicide attempts (Hazel *et al.*, 2002). The National Inquiry into Self-harm among Young People has identified the evidence available and the key issues for improved knowledge and practice (Mental Health Foundation, 2006). The National Institute for Clinical Excellence (NICE) has issued guidelines for the treatment of patients who self-harm, including a section concerning children who self-harm (National Institute for Clinical Excellence, 2004a, 2004b). Self-harm should always be taken seriously, even if the injuries are minor.

Self-harm

For information on self-harm and approaches to supporting young people with this behaviour visit www.selfharm.org.uk.

Guidance on the treatment of patients who self-harm and information for carers and relatives of patients at the NICE (National Institute for Health and Clinical Excellence) web site at www.nice.org.uk/page.aspx?o=213665.

For a summary of evidence and issues, see St John (2004).

CHILDREN OUT OF SIGHT

The children most in need of safeguarding are often those who are least likely to receive it because they are out of sight of the services that should support and protect them. These are children missing from home or from care, living homeless on the streets, abused through child prostitution or victims of child trafficking. Many of these children are victims of calculated exploitation by unscrupulous adults who hold power over them. Most are teenagers, but younger children may have been brought into the country for benefit or housing fraud. Victims of trafficking may be brought here for prostitution or as domestic slaves (Somerset, 2004). Many children described as runaways have in reality not left home of their own accord but have been told to leave by parents or driven out as a result of family conflict or abuse for which no adequate help has been offered (Rees, 2004; Rees and Siakeu, 2004).

These children will often have no contact with health, education or welfare services. All are vulnerable to physical and sexual abuse and exploitation. They may be caught up in crime and selling sex in order to survive. They are vulnerable to drug and alcohol misuse as an escape from their frightening and miserable lives.

Il, aged 17, who had been thrown out of her family home, described how she had been drawn into prostitution. She said:

> I was on the street for four or five days just eating, Oh God I can't talk about this ... this is just ugh. I used to eat food out of the garbage.
>
> Pearce, Williams and Galvin, 2003, p. 45

After this experience Il started going home with men she met in pubs, for the sake of a meal and a bed for the night, offering them sex but leaving before she had to make good her offer.

Shane, aged 15, called ChildLine:

> I've been living in a doss house since I ran away from home. I haven't eaten since Sunday, but I've been taking heroin and speed. I'm on the game and see about six people each night – I work to pay for the drugs and use the drugs to get through the work. I want my life to finish. I want not to wake up again. I want it back to normal. I've been beaten up three times in the last two weeks.
>
> Home Office, 2004, p. 34

Children often become wary and distrustful of professionals, fearing they will be forced to live somewhere that they dislike. They may have been told by their exploiters that they will be seen as offenders rather than victims. Those who are victims of traffickers or under the control of pimps may be locked in to prevent them from seeking help.

How to check if children you have come across are missing from somewhere

The NSPCC National Child Protection Helpline keeps records of children reported for concerns about their safety, and this can include children who are missing. Telephone 0808 800 5000.

The National Missing Persons Helpline is 0500 700 700 and can liaise with missing young people.

For guidance on good practice in relation to children missing from care and from home, see Department of Health (2002a, 2002b).

For further reading, see Social Exclusion Unit (2002).

For guidance on safeguarding children involved in prostitution, see Department of Health *et al.* (2000).

For a summary of recent evidence, see Home Office (2004).

For information on child trafficking in the United Kingdom, see the Unicef (2003) report at www.endchildexploitation.org.uk.

Although, in law, these children have access to the same statutory services as any other children, the research suggests a much more flexible approach, such as outreach or drop-in services, is the most effective way to help them (Department of Health *et al.*, 2000; Rees, 2001; Pearce, Williams and Galvin, 2003). If a child is suspected of being exploited through prostitution or trafficking or is homeless, statutory services and specialist local projects should be alerted quickly. Although most children who leave home stay in their own area, children may move on, or be moved quickly by the adult exploiting them, once questions start being asked.

SAFEGUARDING FROM POOR PRACTICE OR MISCONDUCT BY STAFF

New procedures for checking everyone who works with children through the Criminal Records Bureau have been introduced, and eventually all staff will undergo regular checks. Guidance has been issued to services working with children (Department for Education and Skills, 2002; see Chapter 12 in HM Government, 2006b).

In schools, FE institutions and Local Education Authority education services it is now compulsory to obtain a CRB Disclosure as part of the appointment process (S.I. 2006/1068, S.I. 2006/1067). All the same, only the most complacent would suggest that abuse by staff could never happen now. Many of the past instances of sexual abuse by practitioners have involved staff who had no previous offences identifiable through police records.

Physically abusive practice described in public inquiries often occurred when inexperienced or overworked staff had to cope with challenging children in poorly managed or poorly equipped institutions (Kent, 1997; Utting, 1997). Research and inspection reports suggest that the staff shortages and management problems that created the conditions for poor practice or abuse are far from solved (National Care Standards Commission, 2004). They also show that monitoring and reporting systems can be effective at dealing with poor practice before it becomes endemic or abusive.

ENSURING GOOD PRACTICE

STAFF PRACTICE AND WHISTLE BLOWING

The willingness of staff and others to whistle blow and challenge poor practice is crucial to safeguarding children. Staff can sometimes discount the seriousness of what has happened to children because their primary loyalty is to colleagues or the good name of the institution. ChildLine's analysis of children's calls to the Boarding School Helpline in 1995–1996 found that in some schools, staff sexual abuse of children appeared to have been known and tolerated for many years:

> Regimes of abuse prosper because people turn a blind eye to what is happening, or minimise or rationalise it – 'it is just touching' or 'it will not really do any harm'. Again and again, apparently responsible adults appear to consider it much more serious for a fellow adult to face the ignominy of being found responsible for sexual misconduct than for a child (or many children) to be assaulted.
>
> ChildLine, 1997, p. 39

Utting (1997) noted that the highly competitive world of private education created pressures against openness when problems arose in boarding schools, but also commented that a 'quiet revolution' in improved standards of care for pupils had taken place in recent years as a result of the changing expectations of parents. Stuart and Baines (2004a, p. 82) conclude:

> The state of safeguarding in schools with boarding provision has been transformed since 1997.

A head of care in a school for children with severe learning disabilities said:

> I tell my staff that they have a shared responsibility to whistle blow and I try and talk to them about the fact that child protection isn't just about burns and bruises but it's about how we value, how we talk and how we care for the youngsters.
>
> Paul, Cawson and Paton, 2004, p. 31

Whistle blowing is relevant to all staff behaviour that can harm children. Stephen (in Morris, 1998) described verbal bullying and occasional physical abuse by a care worker in the residential home for disabled young people where he lived. When Stephen complained to another care worker:

> '... she kind of laughed and said I should tell him to stop. Then she said she would tell him I didn't like the things he said. I didn't think it was a good idea.'

> So Stephen didn't tell anyone else. 'Sometimes' he said, 'I thought I was being stupid because he would make a joke out of it, and other people would think it was a joke, the things he said. The worst thing was not knowing when he would decide not to help me go to the toilet. He would say things like "oh you're always wanting a pee, there must be something wrong with you" or "have you been out drinking". They would think it was funny.'

> Morris, 1998, p. 38

Stephen's account shows how important it is that staff know how to challenge practice in a way that does not expose the child to further harm. Managers should ensure that there are safe routes for reporting and that responses give adequate support to the children and to whistle-blowers.

You can find further help for managers in a training resource for corporate parents on safeguarding in residential settings: Towards Safer Care: training and resource pack (Department of Health, 1999).

PRE-CONDITIONS FOR SAFE PRACTICE

A study of special schools identified these conditions for safe practice:

- clear and accessible reporting systems for concerns affecting the safety of children, separate from other normal daily logs or reports, and with a senior manager responsible for checking and acting upon safety or child protection reports;
- a whistle blowing culture in which staff are willing to comment on and report poor practice by colleagues, including seniors;
- a 'no blame' culture in which staff can admit and learn from mistakes;
- support to staff following allegations of bad practice or abuse.

> Paul, Cawson and Paton, 2004

Hands-on involvement by senior managers ensures that staff realise the importance of recording and are confident that action will be taken when they report. In a whistle blowing culture, staff are free to question and report behaviour by colleagues. This needs sensitive handling by management, openness about what will happen in response to reports, and a clear understanding about who should receive reports and act on them. Where there is uncertainty about who to go to or what will happen, staff are reluctant to challenge poor practice.

The 'no blame culture' enables managers to help staff who make genuine mistakes or who do not realise their practice is problematic, and enables staff to ask for help themselves if there is something they are finding hard to cope with. Practice errors can be taken up in training and staff can learn from mistakes. This is especially important in social care and custodial services with a minimally trained workforce, where most learning is 'on the job'.

Support to staff when allegations are made against them is essential in preventing poor practice. If staff see colleagues being treated unfairly or uncaringly by managers following allegations, they are less likely to seek help with their own difficulties and will be reluctant to report colleagues in future. Employers should have fair and open procedures for actions involving staff, and for keeping staff informed of the progress of criminal investigations or disciplinary proceedings (Barter, 1998; Paul, Cawson and Paton, 2004, HM Government, 2006b).

DEALING WITH ALLEGATIONS OF ABUSE OR MISCONDUCT AGAINST STAFF AND FOSTER CARERS

Management practice in dealing with allegations against staff and foster carers requires clarity on how enquiries should be made; how evidence should be protected; when staff should be suspended or other agencies called in; the relationship between employers' disciplinary proceedings and possible criminal investigations; offering appropriate support and making it clear to both children and staff what will happen as a result of an allegation (Barter, 1998).

Guidance on dealing with allegations against people who work with children is given in *Working Together To Safeguard Children* (HM Government, 2006b, 6.20–6.30 and Appendix 5).

First essentials are:

- ensuring safety and support for any children who may have been harmed or may have to act as witnesses in any investigation or legal proceedings;
- managers must consider the possibility that an allegation might indicate a more widespread problem than the one incident complained of – perhaps be only the most recent of several incidents, or indicate collusion by staff.

Working Together To Safeguard Children states that

> parents of affected children should be given information about the concerns, advised on the processes to be followed and the outcomes reached. The provision of information and advice must take place in a manner that does not impede the proper exercise of enquiry, disciplinary and investigative processes.
>
> HM Government, 2006b, Paragraph 6.20

Managers will need to decide whether adults against whom allegations have made can safely be in unsupervised contact with the children concerned or other children (including potential witnesses), at least until it is known whether there is a case to answer. Removal from unsupervised contact does not automatically require suspension and may be possible, for example through deployment to other duties or by temporary leave of absence, but this decision should be based on the specific circumstances of the allegation and initial management evaluation of the situation.

- If you think a child using your service is being abused, whether by staff, other children or outside the placement, make sure you know your organisation's procedures for safeguarding children, and use them.
- Do not ask children leading questions or attempt your own investigation – this may jeopardise any subsequent criminal investigation.
- Know who to contact in children's social care and the police.
- If you make a referral to children's social care about a child's welfare and do not get a response within 3 days, contact them again. Do not give up (see *What To Do If You're Worried A Child is Being Abused*, HM Government 2006a, Paragraph 11.5).
- If urgent action is needed to protect a child's life or prevent serious immediate harm, children's social care and the police should initiate an immediate strategy discussion to discuss plans for emergency action (see *What To Do If You're Worried A Child Is Being Abused*, HM Government, 2006a, Paragraph 22).

THE USE OF EXCEPTIONAL MEASURES TO CONTROL CHILDREN'S CHALLENGING BEHAVIOUR

An area of practice that often raises safeguarding concerns is the management of children's challenging behaviour. This most commonly happens over the use of physical restraint, segregation or separation in single rooms or cells and medication to control behaviour. Action by staff is necessary in dangerous situations. Children are in danger and afraid if staff are not able to protect them from violent behaviour by peers (Barter *et al.*, 2004), or from harming themselves. In custodial settings especially, the inability to restrict or select admissions means that vulnerable children may be detained alongside children who are a serious risk of harm to others. However, in most settings, staff report differences of opinion over when use of these methods of control is necessary, or whether they are used when more positive methods could be tried.

Physical restraint

Physical restraint is permissible for looked-after children only to prevent them from injuring themselves or other people, or preventing serious damage to property. In custodial settings it can also be used to prevent young people from escaping. In schools, staff are able to use reasonable force to restrain students when necessary, but should not use force likely to cause injury (Department for Education and Employment, 1998).

The Youth Justice Board *Code of Practice for Managing the Behaviour of Children and Young People in the Secure Estate* sets out a value base and set of principles for physical intervention across the entire secure estate. There is a strong emphasis on support for young people and encouraging positive behaviour. The Code stresses the importance of minimising the use of physical interventions and restraint and reinforcing other methods of behaviour management. It includes an aspiration to move away from the use of any 'pain compliant' methods of restraining young people, although, at present, these methods are used in Young Offenders Institutions (YOIs).

Restraint is potentially dangerous – people have died while being restrained. Children and staff may be injured. It is essential that staff using restraint are fully trained and have regular refresher courses. Foster carers may also be in situations where they have to restrain children and should be included in training schemes (Hayden *et al.*, 1999).

Staff should be aware that using restraint can increase rather than reduce violence, especially if the young person panics. Hayden (1998) noted that residential staff dislike the word 'restraint' and would often speak instead of 'holding', a word with caring and therapeutic connotations. However, none of the young people interviewed who had experienced restraint had found it a reassuring process. Hart describes a consultation by the Children's Rights Director in which looked-after children commonly saw restraint as a means to secure compliance rather than to protect, and were left feeling 'distressed, hurt and vengeful' (Hart, 2004).

A young person living in a children's home said:

> ... when I was being restrained they wouldn't listen, they said 'when you calm down we'll do it' but it's difficult to calm down when you're in a restraint ... because all you can think about is your parents and what happened to you and you can't stop like that.
>
> Hayden, 1998, Introduction, p. 2

Children who took part in the Children's Rights Director's consultation thought restraint that caused pain or injury was physical abuse (Morgan, 2004c). Morgan found that children accept that restraint is sometimes necessary to prevent injury or major damage to property. The children gave useful suggestions to staff on how to prevent minor incidents from escalating until restraint is used, and how to deal with restraint in the least hurtful way. These included the following:

- use restraint only as a last resort, for example to prevent someone from getting hurt;
- never use restraint as a punishment;
- understand that restraint almost always makes children more worked up than they were before;

- try to avoid using restraint with anyone who has previously been physically or sexually abused, because they would dislike any adult touching or holding them;
- give children time and space to calm down;
- avoid raising the anger level by getting into shouting matches with children;
- find ways to take the heat out of the situation, for example by speaking calmly or taking the child away to somewhere quiet to talk to him or her;
- have individual plans with children's preferred ways of helping them when they lose self-control.

Hayden *et al.* (1999) and Paul, Cawson and Paton (2004) found use of unauthorised and potentially unsafe methods of restraint in children's homes and special schools. It is particularly important that staff who are concerned about restraint practice by colleagues should

- be prepared to use reporting and whistle blowing procedures;
- be aware that staff can easily get into a situation that is difficult to end without someone being hurt.

Regulations and guidance on the use of restraint and segregation with children

For further reading on restraint see:

Children's homes

Children's Homes Regulations 2001.
Web site: www.dh.gov.uk/assetRoot/04/02/12/09/04021209.pdf.
Guidance on permissible forms of control in children's residential care. Department of Health (1993) LAC (93) 13.
Web site: http://www.dh.gov.uk/en/Publicationsandstatistics/Lettersand circulars/LocalAuthorityCirculars/AllLocalAuthority/DH_4003969.

Schools

Department for Education and Employment (1998, Circular 10/98).
Web site: www.dfes.gov.uk/publications/guidanceonthelaw/10_98/summary. htm.

Learning disabled children

Department for Education and Skills and Department of Health (2002)
Web site: www.teachernet.gov.uk/wholeschool/sen/schools/piguide.
See also: Harris *et al.* (1996), Allen (2001) and the British Institute of Learning Disability (2001, 2002, 2004).

Juvenile secure estate

The Young Offender Institution Rules 2000. As amended by The Young Offender Institution (Amendment) Rules 2002.
Web site: http://www.opsi.gov.uk/SI/si1988/Uksi_19881422_en_3.htm.
Youth Justice Board (2006) *Managing the Behaviour of Children and Young people in the Secure Estate*: code of practice. Youth Justice Board for England and Wales, London.
Web site: www.youth-justice-board.gov.uk/Publications.
Prison Service Orders 1600, 1601, 1700 and 4950.
Web site: www.hmprisonservice.gov.uk/resourcecentre/psispsos/listpsos.
Secure Training Centre Rules 1998.
Web site: http://www.opsi.gov.uk/SI/si1998/19980472.htm.

Health services

Code of Practice to the Mental Health Act 1983 (revised 1999).
Web site: http://www.dh.gov.uk/PublicationsAndStatistics/Publications/
PublicationsPolicyAndGuidance/PublicationsPolicyAndGuidanceArticle/
fs/en?CONTENT_ID=4005756&chk=YKlwkm.
See also: Royal College of Nursing (2003) and Hart and Howell (2004).

Segregation or separation

Segregation in a locked room is legal only for children in custody, for looked-after children aged 10 or over in a registered secure unit, or for children detained under the Mental Health Act 1983. Looked-after children may be detained for up to 72 hours without a Secure Accommodation Order but after that an order must be obtained. In YOIs, children may be detained in a special cell to prevent them from harming themselves or anyone else and may have clothing removed. The Chief Inspector of Prisons has criticised the use of segregation, especially of special cells, often known as 'strip cells', for children in custody (Her Majesty's Chief Inspector of Prisons for England and Wales, 2003; Community Care, 2004). Children who are out of control to this extent often have mental health or other needs that are unmet in the institution. Urgent professional support is needed to find alternative ways of working with them. Russell (2004) summarises the legal and practice issues. The *National Service Framework for Children, Young People and Maternity Services* stresses the importance of multi-agency assessment for children with complex needs and serious behaviour disorders (Department of Health and Department for Education and Skills, 2004a).

For further discussion of multi-agency working see Chapter 5; for more information about assessment, see Chapter 8.

Use of medication

The use of medication to control aggressive, hyperactive or other problem behaviour is controversial. There are no regulations and the decision is a matter
for the clinical judgement of the doctor concerned. Medication can normally
be prescribed for children only with a parent or legal guardian's consent, unless
the child is of sufficient age and understanding to make the decision (Fraser
competent), when the child may consent. The exception is if the child is detained under the Mental Health Act 1983.

Mears *et al.* (2003a) found that practitioners in child and adolescent psychiatric units were concerned that 'there is a lack of an evidence base on the use
of medication with young people' (p. 71). Mears *et al.* interviewed staff in secure and forensic in-patient child and adolescent units and noted, 'Most nurses
reported they used rapid tranquillisation when necessary'. Half of them said
there were no written guidelines for its use (Mears *et al.*, 2003a, p. 64, Paragraph 4.7.5.6). They recommended that

> NICE (The National Institute for Clinical Excellence) should produce guidelines
> on the use of medication and other treatment in young people with mental health
> problems. These should also address the use of rapid tranquillisation in in-patient
> services.
>
> p. 82, Paragraph 5.10.7

There was confusion among some psychiatrists over issues of consent to
treatment, particularly over 'Gillick competence' (Mears *et al.*, 2003a, p. 77),
now referred to as 'Fraser competence', and obtaining written rather than verbal consent (Mears *et al.*, 2003a, p. 76).

Few medicines have been tested or standardised for use with children (Department of Health and Department of Education and Skills, 2004b). The *National Service Framework for Children, Young People and Maternity Services*
summarises safety issues in the use of psychoactive medication and includes
standards for the safe use of medication with children (Standard 10). NICE
has developed guidance on the short-term management of disturbed (violent)
behaviour in in-patient psychiatric settings (see www.nice.org.uk/).

THE USE OF EXCEPTIONAL METHODS OF CONTROL: DANGER SIGNS TO WATCH OUT FOR

Managers and anyone else with responsibility for children's safety and welfare
should be challenging frequent use of measures which are intended as a last
resort, and looking at why they are being used. Their use may reflect problems which are beyond the control of the establishment, but research and inspection reports comparing a number of establishments with similar conditions
find great variations in the use of exceptional methods to control behaviour,
indicating that good management of a service can make a difference.

Challenging behaviour can arise in all settings, though in some it is likely to
characterise many, perhaps most, of the children admitted, and in others to be

unusual. Services which rarely admit such children have been found less likely to have clear procedures prepared in advance or staff trained and confident in dealing with challenging behaviour (Hayden *et al.*, 1999; Paul, Cawson and Paton, 2004). In any placement of a child with challenging behaviour it is essential that the placement be carefully planned, with an individual care plan developed to meet possible contingencies and staff given appropriate preparation before the child's admission, and all services should have procedures for responding to challenging behaviour and appropriate training.

Restraint, use of separation and use of sedation (other than treatment for a diagnosed medical condition) to control challenging behaviour are emergency procedures. The following are the practice points to watch out for – they may indicate inappropriate and possibly unsafe practice if

- they are used repeatedly with the same children;
- they are being used as a routine form of control most days;
- they are being used more often than in the past;
- they are used in response to minor incidents;
- some staff are using them a lot more than others;
- restraint is being used by staff who have not recently been trained in safe techniques.

SUPPORT TO RESIDENTIAL SETTINGS FROM COMMUNITY SERVICES

Services for children living away from home, as for children living with their families, depend on good backup from community services. Services of all kinds, however, especially residential services, report difficulties in obtaining support. Problems include

- getting community services to act on safeguarding and welfare issues for disabled children, including those that arose when boarding school pupils were at home for the holidays or children were long-stay hospital patients (Morris, 1995, 1998; Abbott, Morris and Ward, 2000, 2001; National Working Group on Child Protection and Disability, 2003; Stalker *et al.*, 2003; Paul, Cawson and Paton, 2004; Morris, 2006);
- support for looked-after children in custody, including on discharge (Hazel *et al.*, 2002);
- specialist support to care for children with severely challenging behaviour or psychiatric problems (Berridge and Brodie, 1998; Farmer and Pollock, 1998).
- help with safeguarding training needs for private foster carers and independent schools (Holman 2002; Baginsky 2003).

Practitioners in all community settings should be clear about their statutory duties and powers to assist children living away from home. Otherwise, multi-agency working to safeguard children can have no reality for children placed away from their parents. Procedures for safeguarding children described in *Working Together to Safeguard Children* (HM Government, 2006b) apply in residential and foster care settings as elsewhere. If there are child protection concerns, a referral to children's social care should be made and appropriate procedures followed.

The implementation of the *National Service Framework for Children, Young People and Maternity Services* (Department of Health and Department for Education and Skills, 2004a) setting standards for mental health services for children and services for disabled children should improve access to some specialist resources. However, the evidence cited above suggests that practitioner knowledge and expectations are equally important in ensuring good services to children living away from home.

Sources of information on specialist services

British Institute of Learning Disabilities.
Web site: www.bild.org.uk.
Young Minds.
Web site: www.youngminds.org.uk.
National Children's Bureau – National Centre for Excellence in Residential Child Care.
Web site: http://www.ncb.org.uk/Page.asp?originx8797le_11744740243661d 69i111598096.
NSPCC Child Protection Helpline: 0808 800 5000.
Web site: www.nspcc.org.uk/nspcc/helpline.
National Service Framework for Children, Young People and Maternity Services.
Web site: www.dh.gov.uk/PolicyAndGuidance/HealthAndSocialCare Topics/ChildrenServices/ChildrenServicesInformation/fs/en.

ACCESS TO INDEPENDENT SUPPORT

One safeguard for children away from home is through access to an independent person they can trust. Looked-after children with little or no family contact are entitled to independent visitors, who can act as befrienders and representatives. Research suggests that the schemes are underused, especially for disabled children and children in foster care (Knight, 1998; Winn Oakley and Masson, 2000).

Many local authorities now also have Children's Rights Officers, or Advice and Representation schemes provided by independent agencies, which support looked-after children. For children in secure units and young offenders in custody, contact with someone outside the institution is especially crucial to safeguarding them, since they may have no way of directly accessing community-based services if in distress or being abused. Local authority se-cure units will usually have an Independent Representative scheme. The YJB is committed to the principle of independent advocacy services (Youth Justice Board, 2004b) and is developing schemes for children in custody. Advocacy services could be valuable for children in child and adolescent psychiatric units (Mears *et al.*, 2003a). Services now also have standards governing their work (Department of Health, 2002f).

Local advocacy services

Information can be obtained from
National Youth Advocacy Service, NYAS. Telephone: 0151 649 8700.
Web site: www.nyas.net.
Children's Rights Officers and Advocates (CROA). Telephone: 020 7833 2100.
For guidance on children's advocacy services, see Department for Educa-tion and Skills (2004).
Web site: www.dfes.gov.uk/childrensadvocacy/docs/GetitSorted.pdf.

WHAT MAKES GOOD CARE? CHILDREN'S ACCOUNTS

We can ask children about the care they receive. Children's views on their ex-perience reflect the reason they live away from home as well as the quality of the care given. So children who have experienced previous abuse or neglect in their families give high priority to good material care and kindness; good edu-cational opportunities are important to children who are in a boarding school; young offenders often value help to keep out of trouble; and so on.

A 12-year-old respondent to a survey of looked-after children gave a reason for feeling safe in a care placement:

> Where I am, I'm away from the violence and drugs and dangers of the estate where my Mum lives. And now I go to school to keep up my grades.
>
> Timms and Thoburn, 2003, p. 34

A 10-year-old in the same survey said:

> I have a good family and I get looked after well and I don't smell and I have clean clothes.
>
> Timms and Thoburn, 2003, p. 202

Gail, aged 14, and living in a children's home said:

> If they (staff) didn't care about us they wouldn't be here. It's because they care about us that they look after us properly. All the staff are great. I think they're all top.
>
> Barter *et al.*, 2004, p. 202

Children in all settings describe the importance of friends, of having people who listen to them and care for them, of keeping in close contact with their families and of feeling safe. Any children away from home should be able to describe aspects of their current 'home' that they enjoy and help them. It is a simple question to ask, and if children cannot give a good list of things they like about where they live, and name people that they trust and can talk to, there are some safeguarding issues that should be worrying us.

REFERENCES

Abbott, D., Morris, J. and Ward, L. (2000) *Disabled Children and Residential Schools: A Study of Local Authority Policy and Practice*, University of Bristol, Norah Fry Research Centre, Bristol.

Abbott, D., Morris, J. and Ward, L. (2001) *The Best Place to Be? Policy, Practice and the Experiences of Residential School Placements for Disabled Children*, Joseph Rowntree Foundation, York.

Allen, D. (2001) *Training Carers in Physical Interventions: Research Towards Evidence-Based Practice*, British Institute of Learning Disabilities, Kidderminster.

Association of Directors of Social Services, Local Government Association and Youth Justice Board (2003) *The Application of the Children Act (1989) to Children in Young Offender Institutions*, Youth Justice Board, London, www.yjb.gov.uk (accessed 14 September 2008).

Baginsky, M. (2003) *Responsibility Without Power? Local Education Authorities and Child Protection*, NSPCC, London.

Barter, C. (1998) *Investigating Institutional Abuse*, NSPCC, London.

Barter, C. (1999) *Protecting Young People from Racism and Racist Abuse*, NSPCC, London.

Barter, C., Renold, E., Berridge, D. and Cawson, P. (2004) *Peer Violence in Children's Residential Homes*, Palgrave, Basingstoke.

Berridge, D. and Brodie, I. (1998) *Children's Homes Revisited*, Jessica Kingsley, London.

British Institute of Learning Disabilities (2001) *BILD Code of Practice for Trainers in the Use of Physical Interventions*, BILD, Kidderminster.

British Institute of Learning Disabilities (2002) *Easy Guide to Physical Interventions for People with Learning Disabilities, Their Carers and Their Supporters*, BILD, Kidderminster.

British Institute of Learning Disabilities (2004) *Easy Guide to Being Held Safely for Children and Young People with Learning Difficulties and/or Autism, Their Teachers and Parents*, BILD, Kidderminster.

Care Standards Act 2000, Chapter 14, http://www.opsi.gov.uk/acts/acts2000/20000014. htm (accessed 14 September 2008).

Cawson, P., Wattam, C., Brooker, S. and Kelly, G. (2000) *Child Maltreatment in the United Kingdom: A Study of the Prevalence of Child Abuse and Neglect*, NSPCC, London.

ChildLine (1997) *Children Living Away from Home: A Childline Study*, ChildLine, London.

Children Act 1989, Chapter 41, http://www.opsi.gov.uk/acts/acts1989/Ukpga_19890041_en_1.htm (accessed 14 September 2008).

Children Act 2004, Chapter 31, http://www.opsi.gov.uk/acts/acts2004/20040031.htm (accessed 14 September 2008).

Clarke, P. (2002) *By Private Arrangement: Inspection of Arrangements for Supervising Children in Private Foster Care*, Department of Health, London.

Cline, T., Abreu de, G., Fihosy, C. *et al.* (2002) *Minority Ethnic Pupils in Mainly White Schools*, Research Department for Education and Skills, London.

Commission for Health Care Improvement (2004a) *Protecting Children and Young People: Results of an Audit of NHS Organisations in England*, CHI, London, http://www.dfes.gov.uk/acpc/pdfs/Audit-findings_report_web.pdf (accessed 14 September 2008).

Commission for Health Care Improvement (2004b) *Protecting Children and Young People: Results of a Self Assessment Audit of NHS Organisations in Wales*, CHI, London, http://www.wales.nhs.uk/documents/wales_child_prot_english.pdf (accessed 14 September 2008).

Community Care (2004) Owers to watch use of special cells. *Community Care* (1506), 7, http://www.communitycare.co.uk/Articles/2004/01/22/43499/owers-to-watchuse-of-special-cells.html (accessed 14 September 2008).

Curry, D., Knight, V., Owens-Rawle, D. *et al.* (2004) *Restorative Justice in the Juvenile Secure Estate*, Youth Justice Board, London.

Department for Education and Employment (1998) *Section 550A of the Education Act 1996: The Use of Force to Control or Restrain Pupils. Circular 10/98*, Department for Education and Employment, London, http://www.dfes.gov.uk/publications/guidanceonthelaw/10_98/part1.htm (accessed 14 September 2008).

Department for Education and Skills (2002) *Child Protection: Preventing Unsuitable People from Working with Children and Young Persons in the Education Service*, Department for Education and Skills, Darlington, Executive summary, DfES/0278/2002, http://www.teachernet.gov.uk/docbank/index.cfm?id=2172 (accessed 14 September 2008).

Department for Education and Skills (2003) *Bullying – Don't Suffer in Silence: An Anti-Bullying Pack for Schools*, Department for Education and Skills, London, http://www.dfes.gov.uk/bullying/teachersindex.shtml#a (accessed 14 September 2008).

Department for Education and Skills (2004) *Providing Effective Advocacy Services for Children and Young People Making a Complaint under the Children Act 1989 (The Advocacy Services and Representations Procedure (Children) (Amendment) Regulations 2004)*, Department for Education and Skills, London, http://publications.teachernet.gov.uk/eOrderingDownload/GIS04.pdf (accessed 14 September 2008).

Department for Education and Skills (2005a) *Children Looked After by Local Authorities, Year Ending 31 March 2004. England. Volume 1: Commentary and National Tables*, The Stationery Office, London.

Department for Education and Skills (2005b) *Replacement Children Act Guidance on Private Fostering*, Department for Education and Skills, London, www.everychildmatters.gov.uk (accessed 14 September 2008).

Department for Education and Skills (2005c) *Private Fostering: National Minimum Standards for Private Fostering*, Department for Education and Skills, London, www.everychildmatters.gov.uk (accessed 14 September 2008).

Department for Education and Skills (2005d) *Private Fostering: Promoting Awareness of the Notification Requirements*, Department for Education and Skills, London, www.everychildmatters.gov.uk (accessed 14 September 2008).

Department for Education and Skills and Department of Health (2002) *Guidance for Restrictive Physical Interventions: How to Provide Safe Services for People with Learning Disabilities and Autistic Spectrum Disorder*, Department for Education and Skills, Darlington, http://www.teachernet.gov.uk/wholeschool/sen/schools/piguide (accessed 14 September 2008).

Department for Education and Skills and Department of Health (2004) *Guidance on the Delegation of Decisions on 'Overnight Stays' for Looked After Children (LAC (2004) 4)*, Department for Education and Skills, London, http://www.dh.gov.uk/PublicationsAndStatistics/LettersAndCirculars/LocalAuthorityCirculars/AllLocalAuthorityCirculars/LocalAuthorityCircularsArticle/fs/en?CONTENT_ID=4074388&chk=0jOfXB (accessed 14 September 2008).

Department of Health (1993) *Guidance on Permissible Forms of Control in Children's Residential Care (LAC (93) 13)*, Department of Health, London, http://www.dh.gov.uk/en/Publicationsandstatistics/Lettersandcirculars/LocalAuthorityCirculars/AllLocalAuthority/DH_4003969 (accessed 14 September 2008).

Department of Health (1998) *Caring for Children Away from Home: Messages from Research*, John Wiley & Sons, Ltd, Chichester.

Department of Health (1999) *Towards Safer Care: Training and Resource Pack*, Department of Health, London.

Department of Health (2001) *Private Fostering: A Cause for Concern*, Department of Health, London, http://www.dh.gov.uk/PublicationsAndStatistics/Publications/PublicationsPolicyAndGuidance/PublicationsPolicyAndGuidanceArticle/fs/en?CONTENT_ID=4008432&chk=X2G2T4 (accessed 14 September 2008).

Department of Health (2002a) *Children Missing from Care and from Home: A Guide to Good Practice*, Department of Health, London.

Department of Health (2002b) *Children Missing from Care and from Home: Good Practice Guidance (LAC (2002) 17)*, Department of Health, London, http://www.dh.gov.uk/PublicationsAndStatistics/LettersAndCirculars/LocalAuthorityCirculars/AllLocalAuthorityCirculars/LocalAuthorityCircularsArticle/fs/en?CONTENT_ID=4004872&chk=AaEVVh (accessed 14 September 2008).

Department of Health (2002c) *Children's Homes: National Minimum Standards, Children's Homes Regulations*, The Stationery Office, London, http://www.dh.gov.uk/PublicationsAndStatistics/Publications/PublicationsPolicyAndGuidance/PublicationsPolicyAndGuidanceArticle/fs/en?CONTENT_ID=4010076&chk=1q/vZn (accessed 14 September 2008).

Department of Health (2002d) *Fostering Services: National Minimum Standards, Fostering Services Regulations*, The Stationery Office, London, http://www.dh.gov.uk/PublicationsAndStatistics/Publications/PublicationsPolicyAndGuidance/PublicationsPolicyAndGuidanceArticle/fs/en?CONTENT_ID=4005551&chk=PkyT3d (accessed 14 September 2008).

Department of Health (2002e) *Care Standards Act 2000: A Guide for Registered Service Providers*, Department of Health, London, http://www.publications.doh.gov.uk/cebulletin21march.htm (accessed 14 September 2008).

Department of Health (2002f) *National Standards for the Provision of Children's Advocacy Services*, Department of Health, London, http://www.dh.gov.uk/Consultations/ResponsesToConsultations/ResponsesToConsultationsDocumentSummary/fs/en?CONTENT_ID=4017049&chk=vFWybl (accessed 14 September 2008).

Department of Health and Department for Education and Skills (2004a) *National Service Framework for Children, Young People and Maternity Ser-*

vices: Child and Adolescent Mental Health Services (CAMHS), Department of Health, London, http://www.dh.gov.uk/PolicyAndGuidance/HealthAndSocialCare Topics/ChildrenServices/ChildrenServicesInformation/fs/en (accessed 14 September 2008).

Department of Health and Department for Education and Skills (2004b) *National Service Framework for Children, Young People and Maternity Services: Medicines for Children and Young People*, Department of Health, London, http://www.dh.gov.uk/ PolicyAndGuidance/HealthAndSocialCareTopics/ChildrenServices/ ChildrenServicesInformation/fs/en (accessed 14 September 2008).

Department of Health, Home Office, Department for Education and Employment and National Assembly for Wales (2000) *Safeguarding Children Involved in Prostitution: Supplementary Guidance to Working Together to Safeguard Children*, Department of Health, London, http://www.dh.gov.uk/PublicationsAndStatistics/Publications/ PublicationsPolicyAndGuidance/PublicationsPolicyAndGuidanceArticle/fs/en? CONTENT_ID=4006037&chk=WonBkz (accessed 14 September 2008).

Epps, K. (1999) Looking after young sexual abusers: child protection, risk management and risk reduction, in *Children and Young People Who Sexually Abuse Others* (eds M. Erooga and H. Masson), Routledge, London.

Farmer, E. and Pollock, S. (1998) *Sexually Abused and Abusing Children in Substitute Care*, John Wiley & Sons, Ltd, Chichester.

Frosh, S., Phoenix, A. and Pattman, R. (2002) *Young Masculinities: Understanding Boys in Contemporary Society*, Palgrave, Basingstoke.

Gibbs, I. and Sinclair, I. (2000) Bullying, sexual harassment and happiness in residential children's homes. *Child Abuse Review*, **9** (4), 247–56.

Hackett, S., Masson, H. and Phillips, S. (2003) *Mapping and Exploring Services for Young People Who Have Sexually Abused Others*, University of Durham and University of Huddersfield, Durham, http://www.nspcc.org.uk/inform/research/findings/ mappingandexploringservices_wda48266.html (accessed 14 September 2008).

Hagell, A. (2002) *The Mental Health of Young Offenders*, Mental Health Foundation, London.

Harris, J., Allen, D., Cornick, M. *et al.* (1996) *Physical Interventions: A Policy Framework*, BILD, Kidderminster.

Hart, D. (2004) Forcing the issue. *Community Care*, **1519**, 38–40.

Hart, D. and Howell, S. (2004) *Physical Intervention across Children's Services*, National Children's Bureau, London.

Hayden, C. (1998) *The Use of Physical Restraint in Children's Residential Care*, Social Services Research and Information Unit, Portsmouth.

Hayden, C., Goddard, J., Gorin, S. and Van Der Spek, N. (1999) *State Child Care: Looking After Children?* Jessica Kingsley, London.

Hazel, N., Hagell, A., Liddle, M. *et al.* (2002) *Detention and Training: Assessment of the Detention and Training Order and Its Impact on the Secure Estate Across England and Wales*, Policy Research Bureau, London.

Her Majesty's Chief Inspector of Prisons for England and Wales (2003) *Annual Report of HM Chief Inspector of Prisons for England and Wales 2002–2003*, The Stationery Office, London, http://www.inspectorates.homeoffice.gov.uk/hmiprisons/about-us (accessed 14 September 2008).

HM Government (2006a) *What To Do If You're Worried A Child Is Being Abused*, The Stationery Office, London, http://www.everychildmatters.gov.uk/socialcare/ safeguarding (accessed 14 September 2008).

HM Government (2006b) *Working Together to Safeguard Children: A Guide to Inter-Agency Working to Safeguard and Promote the Welfare of Children*, The Stationery Office, London, http://www.everychildmatters.gov.uk/socialcare/safeguarding/workingtogether/ (accessed 14 September 2008).

HM Inspectorate of Prisons and Youth Justice Board (2004) *Juveniles in Custody 2003–2004: An Analysis of Children's Experiences of Prison*, HM Inspectorate of Prisons and Youth Justice Board, London, http://www.yjb.gov.uk/publications (accessed 14 September 2008).

Hobbs, G., Hobbs, C. and Wynne, J. (1999) Abuse of children in residential and foster care. *Child Abuse and Neglect*, **23** (12), 1239–52.

Holman, B. (2002) *The Unknown Fostering: A Study of Private Fostering*, Russell House, Lyme Regis.

Home Office (2004) *Paying the Price: A Consultation Paper on Prostitution*, Home Office, London, http://www.homeoffice.gov.uk/documents/cons-paying-the-price (accessed 14 September 2008).

Hopkins, B. (2004) *Just Schools: A Whole School Approach to Restorative Justice*, Jessica Kingsley, London.

Howard League for Penal Reform (1995) *Banged up, Beaten up, Cutting up (Report of the Howard League Commission of Inquiry into Violence in Penal Institutions for Young People. Chair: Helena Kennedy)*, Howard League for Penal Reform, London.

Howard League for Penal Reform (2002) *Children in Prison – Barred Rights: An In-dependent Submission to the United Nations Committee on the Rights of the Child*, Howard League for Penal Reform, London.

Kendrick, A. (1997) Safeguarding children living away from home from abuse: literature review, in *Children's Safeguards Review* (ed. R. Kent), Scottish Office, Edinburgh.

Kent, R. (1997) *Children's Safeguards Review*, Social Work Services Inspectorate for Scotland, Scottish Office, Edinburgh.

Knight, A. (1998) *Valued or Forgotten? Independent Visitors and Disabled Young People*, National Children's Bureau, London.

Lader, D., Singleton, N. and Meltzer, H. (2000) *Psychiatric Morbidity among Young Offenders in England and Wales: Further Analysis of Data from the ONS Survey of Psychiatric Morbidity among Prisoners in England and Wales carried out in 1997 on Behalf of the Department of Health*, Office for National Statistics, London, http://www.statistics.gov.uk/StatBase/Product.asp?ComboState=Show+Links&More=Y&vlnk=10552&LinkBtn.x=41&LinkBtn.y=13 (accessed 14 September 2008).

Lemos, G. (2005) *The Search for Tolerance: Challenging Racist Attitudes and Behaviour in Young People*, Joseph Rowntree Foundation, York.

Marr, N. and Field, T. (2001) *Bullycide: Death at Playtime*, Success Unlimited, Didcot.

Mears, A., White, R., Banerjee, S., *et al.* (2003a) *An Evaluation of the Use of the Children Act 1989 and the Mental Health Act 1983 in Children and Adolescents in Psychiatric Settings (CAMHA-CAPS). Final Report to the Department of Health*, Royal College of Psychiatrists' Research Unit, London.

Mears, A., White, R., O'Herlihy, A., *et al.* (2003b) Characteristics of the detained and informal child and adolescent psychiatric in-patient populations. *Child and Adolescent Mental Health*, **8** (3), 131–34.

Mental Health Act 1983, Chapter 20, The Stationery Office, London, http://www.dh.gov.uk/en/PublicationsAndStatistics/Legislation/ActsAndBills/DH_4002034 (accessed 14 September 2008).

Morgan, R. (2004a) *Being a Boarder: A Survey of Boarders' and Parents' Views on Boarding Schools*, Commission for Social Care Inspection, Newcastle upon Tyne, www.ofsted.gov.uk (accessed 14 September 2008).

Morgan, R. (2004b) *Safe from Harm: Children's Views Report*, Commission for Social Care Inspection, Newcastle upon Tyne, www.ofsted.gov.uk (accessed 14 September 2008).

Morgan, R. (2004c) *Children's Views on Restraint: The Views of Children and Young People in Residential Homes and Residential Special Schools*, Commission for Social Care Inspection, Newcastle on Tyne, www.ofsted.gov.uk (accessed 14 September 2008).

Morris, J. (1995) *Gone Missing? A Research and Policy Review of Disabled Children Living Away from Home*, Who Cares? Trust, London.

Morris, J. (1998) *Still Missing? Volume 1. The Experiences of Disabled Children and Young People Living Away from their Families*, Who Cares? Trust, London.

Morris, J. (2006) *Safeguarding Disabled Children – A Resource for Local Safeguarding Children Boards*, London Council for Disabled Children, http://www.everychildmatters.gov.uk/resources-and-practice (accessed 14 September 2008).

National Assembly for Wales (2002) *Too Serious a Thing: The Review of Safeguards for Children and Young People Treated and Cared for by the NHS in Wales*, The Carlile Review, National Assembly for Wales, Cardiff, http://www.wales.gov.uk/publications (accessed 14 September 2008).

National Care Standards Commission (2004) *How Do We Care? The Availability of Registered Care Homes and Children's Homes and Their Performance against National Minimum Standards 2002–03*, NCSC, London.

National Inquiry into Self-harm among Young People (2006) *Truth Hurts*, Mental Health Foundation, London, www.selfharm.org (accessed 14 September 2008).

National Institute for Clinical Excellence (2004a) *Self-harm: Short Term Treatment and Management. Understanding NICE Guidance – Information for People who Self-Harm, Their Advocates and Carers, and the Public (Including Information for Young People Under 16 Years)*, NICE, London, http://www.nice.org.uk/Guidance/CG16/PublicInfo/pdf/English (accessed 14 September 2008).

National Institute for Clinical Excellence (2004b) *Self-harm: The Short Term Physical and Psychological Management and Secondary Prevention of Self-Harm in Primary and Secondary Care*, NICE, London, http://www.nice.org.uk/nicemedia/pdf/CG016NICEguideline.pdf (accessed 14 September 2008).

National Working Group on Child Protection and Disability (2003) *'It Doesn't Happen to Disabled Children': Child Protection and Disabled Children*, NSPCC, London.

Oliver, C. and Candappa, M. (2003) *Tackling Bullying: Listening to the Views of Children and Young People*, ChildLine and Department for Education and Skills, London.

Paul, A. and Cawson, P. (2002) Safeguarding disabled children in residential settings: what we know and what we don't know. *Child Abuse Review*, **11** (5), 262–81.

Paul, A., Cawson, P. and Paton, J. (2004) *Safeguarding Disabled Children in Residential Special Schools*, NSPCC, London.

Pearce, J., Williams, M. and Galvin, C. (2003) *It's Someone Taking a Part of You: A Study of Young Women and Sexual Exploitation*, National Children's Bureau, London.

Rees, G. (2001) *Working with Young Runaways: Learning from Practice*, Street Solutions, Children's Society, London.

Rees, G. (2004) Thrown away: young people forced to leave home. *Childright* (208), 14–16, http://www.childrenslegalcentre.com/NR/rdonlyres/1F26DD94-7935-4758-BB3B-2FFBCF55B2F7/0/JULAUG2004.pdf (accessed 14 September 2008).

Rees, G. and Siakeu, J. (2004) *Thrown Away: The Experiences of Children Forced to Leave Home*. Children's Society, London, www.childrenssociety.org.uk (accessed 14 September 2008).

Royal College of Nursing (2003) *Restraining, Holding Still and Containing Children and Young People: Guidance for Nursing Staff*, Royal College of Nursing, London.

Russell, F. (2004) Segregating children in prison. *Childright* (207), 14–15, http://www.childrenslegalcentre.com/NR/rdonlyres/4099E208-0AEB-462F-BF91-AC42A96CD878/0/JUNE2004.pdf (accessed 14 September 2008).

School Standards and Framework Act 1998, Chapter 31, http://www.opsi.gov.uk/acts/acts1998/19980031.htm (accessed 14 September 2008).

S.I. 2006/1067, The School Staffing (England) (Amendment) Regulations 2006.

S.I. 2006/1068, The Education (Pupil Referral Units) (Application of Enactments) (England) (Amendment) Regulations 2006.

Sinclair, I. and Gibbs, I. (1998) *Children's Homes: A Study in Diversity*, John Wiley & Sons, Ltd, Chichester.

Social Exclusion Unit (2002) *Young Runaways: Report by the Social Exclusion Unit*, Office of the Deputy Prime Minister, London, http://www.cabinetoffice.gov.uk/social_exclusion_task_force/~/media/assets/www.cabinetoffice.gov.uk/social_exclusion_task_force/publications_1997_to_2006/young_runaways%20pdf.ashx (accessed 14 September 2008).

Social Services Inspectorate (2000) *Privately Arranged Fostering Placements – Your Council's Responsibilities (CI (2000) 9)*, Department of Health Publications, London.

Solomon, E. (2004) *A Measure of Success: An Analysis of the Prison Service's Performance Against Its Key Performance Indicators*, Prison Reform Trust, London, http://www.prisonreformtrust.org.uk/research1.html (accessed 14 September 2008).

Somerset, C. (2004) *Cause For Concern? London Social Services and Child Trafficking*, ECPAT UK, London, http://www.ecpat.org.uk/publications.html (accessed 14 September 2008).

St John, T. (2004) Self-harm among young people. *Childright* (207), 4–5, http://www.childrenslegalcentre.com/NR/rdonlyres/4099E208-0AEB-462F-BF91-AC42A96CD878/0/JUNE2004.pdf (accessed 14 September 2008).

Stalker, K., Carpenter, J., Phillips, R. *et al.* (2003) *Care and Treatment? Supporting Children with Complex Needs in Health Care Settings*, Joseph Rowntree Foundation and Pavilion, Brighton.

Stuart, M. and Baines, C. (2004a) *Progress on Safeguards for Children Living Away from Home: A Review of Action Since the People Like Us Report*, Joseph Rowntree Foundation, York.

Stuart, M. and Baines, C. (2004b) *Progress on Safeguards for Children Living Away from Home: Three Studies on Abusers, Disabled Children and Children in Prison*, Joseph Rowntree Foundation, York.

Timms, J. and Thoburn, J. (2003) *Your Shout! A Survey of the Views of 706 Young People in Public Care*, NSPCC, London, http://www.nspcc.org.uk/inform (accessed 14 September 2008).

Unicef (2003) *End Child Exploitation: Stop the Traffic*, Unicef, London, http://www.unicef.org/media/media_13034.html (accessed 14 September 2008).

Utting, W. (1997) *People Like Us: The Report of the Review of the Safeguards for Children Living Away from Home*, The Stationery Office, London.

Waterhouse, R. (2000) *Lost in Care: Report of the Tribunal of Inquiry into the Abuse of Children in Care in the Former County Council Areas of Gwynedd and Clwyd Since 1974*, The Stationery Office, London.

Williams, A. (2003) *Staff Guide to the Children's Homes Standards and Regulations*, National Children's Bureau, London.

Winn Oakley, M. and Masson, J. (2000) *Official Friends and Friendly Officials: Support, Advice and Advocacy for Children and Young People in Public Care*, NSPCC, London.

Youth Justice Board (2004a) *National Standards for Youth Justice Services*, Youth Justice Board, London, http://www.yjb.gov.uk/Publications (accessed 14 September 2008).

Youth Justice Board (2004b) *Strategy for the Secure Estate for Juveniles*, Youth Justice Board, London, http://www.yjb.gov.uk/Publications (accessed 14 September 2008).

Youth Justice Board (2006) *Managing the Behaviour of Children and Young People in the Secure Estate*, Youth Justice Board, London, http://www.yjb.gov.uk/ Publications (accessed 14 September 2008).

FURTHER READING

Farrant, F. (2001) *Troubled Inside: Responding to the Mental Health Needs of Children and Young People in Prison*, Prison Reform Trust, London.

Her Majesty's Chief Inspector of Education, Children's Services and Skills, Chief Executive, Healthcare Commission, Chief Inspector of the Commission for Social Care Inspection, Her Majesty's Chief Inspector of Constabulary, Her Majesty's Chief Inspector of the Crown Prosecution Service Inspectorate, Her Majesty's Chief Inspector of Court Administration, Her Majesty's Chief Inspector of Prisons and Her Majesty's Chief Inspector of Probation (2008) *Safeguarding Children 2008: The Third Joint Chief Inspectors' Report on Arrangements to Safeguard Children*, OFSTED, London, http://www.safeguardingchildren.org.uk/content/download/ 2682/16842/file/Safeguarding%20Children%202008.pdf (accessed 14 September 2008).

Jerrom, C. (2004) Campaigners and Inspectors unite over transportation of children. *Community Care*, 18–19, http://www.communitycare.co.uk/Articles/2004/07/15/ 45548/campaigners-and-inspectors-unite-over-transportation-of.html (accessed 14 September 2008).

Kurtz, Z. and James, C. (2002) *What's New: Learning from the CAMHS Innovation Projects*, Department of Health, London, http://www.dh.gov.uk/ PolicyAndGuidance/HealthAndSocialCareTopics/ChildrenServices/ ChildrenServicesInformation/ChildrenServicesInformationArticle/fs/en? CONTENT_ID=4049198&chk=IbLuOk (accessed 14 September 2008).

Social Services Inspectorate (1993) *A Place Apart: An Investigation into the Handling and Outcomes of Serious Injuries to Children and Other Matters at Aycliffe, Centre for Children, County Durham*, Social Services Inspectorate, London.

Thoburn, J., Chand, A. and Procter, J. (2004) *Child Welfare Services for Minority Ethnic Families: The Research Reviewed*, Jessica Kingsley, London.

5 Working Effectively in a Multi-Agency Context

JAN HORWATH

Effective collaborative working is the cornerstone of a successful children's safeguarding system. Indeed, for organisations, safeguarding means:

> ... all agencies working with children, young people and their families take all reasonable measures to ensure that the risks of harm to children's welfare are minimised; and

> where there are concerns about children and young people's welfare, all agencies take appropriate actions to address those concerns, working to agreed local policies and procedures in full partnership with other local agencies.
>
> Cm 5861, 2003, p. 1, Paragraph 5

In this chapter, consideration will be given to the lessons learnt over the past 30 years regarding what works in terms of effective multi-disciplinary safeguarding children practice. The roles and responsibilities of the main agencies and practitioners engaged in safeguarding children will be discussed. The blocks and barriers that prevent effective collaborative endeavours will be explored as well as the specific issues practitioners face when working together to safeguard children.

CORE KNOWLEDGE

- Practitioners and managers use a variety of terms to describe joint working. The terms are frequently used interchangeably to describe collaborative practice.
- There are different forms of collaborative practice. These range from individual practitioners working together on one case to the integration of the whole services working to joint agency management and/or plans.
- All practitioners who come into contact with children and their families have to collaborate with other practitioners to respond to the needs of children and their families. Both practitioners and managers should recognise that

Safeguarding Children   Edited by Hedy Cleaver, Pat Cawson, Sarah Gorin and Steve Walker
Copyright © 2009 by John Wiley & Sons, Ltd

different agencies engaged in safeguarding children have different roles and responsibilities.
- Practitioners and managers should have a clear understanding of the reasons for working together and recognise the barriers that can prevent effective practice, for example, differences in interpretation of thresholds and information that can be shared.
- Collaborative practice involves working in groups. The quality of practice will be influenced by the way in which practitioners and managers work together in these groups. Meaningful communication is key to effective multi-disciplinary working.
- Effective practice is most likely to occur when organisations have systems in place that support collaborative practice.
- Practitioners should identify and address the barriers that have an impact on practice when working together on a particular case.

BACKGROUND TO CURRENT MULTI-AGENCY PRACTICE

The current emphasis on collaborative working in children's services is not new. It has been a theme informing the development of child protection systems in England and Wales for the past 30 years. Issues relating to multi-disciplinary practice were identified in 1974 following the death of Maria Colwell, a 6-year-old who was killed by her stepfather. The report into her death highlighted poor communication between workers from different disciplines and the lack of any systems that facilitated collaborative practice (Department of Health and Social Security, 1974). Because of the report's recommendations, local inter-agency child protection systems were introduced. These were designed to promote working together at a strategic and practice level (Barton, 2002). Since 1974, the government's child protection guidance has been built on this initial guidance. Subsequent guidance has developed and refined systems to support working together at both an operational and a practice level (see, e.g., Department of Health and Social Security, 1986, 1988; Home Office *et al.*, 1991; HM Government, 2006a).

Although this guidance has contributed to improving multi-disciplinary practice, there are still unresolved issues, as highlighted by the Victoria Climbié Inquiry (Cm 5730, 2003). The government has recognised these issues in the Green Paper *Every Child Matters* (Cm 5860, 2003). More specifically, the government recognised that

Our existing system for supporting children and young people who are beginning to experience difficulties is often poorly coordinated and accountability is unclear.

Cm 5860, 2003, p. 21

The government has sought to address these issues in a number of ways – firstly, through the introduction of local safeguarding children boards (LSCBs) and children's trusts. The LSCBs consist of senior representatives from key agencies involved in arrangements to safeguard and promote the welfare of children, including housing, health, the police and the probation services. The LSCBs coordinate and ensure the effectiveness of the work of the partner agencies in relation to safeguarding and promoting the welfare of children. They are the statutory successors to the Area Child Protection Committees (ACPCs), which were formerly responsible for coordinating local practice in relation to safeguarding and promoting the welfare of children. The children's trusts integrate the local arrangements of many of the key agencies that come into contact with children and families. The integration of these services should address many of the structural barriers that have, in the past, affected the quality of multi-disciplinary practice. Secondly, agencies are expected to cooperate in the interests of children under sections 27 and 47 of the Children Act 1989 (see Glossary). The Children Act 2004 (s 10) strengthens collaborative working by placing a duty on each children's services authority in England to make arrangements to cooperate with relevant partners with a view to improving the well-being of children in its area.

Whilst system change should support multi-disciplinary practice, frontline practitioners from different disciplines and professional backgrounds still need to find effective ways of working together. Effective collaborative working to safeguard and promote the welfare of children requires practitioners and agencies to be clear about

- their roles and responsibilities and the reasons for working together in a particular case;
- the legislative basis for the work;
- the protocols and procedures that should be followed;
- the agency, team or professional with lead responsibility;
- timescales-governing practice.

HM Government, 2006b, Paragraph 1

When individual practitioners or senior managers work well together, then their efforts promote better outcomes for children and their families. However, multi-disciplinary practice is complex. Issues of lack of ownership, communication problems, poor understanding of roles and responsibilities, mistrust amongst practitioners and status issues all act as barriers to effective collaboration. This in turn can leave children in vulnerable situations or indeed result in child deaths (Hallett and Birchall, 1992; Department of Health, 1995; Hallett, 1995; Murphy, 1995; Calder and Horwath, 1999; Sinclair and Bullock, 2002; Cm 5860, 2003). In this chapter, we explore some of these issues. However, before doing so it is important to establish what is meant by collaborative working.

COLLABORATIVE WORKING – WHAT IS IN A NAME?

'Communication', 'cooperation', 'coordination' and 'collaboration' are all terms used to describe joint working. Whilst different academics have provided definitions of these terms, there is a lack of consensus in the literature about their meaning (Leathard, 2003). In the experience of the author, this has resulted in practitioners using the terms interchangeably to describe sharing information, coming together for formal multi-disciplinary meetings, such as child protection conferences, and working together on child and family assessments and intervention plans.

Collaborative practice takes place in different arenas. These include the following.

NETWORKS

Practitioners come together to work on a specific case. In England, practitioners are expected to operate in networks when they assess, plan and intervene to safeguard and promote the welfare of children in need. Practitioners come together, usually with family members, to discuss concerns and make and review plans to respond to the identified needs of the children and their family (HM Government, 2006a; Department of Health, Department for Education and Employment and Home Office, 2000).

ONE-STOP SHOPS

These are services delivered from the same building, with service users having one point of access to a range of services. The children's centres and extended schools described in the Green Paper *Every Child Matters* (Cm 5860, 2003) and Sure Start are examples of one-stop shops. Other examples include a multi-agency family centre for disabled children where practitioners from different agencies are based at the centre so that information and services are available at one point of entry (Cigno and Gore, 1999), and multi-agency child care projects that provide coordinated, open access, mainstream services to support families and young children (Wigfall and Moss, 2001).

MULTI-DISCIPLINARY TEAMS

In this setting, previously separated services are combined to provide a new integrated service based at one location. Practitioners from different disciplines come together on a permanent basis and operate as members of one team. They work together, developing a package to identify and/or meet the needs of the service user. The multi-disciplinary teams described in the statutory guidance on inter-agency cooperation to improve the well-being of children (HM Government, 2005), such as youth offending teams and child and adolescent mental health services (CAMHS) teams, are examples of integrated teams.

The difference between the terms 'multi-disciplinary' and 'inter-agency' can also be confusing. Multi-disciplinary collaboration refers to individuals from different disciplines or professions, and possibly agencies, working together at a practice level. In contrast, inter-agency collaboration refers to an organisational commitment to work together. It means that senior managers within agencies or disciplines work together at a strategic level laying down the framework for multi-disciplinary practice (Horwath and Morrison, 1999).

For more information on the different ways in which multi-disciplinary services can be delivered, see Loxley (1997), Lupton, North and Khan (2001), Macdonald and Williamson (2002), Roaf (2002) and Gardner (2003).

THE COLLABORATORS: THE ROLES OF THE KEY AGENCIES ENGAGED IN SAFEGUARDING AND PROMOTING THE WELFARE OF CHILDREN

Collaborative practice in suspected cases of child maltreatment should be informed by *Working Together to Safeguard Children: A Guide to Inter-Agency Working to Safeguard and Promote the Welfare of Children* (HM Government, 2006a) and the *Framework for the Assessment of Children in Need and Their Families* (Department of Health, Department for Education and Employment and Home Office, 2000). This guidance is underpinned by an ecological approach towards child welfare. An ecological approach involves considering not only the developmental needs of the child but also the parent or carer's ability to respond to these needs, the parenting issues that may have an impact on parenting capacity and the family, and environmental factors that influence both the child and family. If this approach is to be effective, practitioners from a range of disciplines have to collaborate to respond to the needs of the child and family. This includes all practitioners who come into direct and indirect contact with children and families and whose work may impact on parental capacity or the home or wider environment in which a parent is bringing up a child (see Chapter 3).

INTER-AGENCY ARRANGEMENTS – ROLES AND RESPONSIBILITIES

As outlined above, effective multi-disciplinary practice amongst practitioners is dependent on appropriate inter-agency arrangements for collaborative work being in place. LSCBs are responsible for these arrangements. Each board consists of senior managers from the different services and professional groups who cooperate and make local arrangements to safeguard and promote the welfare of children in the area, on the basis of national policy and guidance.

Safeguarding Children: A Joint Chief Inspectors' Report on Arrangements to Safeguard Children (Chief Inspector of Social Services *et al.*, 2002) was the first joint inspection report on arrangements to safeguard children. The report summarises the roles and responsibilities of the key agencies engaged in safeguarding children. These agencies include social services, education, police and health bodies. The roles and responsibilities of staff within these agencies, as described in the report, can be divided into those with organisational responsibilities who manage services and those who work directly with service users as listed below. The list also takes into account *What To Do If You're Worried a Child Is Being Abused* (HM Government, 2006b) and *Working Together to Safeguard Children* (HM Government, 2006a) which were written after the first joint inspectors' report.

CHILDREN'S SOCIAL CARE

Organisational

Local authorities, in exercising their children's social care functions, should

- set up the LSCB;
- take a lead role for children in need and ensure that all agencies work together to protect children from significant harm;
- appoint the director for children's services, who is responsible for establishing the LSCB and leading the planning process for children's services.

Practice

Social workers take a lead role in

- undertaking assessments of children in need using the assessment framework and responding by providing support and services;
- undertaking enquiries following allegations or suspicions of abuse, including
  - convening strategy discussions and child protection conferences;
  - initiating court action;
  - coordinating the implementation of child protection plans.
- looking after and planning for children in the care of the local authority and ensuring that they are safeguarded in out-of-home placements.

EDUCATION FUNCTIONS

Organisational

Local authorities, in exercising their education functions, should

- ensure that maintained schools, staff and governors are fully integrated in, and familiar with, local child protection procedures;
- take specific responsibility for the health, safety and welfare of pupils and for related issues such as attendance, behaviour and provision for pupils out of school;

- provide levels of support and advice to independent schools and further education colleges in relation to safeguarding and promoting the welfare of pupils and child protection similar to those of maintained schools;
- ensure that channels of communication are established so that children receive support services promptly and any allegations of abuse are properly investigated.

Practice

There are a range of educational practitioners such as teachers and early years workers who are responsible for

- safeguarding children as well as promoting the health and welfare of children by
  - promoting good attendance,
  - managing behaviour,
  - tackling bullying and other forms of harassment,
  - providing personal, social and health education;
- implementing child protection procedures, including recognising and reporting possible child abuse or neglect, and providing appropriate assessments, reports and services;
- appointing designated child protection staff in schools with responsibility for coordinating action within the school and liaising with other agencies;
- paying specific attention to groups at risk of poor achievement, including looked-after children and those with special needs.

THE POLICE

Organisational

Police should

- be core members of the LSCB;
- provide a child protection unit;
- manage and monitor sex offenders through multi-agency public protection panels (MAPPPs).

Practice

Policing duties include

- protecting children from abuse or neglect;
- protecting the interests of child witnesses;
- exercising powers in connection with child care issues, missing children and children who offend;
- investigating crimes against children or where children are victims;

- proactive operations against those who exploit children, including child sex abusers;
- preventing child prostitution and child pornography.

HEALTH

Organisational

Primary care trusts should

- be core members of the LSCB;
- appoint a designated doctor and nurse for child protection;
- ensure that there are named doctors and nurses in each trust;
- ensure clear service standards for safeguarding and promoting the welfare of children.

The NHS should

- employ designated leads in nursing and paediatric medicine to take a strategic lead in service planning and serve on the LSCB;
- ensure that leads are supported by named doctors and nurses who should assist with internal training, clinical supervision, auditing and implementing new procedures.

Practice

Health practitioners – including general practitioners, midwives, health visitors, school nurses and adult mental health workers – should

- ensure that children receive the care, support and treatment they need in order to promote children's health and development;
- recognise and report situations of possible child abuse or neglect;
- where appropriate, provide assessments, reports and services within the safeguarding children context of local procedures.

OTHER PROFESSIONAL GROUPS

There are many other groups of practitioners who can be involved in safeguarding and promoting the welfare of children. Their roles and responsibilities can be summarised as follows.

Organisational

- Contributing to the LSCB as appropriate.
- Ensuring that staff receive the relevant child protection training as outlined in *Working Together* (HM Government, 2006a).

- Ensuring that staff are familiar with local child protection procedures.
- Providing staff with guidance, supervision and support to contribute to safeguarding children.

Practice

- Identifying and referring potential cases of child abuse or neglect in line with *What To Do If You're Worried a Child Is Being Abused* (HM Government, 2006b).
- Contributing to assessments and providing services to meet child and family needs as appropriate to roles and responsibilities.

For more information regarding the roles and responsibilities of various professional groups, see Murphy (1995), Briggs and Hawkins (1998), Bannon and Carter (2002), HM Government (2006a, 2006b).

For further discussion of inter-agency collaboration when children are living away from home, see Chapter 4; for initial inter-agency consultations and referrals, see Chapter 7; for practitioners' contributions to assessment, see Chapter 8.

WHAT WORKS?

As described above, a wide range of practitioners are engaged in safeguarding and promoting the welfare of children. These practitioners work in a variety of settings, for example, statutory, voluntary and independent agencies or community group settings. They also receive different professional training. In addition, for some practitioners working with children, abuse issues may be central to their role while for others child protection work may be one of many professional activities. These differences will inevitably influence the way in which practitioners work together at both a strategic and practice level. Effective collaboration amongst practitioners is dependent on two factors: the way in which practitioners approach working together and maintain multi-disciplinary relationships and the inter-agency systems created and sustained by organisations at a local level to promote multi-disciplinary working. These are explored in detail below.

INTER-AGENCY SYSTEMS THAT PROMOTE MULTI-DISCIPLINARY PRACTICE

Hudson *et al.* (2003) have developed a framework that describes 10 components for successful 'collaborative endeavour' (p. 253). The components have been adapted below to identify the ingredients for effective working together amongst members of ACPCs or LSCBs.

THE APPROACH TOWARDS COLLABORATION

Effective partnership is dependent on senior managers having a legitimate mandate for collaboration. This is reinforced through the Children Act 2004 that places a duty on children's services authorities to cooperate with their partner agencies and to set up LSCBs, and is outlined in *Working Together* (HM Government, 2005). In addition, senior managers should adopt a local model of collaboration that is likely to benefit all contributing organisations. For example, members of some local ACPCs have negotiated with participating organisations that one or more representatives from all contributing agencies will be on the executive committee. Other ACPCs have reached different arrangements, for example, establishing a small executive group of representatives of key partner agencies that consult with a much larger forum of representatives from all agencies who come into contact with children and families.

THE CONTEXT

Senior managers should recognise that effective collaboration is not easily achieved. This means that managers should be able to recognise and be prepared to address the local issues that arise through partnership working.

ESTABLISHING PURPOSE

Effective collaboration is dependent on senior managers within all contributing agencies being clear about the reasons for working together to safeguard and promote the welfare of children – their aims. The greater the clarity and commitment to the aims, the more effective inter-agency collaboration will be and the less likely issues of power and status will undermine working together (Hogan and Murphy, 2002). For this reason, collaborative partners should have an agreed sense of what they want to achieve, translated into a mission statement, aims and an operational strategy.

DETERMINING PROCESS

This describes the various ways in which the goals are going to be achieved – for example, the ways in which the partners will work together, how services will be delivered and the systems for planning and delivering services. The process is likely to vary depending on local circumstances.

PAYING ATTENTION TO GROUP DYNAMICS

If collaboration is to be effective, attention should be paid to identifying and addressing the issues that arise when individuals work together at both a management and a practice level. This is discussed in more detail below.

For more information about inter-agency systems, consult the Sainsbury Centre for Mental Health (2000), Hudson *et al.* (2003), Miller and McNicholl (2003).

MULTI-DISCIPLINARY COLLABORATION AT A PRACTICE LEVEL: OVERCOMING THE BARRIERS

As described above, multi-disciplinary collaboration is not only dependent on having systems and structures in place that facilitate working together but on practitioners working together as a team, using their individual skills to meet the needs of the child and their family. To achieve this, practitioners must not only understand the rationale for working together with a particular child and family, they should also understand how they contribute towards achieving the overall goal. *What To Do If You're Worried a Child Is Being Abused* is clear – the overall goal is

> working together to promote children's welfare and safeguard them from harm.

With this in mind practitioners should have an understanding of

> the purpose of their activity, what decisions are required at each stage of the process and what are the intended outcomes for the child and family members.
>
> HM Government, 2006b, Paragraph 1

This makes sense, yet workers do not always agree with each other on

- the purpose of the activity
- the outcomes
- the way in which practitioners should work with other practitioners and the family.

When lack of agreement occurs, practice can become subjective and the needs of the child and family are not met. The reasons why this occurs are explored in detail below.

THRESHOLDS AND INTERPRETATIONS

Although *Working Together* (HM Government, 2006a) provides us with standardised definitions of physical abuse, neglect, sexual abuse and emotional abuse, the joint inspectors (Commission for Social Care Inspection *et al.*, 2005) noted considerable concerns about the differing thresholds applied by social work services in their child protection and family support work. Interpreting definitions of abuse and the way they are applied to each child and his or her situation requires the use of professional judgement. One of the challenges of multi-disciplinary practice is recognising that practitioners hold different views about children in need. In addition, the 'thresholds of concern' may vary amongst practitioners. What worries one professional may not concern another to the same extent. Using child neglect as an example, Stone (1998) provided professionals from a range of disciplines with scenarios about child neglect. The professionals agreed on the situations they considered dangerous. However, there was a lack of consensus regarding situations that were safe and there were many areas where they could not agree as to how dangerous the situation was and when to refer to social services. These findings are similar to those of Birchall and Hallett (1995). They noted differences between teachers, health visitors and social workers in assessments of the severity of neglectful situations. Taylor and Daniel (1999) also found differences between health and social care providers' responses and interventions with children who were failing to thrive through non-organic causes.

For further help on identifying worrying situations involving a child, see Chapter 6.

The lack of clarity amongst practitioners about identifying and referring concerns to children's social care means that practitioners are likely to fall back on their professional experience and personal values to decide when to contact social services (Buckley, 2003). If practitioners have had poor experiences of making referrals to other practitioners, this too will influence their approach. For example, the joint chief inspectors who prepared *Safeguarding Children* (Chief Inspector of Social Services *et al.*, 2002; Commission for Social Care Inspection *et al.*, 2005) found teachers reluctant to report concerns to social workers as they had lost confidence in social services' ability to respond positively to the referrals. The inspectors warn of the dangers of this situation noting that

> this left agencies feeling responsible for working with situations that they considered posed high risks of harm to children's welfare.
>
> Chief Inspector of Social Services *et al.*, 2002, Section 6.11, p. 47

There are other situations when practitioners who are anxious about a child and anticipate a negative response from social workers may emphasise the worst aspects of the case in an attempt to get it accepted by children's social services (Dingwall, 1989; Thorpe, 1994; Scott, 1997). Scott noted that social workers can adjust to these types of referrals by discounting what they consider an over-exaggeration of a situation. These responses from social workers do not mean that they are being deliberately difficult or obstructive. Rather they reflect ways in which social workers attempt to manage situations where the demands for services exceed supply. The chief inspectors note that differences over thresholds are far less prominent in areas where multi-agency workshops and training take place on a regular basis. When opportunities are available to discuss case scenarios and gain an understanding of the problems encountered by different practitioners working to safeguard and promote children's welfare, this assists in building up effective working relationships.

Practitioners can clarify their thinking about what to do next when they have concerns about a child in the following ways:

• Discuss concerns with colleagues, managers or, for teachers, the designated member of staff and health workers, the named health professional.
• If these concerns remain, practitioners and/or their manager may discuss these concerns with peers or senior colleagues in other agencies without identifying the child in question.
• Practitioners should also complete a preliminary assessment of the child that makes the concerns explicit and includes evidence to support their concerns. This assessment may assist practitioners in clarifying their concerns about the welfare of a child. In addition, the assessment can assist practitioners in determining whether it is appropriate to refer to children's social care or other services that are better placed than children's social care to meet the needs of the child and family.

HM Government, 2006b

For further discussion of approaching other professionals for help, see Chapter 7. Assessment is discussed in more detail in Chapter 8.

Practitioners in North Lincolnshire use a common assessment framework to identify concerns about the welfare of children. This framework is designed for use by all practitioners who may come into contact with children and families. The assessment assists workers in identifying children's needs and enables them to make referrals regarding these needs to other agencies. It has a number of benefits:

• referrals are appropriate;
• children and families do not have to repeat information;
• services are provided more promptly and coherent packages can be put together;
• assessments are triggered when a concern is raised;
• further assessments build on this common assessment.

Cm 5860, 2003, p. 5

WORKING IN A GROUP: TENSIONS AND DILEMMAS

As highlighted above, effective collaboration frequently involves working in groups. For example, practitioners may come together in a group by working together on a particular case through strategy discussions, case planning meetings and core groups. These groups are also likely to include children, parents, caregivers and other family members. Alternatively, a multi-disciplinary team may work together to deliver the children's services. Whether practitioners come together to work on one case or many, the quality of practice will depend on the attention paid to group dynamics (Payne, 2000). There are some specific issues that managers and practitioners should consider.

GROUP SIZE

Determining membership of a multi-disciplinary group is crucial. Kolbo and Strong (1997) found that the effectiveness of multi-disciplinary child sexual abuse teams is enhanced through broad representation and participation of professionals. Bell (2001), in her study of network teams, noted that the size and composition of the group influenced the amount of communication by individual members, and in large groups a single individual dominated. She also found that where a group included a large number of staff from one agency, only one or two agency representatives actually participated. Bell concludes that active participation is encouraged if membership is kept to no more than eight members. It is particularly important to pay attention to the size of the group when children and families are involved. If the group is too large, the family members are likely to be inhibited and their level of participation will be affected.

GROUP THINK

When people come together to form a group, norms regarding the way in which the group operates develop. These can affect the way in which the group members make decisions. Certain ideas become accepted and are not challenged even in the light of new information. This is referred to as 'group think'. In these situations distorted assessments of the child and family situation can occur. For example, beliefs and assumptions may exist amongst group members that a child should remain with his or her parents that are not challenged in light of changing circumstances. Reder, Duncan and Gray (1993) describe how 5-year-old Richard Fraser was murdered by his father. The report into his death highlighted the fact that, despite evidence to the contrary, professionals did not shift from their original belief that the child was safe when his father was there. Janis (1972) believes groups that are most vulnerable to 'group think' are those which

- are very cohesive;
- are insulated from information outside the group;
- rarely search systematically through alternative options;
- are often working under stress and are dominated by a directive group leader.

PROFESSIONAL TRADITIONS AND PRECONCEPTIONS

Differences in professional training and professional socialisation mean that practitioners have different philosophies and approaches to their work that can have an impact on the way in which the practitioners work together. Lupton, North and Khan (2001) note that a lack of consensus exists amongst professionals on two dimensions: 'who does what' and 'how it is done'.

WHO DOES WHAT?

A difference about who does what can result in disputes regarding geographical turf. For example, different geographical boundaries may exist between the primary care trust and the police force, with a primary care trust straddling two different police force areas. This can lead to confusion as the police may operate differently in each force and health staff may not know which police force should be contacted with regard to which patient (Commission for Health Improvement, 2004).

Differences may also exist regarding professional turf. Practitioners may hold different views as to who does what work with the child and family. For example, staff in the family centre may consider that it is the social worker's role to discuss parenting skills with a parent, whilst the social worker may believe staff at the family centre should be doing this. Issues regarding who does what are most likely to occur when

- practitioners are working in a climate where there are fears of job losses;
- funding is limited or new arrangements are being established;
- workers have heavy workloads;
- lack of clarity exists amongst practitioners regarding roles and responsibilities;
- conflicting demands are made on workers' time.

Roaf, 2002

HOW IT IS DONE

How the work is done will depend on a number of factors:

- The theoretical approach taken by the different practitioners – variations may exist depending on whether practitioners take a medical, psychodynamic, behavioural or cognitive approach to understanding child maltreatment. This can lead to different interpretations of the problem and ideas about appropriate interventions.
- The practitioner's specialist area of practice – many practitioners during qualification training or early into their careers specialise in one practice area. This means that practitioners who, for example, specialise in work with children can be relatively uninformed about work with adults and

vice versa. This has been well documented in relation to professio
working with parents who are misusing alcohol and drugs (Cleaver, Un
and Aldgate, 1999), adults with mental health issues (Falkov, 1996; Rede
McClure and Jolley, 2000) and more recently in relation to young people who offend, where the focus is on their offending behaviour and issues related to maltreatment can be marginalised (Chief Inspector of Social
Services *et al.*, 2002).

- Practitioners are in jobs where safeguarding children is considered to be only
  a minor part of their work – in this situation, workers may be less alert to
  factors that may be harmful or abusive to children. For example, ambulance
  crews can be the first people to see a child in his or her home environment.
  Ambulance trusts have policies for reporting 'incidents'. However, the level
  of reporting of information not classed as an incident is unclear. The crew
  may decide not to take a child to hospital but remain concerned about the
  child's home environment and not be clear whether this is a safeguarding
  matter (Commission for Health Improvement, 2004).

If practitioners are to work together in a way that promotes better outcomes
for children and families, then differences in perspectives and approaches have
to be acknowledged and addressed.

PERCEPTIONS OF POWER AND STATUS

Practitioners' perceptions of their own power and status and those of other
group members will influence practitioners' engagement in collaborative practice. Authority within the group will be influenced by the status attached to
different professional groups and their knowledge. For example, medicine has
traditionally been regarded as a high-status profession and greater weight has
usually been given to medical knowledge than to social welfare knowledge.
Hence, medical practitioners may have a disproportionate influence in collaborative working. Power may also derive from the perceived centrality of the
professional's agency to the work (Sinclair and Bullock, 2002). For example,
Calder and Horwath (1999) note that core group members often deferred to
the social worker because of the central role played by social services. In these
situations, if practitioners do not consider themselves to be as important as
other practitioners, they may remain less committed to working together and
may be susceptible to the pull from other agendas within their agency. Alternatively, individuals may be unsure of the value of their contribution and
consequently leave the work to others or they may liaise only with those professionals with whom they feel comfortable (Hall, 1999; Bell, 2001).

If power and status influence practitioners' involvement in collaborative
working, consideration should also be paid to the impact on children and families. It is important to recognise that just as practitioners may feel daunted,
inhibited and reluctant to participate in multi-disciplinary working so may

ence, when working with children and families, prac-
...r ways in which to promote child and family participa-
...a the power and status issues that are likely to be present
...e Chapter 2).

...MMUNICATION

Effective multi-disciplinary working will also be influenced by the way in which practitioners communicate with each other. Reder and Duncan (2003) identify two key issues that negatively influence communication when working to safeguard children. These are

- an uncertain knowledge base, such as lack of understanding regarding issues of confidentiality and the referral process;
- a lack of respect or mistrust of different professional perspectives.

Reder and Duncan argue that effective communication is the responsibility of both message initiator and receiver. Each will put a meaning on the content of the message, which is influenced by their personal values, beliefs and emotional state. In addition, agency context such as policies, workload and inter-agency relationships will also influence the way in which a practitioner delivers or interprets a communication. This is illustrated in the telephone conversation below, which describes poor practice.

Designated teacher to social worker: I want to make a referral regarding a 5-year-old girl called Rosie. She has told her teacher she does not want to go home from school as mum's boyfriend keeps hitting her and locked her in a cupboard where she spent the whole night. Mother and her boyfriend are known drug users and we have had concerns for some time about their parenting, but this is the last straw.

Teacher's thoughts: I will only report the negative things about this case and exaggerate a little. I want the social worker to take me seriously and if I tell her that grandma lives next door, she may not do anything. It is coming up to the weekend and I know I'll have sleepless nights if this is not sorted.

Social worker to teacher: Have you talked to Rosie's mum about this? Perhaps you could do that and get back to us on Monday if you are still worried.

Social worker's thoughts: I've been caught out by staff from this school before. They get panicky about anything. It's typical for them to dump this at the door of children's social care on a Friday. I really want to leave early today and the last thing I need is to go out. In addition, there is that other referral that is likely to need following up before I go.

Interpretation of the content of a dialogue such as the one above will also be influenced by

- the tone of voice of the communicators (Do they sound worried?);
- the non-verbal communication (Do they have information at hand? Have they made a written referral?);
- the time of day and day of the week (Has this been left to a Friday afternoon?);
- the status of the referrer.

The actual words used will also influence the outcome of the communication. For example, a referrer may describe a child as 'inappropriately dressed'. There is no guarantee that one worker's view of inappropriately dressed is the same as another worker's. In addition, one practitioner may use professional jargon that is not understood by the other practitioner. The recipient of the information may lack the confidence to ask for clarification or misinterpret the meaning of the term. The introduction of a common assessment framework signalled in the Green Paper *Every Child Matters* (Cm 5860, 2003) and taken forward in practice guidance (Department for Education and Skills, 2005; HM Government 2006c,d) should go some way towards ensuring that practitioners speak a common language and have a framework for specifying vague concerns.

WORKER ANXIETY

Work to safeguard children can provoke anxiety. A study recently completed by the author in the Republic of Ireland highlighted some of the anxieties held by practitioners who refer cases of child neglect to social work services. These anxieties included

- apprehension about the response from social workers – this included fear of being ignored, having concerns dismissed or views not being taken seriously;
- worry about what the referral will mean for a family – potential referrers were concerned that families will experience considerable distress but with few if any services likely to improve their situation;
- repeating previous negative experiences;
- lack of feedback – practitioners described being left living with uncertainty, as they had no idea what had happened to a child as a result of the referral;
- fears of verbal and physical aggression from parents and carers;
- concerns about the way in which the community will perceive the referrer – this was prevalent amongst practitioners who work and live in the same community or run independent concerns such as private nurseries.

Horwath and Sanders, 2003

Worker anxiety can have a significant impact on practice as practitioners may use a number of defence mechanisms to manage this anxiety, which can distort their perceptions of the needs of the child. These defence mechanisms include

- problem avoidance – denying or minimising the problem;
- wishful thinking – being over-optimistic about a situation;
- collusion – over-identification with the carers.

                    Morrison, 1993; Reder, Duncan and Gray, 1993; Reder and
                                                          Duncan, 1999

INFORMATION SHARING

The joint chief inspectors in the *Safeguarding Children* inspection (Chief Inspector of Social Services *et al.*, 2002) found that staff from all agencies were confused and unclear about their responsibilities in respect of confidentiality and information sharing around child welfare concerns. This can impact on working together to safeguard children. Firstly, decisions may be made about children without crucial information. Secondly, practitioners can become frustrated with and marginalise practitioners who are perceived as being reluctant to share information. The law is not a barrier to sharing information to protect a child from harm. Appendix 3 on Information Sharing in *What To Do If You're Worried a Child Is Being Abused* (HM Government, 2006b) is clear that practitioners should both be aware of the law and comply with the code of conduct or other guidance applicable to their profession. These rarely provide an absolute barrier to the disclosure of information. Hence, practitioners should be prepared to exercise judgement about what to disclose, for what purpose and to whom in the course of their work with children and families. As highlighted in the government's response to the *Victoria Climbié Inquiry* (Cm 5730, 2003, p. 43, Paragraph 2), 'failure to pass on information that might prevent a tragedy can expose professionals to criticism in the same way as an unjustified disclosure.'

It is all too easy to state how practitioners should share information without considering the process that they have to go through before reaching a decision to share information. At a seminar held on 11 December 2003 by the Royal College of General Practitioners, seminar members considered the questions GPs are likely to ask themselves in deciding when to share information. These questions, summarised below, are likely to resonate with other groups of practitioners:

- How long do I wait to make sure that I have sufficient evidence that this child's needs are not being met?
- How do I balance the needs of the child with those of the parent/carer?
- How do I share information while maintaining the trust and confidence of the parent and child?

- How do I reconcile sharing information with the code of conduct of my regulatory body?
- Is there a difference in sharing information with members of my immediate team and the broader child welfare network?

Bastable and Horwath, 2004

Supervision, consultation and support are key in terms of assisting practitioners to answer these questions. Named health practitioners and designated staff in schools have a crucial role to play. Practitioners can also seek assistance from their managers, peers or senior colleagues in other agencies by discussing concerns without identifying the child in question (HM Government, 2006b).

For more information, see Reder, Duncan and Gray (1993), Scott (1997), Reder and Duncan (1999), Munro (2002), Reder and Duncan (2003).

ESSENTIALS FOR EFFECTIVE PRACTICE

Practitioners can promote their own multi-disciplinary practice by identifying and addressing the barriers that have an impact on practice when they work together on a particular case. The following list of questions is designed to assist practitioners working together to meet the needs of children.

CLARIFYING THE TASK

- What is my approach towards children suffering harm and children in need?
- Do I understand my role in terms of identifying and assessing children in need?
- How do I respond to concerns raised by family members and the community?
- Am I familiar with current guidance regarding working together, including working with children and families?
- Are there issues regarding information sharing and confidentiality which are having an impact on my work?
- Do I know whom to contact within my agency if I have concerns about a child or the impact of parenting issues on a child?
- Do I understand the agency procedure for making a referral to children's social care?
- Am I clear about the kind of information I should be sharing with children's social care and other practitioners and the questions I am likely to be asked?
- What are my fears and anxieties about this situation? How could these impact on my practice?

- If a referral to children's social care is not appropriate how can I work with practitioners from other agencies to ensure we focus on the child in the context of the family and the community?

PLANNING MULTI-DISCIPLINARY MEETINGS

- Who is working with this child and family?
- What is the nature of their involvement?
- Are there key agencies who should be involved but do not appear to be working with this family?
- Is there more than one person from the same agency involved with the family? If yes, is it necessary for all those representatives to attend meetings?
- Is there a key group of people who should be working together with the child and family?
- Are there other practitioners that this group can call on when necessary?
- How should we work with the child and family to ensure an appropriate level of participation?

WORKING TOGETHER

- Do we recognise how practitioners from both adult and children's services may be able to contribute to identifying and meeting the needs of this child and family?
- Who holds the power in the multi-professional group working with this family?
- What impact does this have on my contribution to the work?
- How can this distort assessments?
- What are the views emerging about the child and his or her situation? Do they have an evidence base?
- How effectively do we communicate with each other?
- Are there organisational issues that are affecting the work with this child and family?
- How do we work with and engage the family?

MULTI-DISCIPLINARY TRAINING

Multi-disciplinary training is also a very effective method for promoting multi-disciplinary working. It is particularly effective if training is delivered locally so that those who work together have an opportunity to train together. This type of training enables participants to explore the local tensions and dilemmas that practitioners encounter in their everyday practice. Multi-disciplinary training should take place at every level within the organisation. A project developed at the University of Salford for the Department of Health and the General

Social Care Council has published model standards for training staff in inter-agency working (Shardlow *et al.*, 2004).

CONCLUSIONS

As can be seen in this chapter, working together is not easily achieved. If practitioners are to safeguard and promote the welfare of children, they need to operate in agencies that give the message that collaborative practice is important and that it is supported by both senior and middle managers within the organisation. This support has to be more than words. It means having systems in place that support collaborative practice, and most of all it is dependent on senior managers demonstrating good practice by example.

REFERENCES

Bannon, M. and Carter, Y. (2002) *Protecting Children from Abuse and Neglect in Primary Care*, Oxford University Press, Oxford.

Barton, A. (2002) *Managing Fragmentation: An Area Child Protection Committee in a Time of Change*, Ashgate, Aldershot.

Bastable, R. and Horwath, J. (2004) Grasping the Nettle: The GP, the Child and Information Sharing. Unpublished report of a workshop held on 12 December 2004 at the Royal College of General Practitioners.

Bell, L. (2001) Patterns of interaction in multi-disciplinary child protection teams in New Jersey. *Child Abuse and Neglect*, **25**, 65–80.

Birchall, E. and Hallett, C. (1995) *Working Together in Child Protection*, HMSO, London.

Briggs, F. and Hawkins, R. (1998) *Child Protection: A Guide for Teachers and Child Care Professionals*, Allen and Unwin, St Leonards.

Buckley, H. (2003) *Child Protection Work: Beyond the Rhetoric*, Jessica Kingsley, London.

Calder, M. and Horwath, J. (eds) (1999) *Working for Children on the Child Protection Register: An Inter-Agency Guide*, Arena, Aldershot.

Chief Inspector of Social Services, Director for Health Improvement, Commission for Health Improvement, Her Majesty's Chief Inspector of Constabulary, Her Majesty's Chief Inspector of the Crown Prosecution Service, Her Majesty's Chief Inspector of the Magistrates' Courts Service, Her Majesty's Chief Inspector of Schools, Her Majesty's Chief Inspector of Prisons and Her Majesty's Chief Inspector of Probation (2002) *Safeguarding Children: A Joint Chief Inspectors' Report on Arrangements to Safeguard Children*, Department of Health, London, http://www.dh.gov.uk/PublicationsAndStatistics/LettersAndCirculars/ChiefInspectorLetters/ChiefInspectorLettersArticle/fs/en?CONTENT_ID=4004286&chk=PZKIDJ (accessed 4 September 2008).

Children Act 1989, Chapter 41, HMSO, London, http://www.opsi.gov.uk/acts/acts1989/Ukpga_19890041_en_1.htm (accessed 4 September 2008).

Children Act 2004, Chapter 31, HMSO, London, http://www.opsi.gov.uk/acts/acts 2004/20040031.htm (accessed 4 September 2008).

Cigno, K. and Gore, J. (1999) A seamless service: meeting the needs of children with disabilities through a multi-agency approach. *Child and Family Social Work*, **4**, 325–35.

Cleaver, H., Unell, I. and Aldgate, J. (1999) *Children's Needs – Parenting Capacity: The Impact of Parental Mental Illness, Problem Alcohol and Drug Use, and Domestic Violence on Children's Development*, The Stationery Office, London.

Cm 5730 (2003) *The Victoria Climbié Inquiry – Report of an Inquiry by Lord Laming*, The Stationery Office, London, http://www.victoria-climbie-inquiry.org.uk/ finreport/finreport.htm (accessed 4 September 2008).

Cm 5860 (2003) *Every Child Matters*, The Stationery Office, London, www.everychild matters.gov.uk/ (accessed 4 September 2008).

Cm 5861 (2003) *Keeping Children Safe – The Government's Response to the Victoria Climbié Inquiry Report and Joint Inspectors' Report Safeguarding Children*, The Stationery Office, London, http://www.everychildmatters.gov.uk/publications (accessed 4 September 2008).

Commission for Health Improvement (2004) *Protecting Children and Young People: Results of an Audit of NHS Organisations in England*, Commission for Health Improvement, London.

Commission for Social Care Inspection, Her Majesty's Inspectorate of Court Administration, The Healthcare Commission, Her Majesty's Inspectorate of Constabulary, Her Majesty's Inspectorate of Probation, Her Majesty's Inspectorate of Prisons, Her Majesty's Crown Prosecution Service Inspectorate and The Office for Standards in Education (2005) *Safeguarding Children: The Second Joint Chief Inspectors' Report on Arrangements to Safeguard Children*, Commission for Social Care Inspection, London, www.safeguardingchildren.org.uk (accessed 4 September 2008).

Department for Education and Skills (2005) *Common Assessment Framework for Children and Young People*, Department for Education and Skills, London, http://www.everychildmatters.gov.uk/deliveringservices/caf (accessed 4 September 2008).

Department of Health (1995) *Child Protection Messages from Research*, HMSO, London.

Department of Health, Department for Education and Employment and Home Office (2000) *Framework for the Assessment of Children in Need and Their Families*, The Stationery Office, London, http://www.dh.gov.uk/en/Publications andstatistics/Publications/PublicationsPolicyAndGuidance/DH_4003256 (accessed 4 September 2008).

Department of Health and Social Security (1974) Report of the Committee of Inquiry into the Care and Supervision Provided in Relation to Maria Colwell. Department of Health and Social Security, London.

Department of Health and Social Security (1986) *Child Abuse and Working Together: A Draft Guide for Arrangements for Inter-Agency Cooperation for the Protection of Children from Abuse*, HMSO, London.

Department of Health and Social Security (1988) *Working Together: A Guide to Arrangements for Inter-Agency Cooperation for the Protection of Children from Abuse*, HMSO, London.

Dingwall, R. (1989) *Some Problems about Predicting Child Abuse and Neglect*, Harvester Wheatsheaf, Hemel Hempstead.

Falkov, A. (1996) *Study of Working Together 'Part 8' Reports: Fatal Child Abuse and Parental Psychiatric Disorder: An Analysis of 100 Area Child Protection Committee Case Reviews Conducted under the Terms of Part 8 of Working Together under the Children Act 1989*, Department of Health, London.

Gardner, R. (2003) Working together to improve children's life chances: the challenge of interagency collaboration, in *Collaboration in Social Work Practice* (eds J. Wienstein, C. Whittington and T. Leiba), Jessica Kingsley, London.

Hall, C. (1999) Integrating services for children and families: the way forward? *Children and Society*, **13**, 216–22.

Hallett, C. (1995) *Interagency Coordination in Child Protection*, HMSO, London.

Hallett, C. and Birchall, E. (1992) *Coordination in Child Protection*, HMSO, London.

HM Government (2005) *Statutory Guidance on Inter-Agency Cooperation to Improve the Wellbeing of Children: Children's Trusts*, Department for Education and Skills, London, http://www.everychildmatters.gov.uk/strategy/guidance (accessed 4 September 2008).

HM Government (2006a) *Working Together to Safeguard Children: A Guide to Inter-Agency Working to Safeguard and Promote the Welfare of Children*, The Stationery Office, London, http://www.everychildmatters.gov.uk/socialcare/safeguarding/workingtogether (accessed 4 September 2008).

HM Government (2006b) *What To Do If You're Worried a Child Is Being Abused*, Department for Education and Skills, London, http://www.everychildmatters.gov.uk/socialcare/safeguarding (accessed 4 September 2008).

HM Government (2006c) *Common Assessment Framework for Children and Young People: managers' guide*, The Stationery Office, London, http://www.everychildmatters.gov.uk/caf (accessed 22 August 2008).

HM Government (2006d) *Common Assessment Framework for Children and Young People: practitioners' guide*, The Stationery Office, London, http://www.everychildmatters.gov.uk/caf (accessed 22 August 2008).

Hogan, C. and Murphy, D. (2002) *Outcomes: Reframing Responsibility for Well Being*, The Annie Casey Foundation, Baltimore.

Home Office, Department of Health and Department for Education (1991) *Working Together Under the Children Act 1989: A Guide to Arrangements for Inter-Agency Cooperation for the Protection of Children from Abuse*, HMSO, London.

Horwath, J. and Morrison, T. (1999) *Effective Staff Training in Social Care: From Theory to Practice*, Routledge, London.

Horwath, J. and Sanders, T. (2003) *Do You See What I See? Multi-Professional Perspectives on Child Neglect*, North Eastern Health Board and the University of Sheffield, Dunshaughlin.

Hudson, B., Hardy, B., Henwood, M. and Wistow, G. (2003) In pursuit of interagency collaboration in the public sector: what is the contribution of theory and research? in *The Managing Care Reader* (eds J. Reynolds, J. Henderson, J. Seden, J. C. Worth and A. Bullman), Routledge, London.

Janis, I. (1972) *Victims of Group Think*, Houghton Mifflin, Boston.

Kolbo, J. and Strong, E. (1997) Multi-disciplinary team approaches to the investigation and resolution of child abuse and neglect: a national survey. *Child Maltreatment*, **2** (1), 61–72.

Leathard, A. (ed.) (2003) *Interprofessional Collaboration: From Policy to Practice in Health and Social Care*, Brunner-Routledge, Hove.

Loxley, A. (1997) *Collaboration in Health and Welfare*, Jessica Kingsley, London.

Lupton, C., North, N. and Khan, P. (2001) *Working Together or Pulling Apart?* Policy Press, Bristol.

Macdonald, G. and Williamson, E. (2002) *Against the Odds: An Evaluation of Child and Family Support Services*, National Children's Bureau, London.

Miller, C. and McNicholl, A. (2003) *Integrating Children's Services: Issues and Practice*, Office of Public Management, London.

Morrison, T. (1993) *Staff Supervision in Social Care*, Pavilion, Brighton.

Munro, E. (2002) *Effective Child Protection*, Sage, London.

Murphy, M. (1995) *Working Together in Child Protection*, Arena, Aldershot.

Payne, M. (2000) *Teamwork in Multiprofessional Care*, Palgrave, Basingstoke.

Reder, P. and Duncan, S. (1999) *Lost Innocents? A Follow-Up Study of Fatal Child Abuse*, Routledge, London.

Reder, P. and Duncan, S. (2003) Understanding communication in child protection network. *Child Abuse Review*, **12** (March–April), 82–100.

Reder, P., Duncan, S. and Gray, M. (1993) *Beyond Blame – Child Abuse Tragedies Revisited*, Routledge, London.

Reder, P., McClure, M. and Jolley, A. (eds) (2000) *Family Matters: Interfaces Between Child and Adult Mental Heath*, Routledge, London.

Roaf, C. (2002) *Coordinating Services for Included Children: Joined Up Action*, Open University, Buckingham.

Sainsbury Centre for Mental Health (2000) *Taking Your Partners: Using Opportunities for Inter-Agency Partnership in Mental Health*, SCMH, London.

Scott, D. (1997) Inter-agency conflict: an ethnographic study. *Child and Family Social Work*, **2**, 73–80.

Shardlow, S., Davis, C., Johnson, M. *et al.* (2004) *Education and Training for Inter-Agency Working: New Standards*, Salford Centre for Social Work Research, University of Salford, http://www.ihscr.salford.ac.uk/SCSWR/interagency_working_.pdf (accessed 4 September 2008).

Sinclair, R. and Bullock, R. (2002) *Learning from Past Experience – A Review of Serious Case Reviews*, Department of Health, London.

Stone, B. (1998) Practitioners' perspectives on child neglect. *Childright*, **151** (Nov.), 6–8.

Taylor, J. and Daniel, B. (1999) Interagency practice in children with nonorganic failure to thrive: is there a gap between health and social care? *Child Abuse Review*, **8**, 325–38.

Thorpe, D. (1994) *Evaluating Child Protection*, Open University Press, Buckingham.

Wigfall, V. and Moss, P. (2001) *More Than the Sum of Its Parts? A Study of a Multi-Agency Child Care Network*, National Children's Bureau, London.

II The Process of Safeguarding

6 Should I Be Worried?

MARGARET A. LYNCH

Everyone has a responsibility to take action if they are worried about a child's welfare. The report into the death of Victoria Climbié (Cm 5730, 2003) highlighted the need for organisations to take safeguarding children seriously. This responsibility was endorsed in the government's response, *Keeping Children Safe* (Cm 5861, 2003), and in the Green Paper, *Every Child Matters* (Cm 5860, 2003). The Children Act 2004 places new duties on agencies to make arrangements to safeguard and promote the welfare of children. Agencies, however, are made up of individuals, and children will only be protected if everyone within an organisation knows when and how to respond to their concerns. How to act has been set out in the government's practice guidance *What To Do If You're Worried a Child Is Being Abused* (HM Government, 2006d).

This chapter aims to help all frontline workers think through what might make them concerned about a child's welfare in the first place. The triggers for concern will depend on the circumstances in which individuals are working and on the frequency with which they see individual children or their carers. Everyone coming into contact with children, whether this is a core component of their work or because of their work with adults (some of whom may care for children), should be prepared to be worried and know with whom they can discuss concerns. This chapter does not attempt to provide a comprehensive list of worrying symptoms and signs. Rather it seeks, using case examples, to illustrate how concerns can arise and the effect our response can have on the outcomes for the child.

CORE KNOWLEDGE

- Everyone who works in any capacity with children can become worried about a child's welfare or safety.
- Those working with adults who care for children may become aware of characteristics or circumstances that should make them worry about their parenting capacity.

Safeguarding Children   Edited by Hedy Cleaver, Pat Cawson, Sarah Gorin and Steve Walker
Copyright © 2009 by John Wiley & Sons, Ltd

- Carefully thinking through what is making you concerned will help with decisions about what to do next.
- Communicating with the child and family and with others who know them will help clarify the validity of your worries.

DECIDING WHAT HAS MADE YOU WORRIED

Sometimes the cause of a worry about a child is obvious. For example, the child has an injury that may well have been inflicted or the parent who arrives to collect the child is drunk and verbally abusive to staff. On other occasions, however, the worry starts with a less well-defined sense of unease, a feeling that all is not well with or for the child or that something has changed in the family that is distressing the child. Whenever you feel worried in this way about a child it is helpful to think through why you are worried. Is it the way the child looks, what the child has said or the way in which the child is behaving or perhaps even a combination of these observations? Is it that there has been a sudden or gradual change in the child over the time you have known the child? Is it that the child looks physically uncared for?

Ask yourself similar questions when it is something about a parent that triggers your worry. If both the parent and child are known to you, reflect on whether there are things about both of them that are concerning or that have recently changed. Can you make any observations about the way they interact with each other or with other members of the family? Have others expressed worries about the child or family? Is there a colleague who knows the child or family whom you could talk to in order to check out your worries?

Consideration should always be given to communicating with the family and child about your worries. A discussion with the parent may reveal that they too have worries about the child or themselves or there may be a very good reason why things have changed. Together you may be able to plan a referral or intervention that will help the child. Sometimes it will be a parent or other carer who first voices, directly or indirectly, concerns about a child. It is important to be receptive to such approaches and be prepared to listen to worries that may implicate the behaviour of fellow practitioners.

For further discussion of communicating with parents, see Chapter 2.

It may be appropriate to enquire of the child why his or her behaviour has changed or why, for example, he or she seems miserable or anxious. In some circumstances it will be the child who brings a concern to a practitioner. This is more likely to occur in settings where there is an opportunity for a relationship of trust to build up and includes all everyday services for children. Other settings will include out-of-school activities such as church groups, sports and drama clubs (all likely to involve volunteers). Research has demonstrated the importance of the initial response to a child who is trying to share a concern with an adult (Roberts and Taylor, 1993; Prior, Lynch and Glaser, 1994). It is important the adult conveys a willingness to listen and shows interest in what the child has to say without in any way cross-examining the child.

For more detailed discussion of communicating with children, see Chapter 1.

Those with ongoing contact with a group of children over time, such as teachers and health visitors, will not only be alert to changes in individual children but will also have their knowledge of a population of similar children to draw on when deciding why they have become concerned.

Knowledge that allows worries to be put into context is particularly important for both minority ethnic and disabled children. When working with children from minority ethnic families it is important to acknowledge and respect cultural diversity while at the same time not using 'culture' as a reason for dismissing feelings of unease about a child's well-being.

Disabled children are at greater risk than non-disabled children of maltreatment. The main reasons for this can be summarised as dependency, institutionalisation and communication (Westcott and Jones, 1999). All professional staff who work with them and their families should be able and willing to recognise worrying signals and to encourage parents, support staff and volunteers to do the same.

A professional's training and areas of expertise will influence the nature of their worries and the evidence they will have to support any concerns. Thus, a paediatrician may well be able to explain in detail why they find an injury worrying but should not be expected to provide the same expert interpretation when it comes to expressing their worries about a parent with erratic or unpredictable behaviour. This should not inhibit them from sharing their observations in a way that will initiate appropriate consideration of the needs of both the child and the family members.

For more detailed discussion of multi-agency working, see Chapter 5.

It is not necessary to know a child or carer well before allowing yourself to feel uneasy nor, as the example below demonstrates, do you have to be an experienced child care professional to have well-founded worries about the welfare of a child.

The dermatologist was uneasy because she considered the child's skin looked poorly cared for; the child was black and the 'mother' was white and did not talk to the child as she pulled off her clothes, nor did she know much about the child's early history. In conversation with the 'mother', the dermatologist learnt that the child was living with the woman in some sort of private arrangement. Unsure what she should do, she discussed her worries with the named doctor for child protection. The named doctor consulted with children's social care who, after enquires, confirmed that this was a private foster placement about which they had no knowledge. In the past, however, there had been a referral about one of the family's own children. When the birth family was traced it was discovered that both parents were students. The child returned to their care and, with the support of a community organisation, appropriate day care was arranged for the child.

Indeed, sometimes it is someone who is seeing a child and family for the first time who will pick up worrying characteristics that have been accepted or not noticed by others who have been in contact with the child and/or family for a long time. Where, for example, a child has gradually become more and more withdrawn in class or slowly lost weight, those in regular contact may not become particularly worried (perhaps even feeling relieved that this child is at least quiet in class). This means we should always be willing to hear the worries of others (e.g. the locum doctor or supply teacher) in relation to children and families we consider we know well or, in the language of some doctors, to be 'our patients'. Those perceived to be in positions of authority should behave in a way that gives others the confidence to raise worries without the fear that they will be dismissed as irrelevant.

The domains and dimensions for assessing children's needs and circumstances (Department of Health, Department for Education and Employment and Home Office, 2000a; HM Government, 2006b; 2006c), described in Chapter 8, provide us with a useful approach to developing our thinking beyond our initial concerns about a child or parent. Thus, they help us focus on what we know about how well the child's developmental needs are being met and the parent's capacity to parent the child, as well as helping us look more generally at the family and the environment in which they live. Linking our thinking to the Assessment Framework dimensions at this early stage will help us identify both worrying and protective features and help us and others plan the actions required to promote the child's development and safeguard their welfare (including referral to children's social care).

Obviously, lack of knowledge about a child or family should not deter us from making an immediate referral if we are concerned the child is at risk of significant harm. The threshold for discussing any worries with your line manager or named child protection colleague should be low.

For further discussion about approaching someone for help, see Chapter 7. For reading on first responses by frontline workers to children's concerns, see Jones (2003) and Chapter 9.

For further reading on working with minority ethnic and disabled children, see Cross et al. (1993), Marchant et al. (1999), Dutt and Phillips (2000), Marchant and Jones (2000), Koramoa, Lynch and Kinnair (2002) and Jones (2003); and Chapter 5.

RECORDING WHAT MAKES YOU WORRIED

Having decided why you are worried, those worries should be carefully recorded. There is a tendency to sum up an observation with an interpretive phrase and to leave out detail of the action or behaviour that is worrying us. The following case example illustrates the potential danger in such an approach.

'Reluctant to go home' read the nursery report for the child protection conference. Unfortunately, the nursery worker who knew Linda best was off sick on the day of the conference so could not explain why she found the 'reluctance' so worrying. Many children are reluctant to leave an activity when mother arrives at nursery to pick them up. Linda, however, would always stop playing whenever she saw her mother arrive and hide under a table. When her mother attempted to retrieve her she would hold on to the table leg and cry in distress. Linda was frightened to go home with good reason; she was soon to die at the hands of her father and become the subject of a serious case review.

For this particular case, the child's reluctance to go home was one of a number of clues to the seriousness of the child's predicament that were missed and, on its own, probably had little influence on the outcome. It does, however, illustrate the importance of recording in some detail anything which worries us and in a way that will be understood by others even if we are not available to explain what lies behind a summarising phrase.

In some instances, we may not have the necessary knowledge of the child and family or the specialised expertise necessary to interpret the significance of our observations. In such circumstances, however, an accurate descriptive account can make it possible for others to use the information in their assessment. We should not only record those things we feel to be potentially worrying but also those which might indicate strengths. If there has been a conversation with the child or carer the content of this should be recorded, as should an accurate description of any non-verbal communication.

CHILDREN WHO MAKE YOU WORRIED

This section explores some of the main groups of children who cause front-line workers to worry about their welfare and in some instances their safety. Additional material is recommended for those who are considering a child's particular circumstances in more depth.

Table 6.1 Psychological impairments and problems associated with childhood abuse

Affective symptoms	Fears
	Post-traumatic stress disorder
	Depression
Behaviour problems	Conduct disorder
	Sexualised behaviour
	Self-destructiveness
	Hyperactivity
Cognitive functioning	Educational problems
	Language difficulties
Personal and social adjustment	Self-esteem
	Attachment
	Peer relations

Source: Adapted version of Table 1 (p. 1827) from Jones (2000) by permission of Oxford University Press.

THE DISTRESSED CHILD

Children exposed to what has been described as victimisation experiences (Finkelhor and Kendall-Tackett, 1997) may well manifest a range of psychological impairments and problems (see Table 6.1).

Given that more than one form of violence may well take place in an abusive household, it is not surprising that similar difficulties are experienced by children exposed to domestic violence. This should always be considered as a possibility for a child exhibiting aggressiveness or who clearly has problems controlling and regulating emotion (anger but also fear) in an age-appropriate way (Jouriles *et al.*, 2001). To a degree, the symptoms shown by the victimised child are dependent on developmental age.

Children under 3 years old

With young children abuse, neglect and family violence can affect their ability to form normal attachments. The result can be a child who is excessively clingy or one who is showing no attachment to any adult figure. Such children may be indiscriminate in their affections. Even at this early stage the abused children may themselves be exhibiting excessive aggression and prolonged periods of loss of control. Other symptoms of distress may include excessive fearfulness and waking at night.

Three- to seven-year-olds

By this age the child is likely to show evidence of poor adjustment to nursery or school. This includes aggressiveness and oppositional behaviour. The child may be excessively anxious and fearful and may even show signs of post-traumatic stress. Poor self-esteem may already be apparent. This is the age group most likely to suffer distress as the result of physical neglect. The scruffy, smelly children will find themselves without friends.

Children over 7 to teenagers

The behavioural and emotional difficulties experienced by the younger children are likely to continue. Older children may also show evidence of depression and overwhelming feelings of worthlessness and helplessness. Self-blame can lead to self-harm. They may be indiscriminate in forming relationships and/or isolated from their peer group. They are unlikely to trust anyone.

Teenagers

For the teenager these manifestations of distress may become more extreme with suicide attempts, eating disorders, alcohol and drug abuse, risky sexual activity and involvement in peer violence and criminal activity. A number of these troubled young people will find themselves in secure accommodation (Stein and Lewis, 1992; Hamilton, Falshaw and Browne, 2002; Bailey, 2004). Some young people will vote with their feet and leave an abusive or neglectful home, making running away another important signal of distress (Stein, Rees and Frost, 1994).

For further discussion of children in secure accommodation and who run away from home, see Chapter 4.

While the manifestations described above are not found exclusively in abused and neglected children, they are indicators that the child is troubled and justification for practitioners to be worried and to take action to ascertain the cause of the child's distress.

School-age children who are suffering abuse and neglect might well have educational problems, including poor performance, due to lack of concentration and school non-attendance or lateness. This had been reported as a concern in 20% of children on the child protection register for emotional abuse (Glaser, Prior and Lynch, 2001). Others will drop out of school completely.

However, as illustrated by the example below, occasionally, a child who is suffering at home will present no overt problem at school, using immersion in academic or sports activities as a way of escaping and temporarily forgetting the abuse. In such circumstances it may come as a surprise to a school that others are worried about the child's welfare.

The young South American simultaneous interpreter was doing an excellent job at the child protection workshop. However, it soon became clear to the visiting presenter that she was also very interested in the sexual abuse material that was being discussed. In response to the presenter's commenting on this, the interpreter said that this was easily explained: she had suffered long-term abuse herself as a child and in order to spend as little time as possible at home she had signed up for every extra language course available in her home town. She had become a fluent speaker of several languages and won a scholarship to the best school for interpreters in the capital.

For reading on first responses by frontline workers to children's concerns, see Jones (2003).

For more on psychological manifestations read Jones (2003), Chapter 4 of this book.

THE CHILD WITH AN INJURY

If a child is seriously injured or their carer thinks they need medical attention, they are likely to present directly to a doctor or hospital. Whenever the injury has no obvious explanation the possibility of harm due to abuse or lack of care must be considered. Figure 6.1 shows a flow diagram designed to help staff in Accident and Emergency decide if they should take further steps to exclude abuse as a cause of the injury. It was attached in the form of a sticky label to the notes of every pre-school child seen in the department. An audit demonstrated its effectiveness in increasing awareness and referrals, and the authors now recommend its use for all children presenting with an injury. The principles could also be applied in primary health care.

Often, it does not require a professional perspective to be suspicious about an injury. Anyone in contact with children will be familiar with the appearance of minor accidental injuries and is likely to recognise when an injury may have been inflicted. For example, one expects an active toddler frequently to have a few bruises while bruises on a non-mobile child should raise a question in our minds about the origin of these injuries. The chance sighting of an injury can happen in a variety of settings. For example, the child comes into nursery, playgroup or school with a bruise, or the health visitor or social worker catches sight of a minor injury on a home visit. The decision about whether there is cause for worry will depend on a number of factors, some similar to the issues flagged up in the Accident and Emergency flow diagram. The parent may of course volunteer a completely plausible explanation, as may the child.

For further information on injuries, see Hobbs and Wynne (2001).

For further information on bruising, see Maguire *et al.* (2005).

THE NEGLECTED CHILD

Sometimes one becomes worried that a child's appearance indicates that they are being physically neglected. In deciding what action should be taken helps

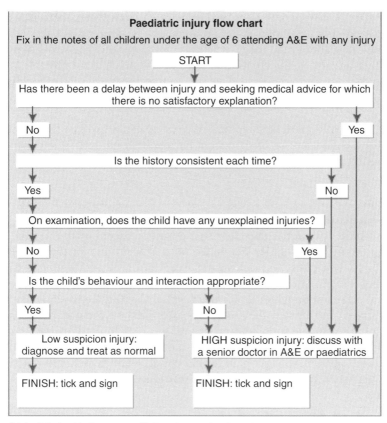

Figure 6.1 caption within image:

Sticky label added to notes of injured pre-school children to increase awareness of intentional injury in emergency department

Figure 6.1 Paediatric injury flow chart
Source: Benger and Pearce (2002); reproduced with permission from the BMJ Publishing Group.

to consider the impact any suboptimal care is having on the child together with what else one knows about the family:

- Are the children showing signs of distress?
- Is their appearance or smell causing other children to avoid or bully them?
- Are they coming to school hungry and/or late?
- Has there been a recent change in the quality of care?
- Does the mother also look neglected?
- Could it be that the parents have learning disabilities and are in need of support and guidance?

There are a number of reasons a child might be neglected. Parents may be overwhelmed by their own or family problems or have difficulties which compromise their parenting ability (see section 'Parents and Other Carers

Who Make You Worried' later in this chapter). Sometimes there is a simple explanation. For example, a parent may not be feeding a baby correctly because they cannot read the instructions on the packet. The stress of poverty and other adverse social conditions can make it much more difficult for parents to care for their children. A gentle enquiry of the parent of a child who looks neglected may be the first step in helping a family to get the necessary help.

For some children the recognition of physical neglect will be the first indication that a child is at risk of significant harm, either because of impairment of their health and development as a result of the neglect or because of coexisting abuse.

The paediatrician asked the little girl to take off her slightly grubby jeans and T-shirt. It then became clear that despite a recent wash the child had longstanding grime under her nails, on her scalp and in the creases of her body. Her pants were clean but were too large and belonged to her brother. Gentle questioning of the mother revealed that she had done her best to clean her daughter up for the hospital visit but the washing machine was broken and anyway they could not afford to heat the water. The father had left his wife and four children several weeks before, following a violent domestic dispute. Not surprisingly the mother had become depressed. She was unsure how best to get help for her children and herself and welcomed the suggestion that the paediatrician introduce her to the hospital social worker.

Neglect of a child's health care needs should be a reason to worry as should the circumstances of some 'accidents'. Has an accident occurred because of lack of supervision? For example, how was the 3-year-old able to get out onto the main road? How did the 14-month-old climb out on to the windowsill or the 12-month-old walk off the pub roof in his baby walker? Why was the 2-year-old able to swallow his mother's anti-depressants? In some cases asking such questions will result in worries over family functioning; in others deficiencies in building design or traffic control will come to light. Both require a response.

For further information on the effect of neglect on children's development, see Hildyard and Wolfe (2002).

For further information on the effect of failure to thrive in young children, see Batchelor (1999).

THE CHILD WITH PUZZLING ILLNESSES

Occasionally, worrying discrepancies between a parent's reports of their child's state of health and the findings or observations of others who know the child may trigger concerns over the welfare of a child. A doctor may begin to become worried if

- examination and investigation repeatedly fail to explain reported signs and symptoms;
- response to treatment is inexplicably poor;
- over time the child is repeatedly reported to have a wide range of new symptoms;
- the child's daily life is restricted beyond that which might be expected for any illness from which the child is known to suffer.

Sometimes it will be someone other than the doctor who first becomes uneasy. Anyone working with the child may become aware of puzzling discrepancies between what they have been told about a child's health and what they themselves observe. For example, a child reported to have frequent fits when in the care of the parent may have none while in the nursery. When worries such as these occur they will need to be shared and sensitive discussions take place to consider possible explanations. If, after discussion at a senior level, it is thought that fabricated or induced illness is a possibility then the government's guidance should be followed (Department of Health *et al.*, 2002).

For further information, see Department of Health *et al.* (2002) and Royal College of Paediatrics and Child Health (2002).

CHILDREN AND YOUNG PEOPLE REFERRED TO ADULT (OR GENERIC) SERVICES

As with the child who worried the dermatologist, many children are referred to and seen in specialist health services that are not specifically for children. This will include orthopaedic, ear, nose and throat, ophthalmology, general surgical and dental services. (Concerns where the parent is the client or patient are dealt with later in this chapter.) Practitioners, such as a general practitioner, health visitor or paediatrician, with access to opinions (e.g. in letters) from such services should be alert to anything that might trigger concerns about a child's welfare or safety and be willing to acknowledge the need for concern even if this has not been articulated by the specialist professional.

Nor should it be forgotten that sexually abused children may first come to notice when pregnant, seeking contraceptive advice or presenting for treatment of a sexually transmitted disease. It is important that services seeing these young people have a protocol which encourages staff to be alert to worrying factors and makes it clear with whom to discuss those worries. Whenever it is possible young people should be seen in separate 'young people clinics' within genitourinary medicine services. It is in such services that children abused through prostitution may first come to notice.

For further information, see Department of Health *et al.* (2000b), Thomas *et al.* (2003) and HM Government (2006a).

THE CHILD WHO IS NOT THERE

Non-attendance, whenever and wherever it occurs, should be taken seriously and may indicate a need to worry over the welfare of the child. It may be caused by family stress or be an indication that a parent is failing to recognise or to meet a child's needs. Unfortunately, many services, especially within health (e.g. speech therapy or hospital paediatric follow-up clinics), use failure to attend as a reason to terminate contact with the family with or without a letter to the original referrer. These may be the very children whose development is being impaired by abuse or neglect, and a system needs to be in place to identify when this is the case. In the main, the younger child who fails to attend for immunisation, routine child health surveillance or specialist clinics will be followed up by the health visitor provided they are made aware of the no show.

As the tragedy of Victoria Climbié demonstrated, some of the most worrying children and their families are not registered with a general practitioner (GP). While there is no statutory requirement for a child to be registered with a GP it is generally accepted that this is something a caring parent tries to do for their child. Failure to register should be picked up by other health practitioners, and by education and social care practitioners, provided the question is asked in the first place.

While it should be possible to track the majority of older children through schools, some of the children who give most cause for worry are not in school whether this is because they have never been registered, or they are truanting or they have been excluded.

If a child is taken out of school to visit relatives, at home or abroad, some schools will, without enquiring as to whether the child is back in the local area, remove the child from the school roll if the child does not return within a set period of time. Once again, routine enquiry by those seeing children in other settings (e.g. Accident and Emergency departments, walk-in primary care clinics and other health facilities) should identify those out of school. If the child is reported to have moved to another area every effort should be made to transfer the records.

For girls from some cultures, removal from school to visit the family's country of origin may provoke concern that the visit may have been planned in order to submit the girl to female genital mutilation or, if older, to be married. Particular attention needs to be paid to the girl who is upset at the proposed trip. Gentle enquiry about her worries may avoid jumping to conclusions and may provide an explanation such as fear of flying or distress at missing an important examination.

For further information, see the government guidance on female genital mutilation (LASSL, 2004; Home Office Circular 010/2004).

On forced marriage, see Foreign and Commonwealth Office *et al.* (2004), summarised in HM Government (2006a, Paragraphs 6.11–6.19).

Children who miss long periods of schooling or who are recurrently late are also a cause for concern. As mentioned above, one study of children on the child protection register for emotional abuse found 20% were exhibiting problems at school that included underachievement, absences and lateness (Glaser, Prior and Lynch, 2001). Even authorised absences can be worrying if they are for an apparently well child to attend multiple doctors' appointments or for vague symptoms, for example headaches, dizzy spells and tummy aches, never complained of in school. As indicated in section 'The Child with Puzzling Illnesses' earlier in this chapter, careful consideration needs to be given for the reasons for such absences and, if they continue, teachers should discuss their concerns with the designated teacher for child protection (Department of Health *et al.*, 2002; Department for Education and Skills, 2006).

PARENTS AND OTHER CARERS WHO MAKE YOU WORRIED

Links between child abuse and neglect and parental mental illness, substance misuse and domestic violence are well established. On occasions the manifestation in the parent is so florid that urgent action is required, as the case below demonstrates.

One afternoon a toddler's father, who was a known substance abuser, was seen by a nursery assistant supporting himself against the wall as he slowly made his way into the nursery to collect his child. It quickly became obvious that he was under the influence of drugs and/or drink and the staff were worried about his capacity to look after the child. A call to the family social worker resulted in an emergency placement with the maternal grandmother. A week later the flat where the child had lived with his parents and their addict friends was destroyed by a fire. Only the mother, who was badly burnt, escaped with her life.

For further details, see Oates (1997), Cleaver, Aldgate and Unell (1999), Dearden and Becker (2001), Royal College of Psychiatrists (2002) and Advisory Council on the Misuse of Drugs (2003).

Experience also tells us that physically ill parents and those with learning disabilities may also have reduced capacity to care for their children and therefore require extra support (Cotson *et al.*, 2001; Dearden and Becker, 2001; Cleaver and Nicholson, 2007a). In some of these families the child will have taken on the role of carer.

Parental attributes can on their own be enough to cause worry and to trigger action to ensure the family are receiving appropriate support. Indeed, some parents will themselves be worried that their condition means that without appropriate support they will be unable to care for their child as well as they might wish. Those working with parents should be prepared to identify and discuss worries about the children. Just because a parent is doing well does not necessarily mean all is well with the child. Those working with children should be alert to signs that a child's carer may have attributes that will affect his or her ability to parent the child. Often concerns about a parent and worries about a child occur together, making referral for a holistic assessment all the more appropriate. Those working primarily with mentally ill parents or adult substance misuse need to consider the impact of the adult's condition on their capacity to parent and be prepared to worry about the welfare of the child. Failure to do so can lead to fatal consequences for the child, as can failure to share information with those with lead responsibility for safeguarding the child. This has been dramatically illustrated in a number of serious case reviews (Falkov, 1996) of which the following case is one example. This child survived thanks to the quick action of the river police who happened to be passing.

> During her hospitalisation for severe mental illness, the mother had talked of voices telling her to harm her baby daughter. This daughter had been placed with a relative by social services but neither the social worker nor the relative were fully aware of the extent of the mother's delusional state. Thus, when at home on leave from the hospital, she asked to take her daughter out unsupervised, the relative handed the child over. An hour later the child was pulled from the river having been thrown in from a bridge by her mother.

It is important that professional staff who only see children in passing are willing to be worried and to take action.

> An 18-month-old boy was referred to the child development centre because of delay in all areas of his development. It was reported that he was cared for every day by a grandmother while his mother worked. When this was explored further it was discovered that the grandmother was immobilised with leg ulcers and receiving regular treatment in the home from the district nurse. Because the grandmother was unable to move around freely she kept her grandson strapped into his buggy all day 'to keep him safe'.
>
> Unfortunately, the district nurse who had observed this on her visits had not felt it was her place to be worried and in any case was unaware of what she should do or to whom she should speak about her observations.

This example highlights the need to ensure all staff going into homes, for whatever reason, are encouraged to be observant in relation to any children who may be there. This should include police being called out to domestic disputes and ambulance crew and paramedics attending adults (e.g. for drug overdoses). Other staff who may find themselves visiting the home include housing officers, probation officers and those reading meters or undertaking repairs. They all need to be willing to be worried and to know who they can go to with concerns over child welfare or well-being. If the example given above happened today one would hope that the district nurse would go to her line manager who would be likely to advise discussion with the family health visitor. This could well result, as happened eventually in the case above, in the fast-tracking of a day care place for the child.

For more discussion of multi-agency working, see Chapter 5.

For discussion of the role of services in contact with the family, see Chapter 2.

EMPOWERING SUPPORT STAFF TO WORRY

> The paediatrician already knew some of the difficulties the family was having with the behaviour of their 5-year-old who was being assessed for likely autism. At their next appointment she was running late and, while the family waited to be seen, the receptionist observed the father becoming upset as the boy threw toys around the waiting room. In his attempt to control the boy he hit him hard and deliberately around the head. Intercepting the paediatrician between patients the receptionist, who had been on a recent child protection awareness study day, described what she had seen. The paediatrician was able immediately to discuss the matter in a sympathetic manner with the parents and, with their full agreement, make a referral to children's social care. This led to a full assessment of the needs of the child and family and resulted in a package of intervention including advice on behaviour management for the parents and provision of respite care.

The example above shows the value of providing administrative and support staff with training on the recognition of worrying circumstances that might indicate a child could be suffering abuse or neglect. Together with this basic awareness staff must feel supported and know how to share worries about a child's welfare. Having passed on their concerns some feedback on outcome is essential. The positive outcome in the example given above reinforced the receptionist's willingness to play her part in the future protection of children. It is not just those with face-to-face contact that can pick up concerns about children or parents.

Secretaries and administrative staff may well find themselves dealing with very distressed or disturbed parents or other relatives on the telephone and need to feel confident about what to do in such circumstances. Occasionally, they may find themselves talking directly to a child. Admitting you are worried can be the first step in involvement in the safeguarding process; seen as 'something to be avoided' by many practitioners. Yet, as we have seen in the case examples in this chapter, early acknowledgement of concerns can result not only in children being protected from harm but also provide an opportunity to promote their welfare. In some circumstances it is easier to explain away your worries than take action. The following are some examples:

- 'Physical discipline is accepted in the culture from which the child comes and the child was very naughty so it would be unfair to call children's social care over the bruising.'
- 'The mother is ill and intervening would make her condition worse.'
- 'We only found out about this by chance so it would break confidentiality to tell anyone.'
- 'Given the surroundings the family live in, what do you expect?'
- 'I have known this family for generations and the children have always looked undersized and neglected.'
- 'I only refer when it has become a clear-cut child protection issue.'

ANTICIPATING WORRYING CIRCUMSTANCES NEEDING IMMEDIATE ACTION

Whenever tempted to dismiss worries we need to remind ourselves that all children have a right to optimal health and development and to be protected from abuse and neglect. This is going to be possible only if all are prepared to put the best interests of the child as their primary consideration. Ignoring worries when they concern the welfare of a child cannot be an option. When a child is identified as suffering an injury or has made a clear disclosure of abuse, staff are likely to be clear about the procedure to follow. There are other worrying circumstances requiring immediate action where they may be less clear. For many services, these types of situations can be anticipated and responses usefully rehearsed before staff are confronted with the problem of what to do. For example, anyone undertaking home visits, whether their role is focused on children or adults, will sooner or later come across a child 'home alone' or in surroundings that are too dangerous for a child (or anyone else) to continue to live in. In situations where parents come to pick up their children (such as from nursery school) staff need to know what to do if parents arrive drunk, clearly under the influence of drugs or too mentally disturbed to care safely for their child. A similar problem also exists for those working with an adult who has care of a child when it becomes apparent that he or she is an immediate threat to the child's safety. Managers responsible for delivering services to children and families or to adults who care for a child could usefully proactively consider with their staff any circumstances they might come across in the course of their day-to-day work that might require immediate action to safeguard a child. They should, when necessary, be willing and able to make direct contact with children's social care or the police.

CONCLUSION

The purpose of this chapter is to help all frontline workers to think through what could and should make them worried about a child's welfare or safety. Most of us can prepare ourselves in advance for the way in which most of the concerns about a child's welfare will come to our attention. Sometimes the cause of the worry is obvious, though more often our initial reaction is one of not very well-defined uneasiness.

For whatever reason we initially become worried it is important that we think through the reasons for our concern carefully and, whenever possible, also document them carefully. We will then be in a position to share our worries constructively with others. Details about how to raise worries about a child both within our own organisation and with colleagues from other organisations is the subject of the next chapter.

REFERENCES

Advisory Council on the Misuse of Drugs (2003) *Hidden Harm: Responding to the Needs of Children of Problem Drug Users*, Home Office, London.

Bailey, S. (2004) Adolescence and beyond: 12 years onward, in *The Developing World of the Child* (eds J. Aldgate, D. Jones, W. Rose and C. Jeffery), Jessica Kingsley, London.

Batchelor, J. (1999) *Failure to Thrive in Young Children: Research and Practice Evaluated*, The Children's Society, London.

Benger, J. and Pearce, A. (2002) Simple intervention to improve detection of child abuse in emergency departments. *British Medical Journal*, **324**, 780–82.

Cleaver, H., Aldgate, J. and Unell, I. (1999) *Children's Needs – Parenting Capacity: The Impact of Parental Mental Illness, Problem Alcohol and Drug Use, and Domestic Violence on Children's Development*, The Stationery Office, London.

Cleaver, H. and Nicholson, D. (2007a) *Parental Learning Disability and Children's Needs: Family Experiences and Effective Practice*, Jessica Kingsley, London.

Cm 5730 (2003) *The Victoria Climbié Inquiry: Report of an Inquiry by Lord Laming*, The Stationery Office, London, http://www.victoria-climbie-inquiry.org.uk/finreport/finreport.htm (accessed 22 August 2008).

Cm 5860 (2003) *Every Child Matters*, The Stationery Office, London, http://www.everychildmatters.gov.uk/_content/documents/EveryChildMatters.pdf (accessed 22 August 2008).

Cm 5861 (2003) *Keeping Children Safe. The Government's Response to The Victoria Climbié Inquiry Report and Joint Chief Inspectors' Report Safeguarding Children*, The Stationery Office, London.

Cotson, D., Friend, J., Hollins, S. and James, H. (2001) Implementing the framework for the assessment of children in need and their families when a parent has a learning disability, in *The Child's World: Assessing Children in Need* (ed. J. Horwath), Jessica Kingsley, London.

Cross, M., Gordon, R., Kennedy, M. and Marchant, R. (1993) *The ABCD Pack: Abuse and Children Who Are Disabled: A Resource and Training Pack*, NSPCC, Leicester.

Dearden, C. and Becker, S. (2001) Young carers: needs, rights and assessments, in *The Child's World: Assessing Children in Need*. (ed. J. Horwath), Jessica Kingsley, London.

Department for Education and Skills (2006) *Safeguarding Children and Safer Recruitment in Education*, Department for Education and Skills, London, http://www.everychildmatters/safeguarding (accessed 22 August 2008).

Department of Health, Department for Education and Employment and Home Office (2000a) *Framework for the Assessment of Children in Need and Their Families*, The Stationery Office, London, http://www.dh.gov.uk/prod_consum;_dh/groups/dh_digitalassets/@dh/@en/documents/digitalasset/dh_4014430.pdf (accessed 22 August 2008).

Department of Health, Home Office, Department for Education and Employment and National Assembly for Wales (2000b) *Safeguarding Children Involved in Prostitution: Supplementary Guidance to Working Together to Safeguard Children*, Department of Health, London, http://www.dh.gov.uk/prod_consum_dh/groups/dh_digitalassets/@dh/@en/documents/digitalasset/dh_4057858.pdf (accessed 22 August 2008).

Department of Health, Home Office, Department for Education and Skills and Welsh Assembly Government (2002) *Safeguarding Children in Whom Illness Is Fabricated or Induced*, Department of Health, London, http://www.dh.gov.uk/prod_consum_dh/groups/dh_digitalassets/@dh/@en/documents/digitalasset/dh_4056646.pdf (accessed 22 August 2008).

Dutt, R. and Phillips, M. (Department of Health) (2000) Assessing black children in need and their families, in *Assessing Children in Need and Their Families: Practice Guidance*, The Stationery Office, London, http://www.dh.gov.uk/prod_consum_dh/groups/dh_digitalassets/@dh/@en/documents/digitalasset/dh_4079383.pdf (accessed 22 August 2008).

Falkov, A. (1996) *A Study of Working Together Part 8 Reports: Fatal Child Abuse and Parental Psychiatric Disorder*, Department of Health, London.

Finkelhor, D. and Kendall-Tackett, K. (1997) The developmental perspective on the childhood impact of crime, abuse, and violent victimisation, in *Development Perspectives on Trauma: Theory, Research and Intervention* (eds D. Cicchetti and S. Toth), University of Rochester Press, New York.

Foreign and Commonwealth Office, Association of Directors of Social Services, Home Office, Department for Education and Skills and Department of Health (2004) *Young People and Vulnerable Adults Facing Forced Marriage: Practice Guidance for Social Workers*, Foreign and Commonwealth Office, London, http://www.adss.org.uk/publications/guidance/guidance.shtml (accessed 22 August 2008).

Glaser, D., Prior, V. and Lynch, M. (2001) *Emotional Neglect: Antecedents, Operational Definitions and Consequences*, BASPCAN, York.

Hamilton, C., Falshaw, L. and Browne, K. (2002) The link between recurrent maltreatment and offending behaviour. *International Journal of Offender Therapy and Comparative Criminology*, **46** (1), 75–94.

Hildyard, K. and Wolfe, D. (2002) Child neglect: developmental issues and outcomes. *Child Abuse and Neglect*, **26** (6–7), 679–95.

HM Government (2006a) *Working Together to Safeguard Children: A Guide to Inter-Agency Working to Safeguard and Promote the Welfare of Children*, The Stationery Office, London, http://www.everychildmatters.gov.uk/safeguarding (accessed 22 August 2008).

HM Government (2006b) *Common Assessment Framework for Children and Young People: Managers' Guide*, Department for Education and Skills, London, http://www.everychildmatters.gov.uk/caf (accessed 22 August 2008).

HM Government (2006c) *Common Assessment Framework for Children and Young People: Practitioners' Guide*, Department for Education and Skills, London, http://www.everychildmatters.gov.uk/caf (accessed 22 August 2008).

HM Government (2006d) *What To Do If You're Worried A Child Is Being Abused*, Department for Education and Skills, London, http://www.everychildmatters.gov.uk/safeguarding (accessed 22 August 2008).

Hobbs, C. and Wynne, J. (2001) *Physical Signs of Child Abuse*, WB Saunders, London.

Home Office Circular 010/2004, *The Female Genital Mutilation Act 2003*, http://www.knowledgenetwork.gov.uk/HO/circular.nsf/79755433dd36a66980256d4f004d1514/1b9ac55f598c73f780256e280040c40d?OpenDocument&Click= (accessed 22 August 2008).

Jones, D. (2000) Child abuse and neglect, in *The New Oxford Textbook of Psychiatry* (eds M. Gelder, J. Lopez-Ibor and N. Andreasen), Oxford University Press, Oxford.

Jones, D. (2003) *Communicating with Vulnerable Children: A Guide for Practitioners*, Gaskell, London.

Jouriles, E., Norwood, W., McDonald, R. *et al.* (2001) Domestic violence and child adjustment, in *Interparental Conflict and Child Development: Theory, Research and Applications* (eds J. Grych and F. Fincham), Cambridge University Press, Cambridge.

Koramoa, J., Lynch, M.A. and Kinnair, D. (2002) A continuum of child-rearing: responding to traditional practices. *Child Abuse Review*, **11** (6), 415–21.

LASSL (2004) *4: Female Genital Mutilation Act 2003*, Department for Education and Skills, London, http://www.dh.gov.uk/en/Publicationsandstatistics/Lettersandcirculars/Localauthoritysocialservicesletters/AllLASSLs/DH_4074779 (accessed 22 August 2008).

Maguire, S., Mann, M.K., Sibert, J. and Kemp, A. (2005) Are there patterns of bruising in childhood which are diagnostic or suggestive of abuse? A systematic review. *Archives of Disease in Childhood*, **90** (2), 182–86.

Marchant, R. and Jones, M. (Department of Health) (2000) Assessing the needs of disabled children and their families, in *Assessing Children in Need and Their Families: Practice Guidance*, The Stationery Office, London.

Marchant, R., Jones, M., Giles, A. and Julyan, A. (1999) *Listening on All Channels: Consulting with Disabled Children*, Triangle, Brighton.

Oates, M. (1997) Patients as parents: the risk to children. *British Journal of Psychiatry*, **170** (32), 22–7.

Prior, V., Lynch, M. and Glaser, D. (1994) *Messages from Children: Children's Evaluation of the Professional's Response to Child Sexual Abuse*, NCH Action for Children, London.

Roberts, J. and Taylor, C. (1993) Sexually abused children speak out, in *Child Abuse and Child Abusers* (ed. L. Waterhouse), Jessica Kingsley, London.

Royal College of Paediatrics and Child Health (2002) *Fabricated or Induced Illness by Carers*, RCPCH, London.

Royal College of Psychiatrists (2002) *Patients as Parents: Addressing the Needs, Including the Safety, of Children of Parents Who Have Mental Illness*, Council Report CR105, http://www.rcpsych.ac.uk/files/pdfversion/cr105.pdf (accessed 22 August 2008).

Stein, A. and Lewis, D. (1992) Discovering physical abuse: insights from a follow-up study of delinquents. *Child Abuse and Neglect*, **16** (4), 523–31.

Stein, M., Rees, G. and Frost, N. (1994) *Running the Risk: Young People on the Streets of Britain Today*, Children's Society, London.

Thomas, A., Forster, G., Robinson, A. and Rogstad, K. (2003) National guidelines for the management of suspected sexually transmitted infections in children and young people. *Archives of Disease in Childhood*, **88**, 303–11.

Westcott, H. and Jones, D. (1999) Annotation: the abuse of disabled children. *Journal of Child Psychology and Psychiatry*, **40** (4), 497–506.

FURTHER READING

C I (99)24: Home Office Working Party on Forced Marriages: Mapping Exercise, http://www.dh.gov.uk/PublicationsAndStatistics/LettersandCirculars/ChiefInspector LettersArticle/fs/en?CONTENT_ID=4004588&chk=QiQi9W (accessed 22 August 2008).

7 Approaching Someone for Help

MARY ARMITAGE
STEVE WALKER

This chapter explores the actions that practitioners should take when approaching someone for help if they are concerned about a child's welfare. The role of recording and the importance of preparation in clarifying concerns and supporting effective communication are discussed. The use of procedures in identifying the most appropriate person for practitioners to approach and involving children and families are considered. Finally, some of the issues that can prevent a practitioner from approaching someone for help are reviewed and some strategies to overcome these are suggested.

CORE KNOWLEDGE

- Take responsibility for knowing who to approach for help about a child within your own organisation or if necessary outside of it. Familiarise yourself with the content and location of your agency's procedures and the practice guidance *What To Do If You're Worried a Child Is Being Abused* (HM Government, 2006d).
- If you have a concern, discuss it as soon as possible with a colleague, manager or the designated person within your agency, or with a colleague in another agency.
- Think about the child and family and consider the appropriateness of discussing your concerns with them and explaining what will happen.
- When you are discussing a concern or making a referral, be clear about the nature and extent of your concerns, think through what you need to say, and record your concerns in writing, following your agency's procedures.
- Clarify what will be done with the information you pass on and share any expected outcomes that you might have.
- Follow up any verbal referral in writing within 24 hours.

Safeguarding Children Edited by Hedy Cleaver, Pat Cawson, Sarah Gorin and Steve Walker
Copyright © 2009 by John Wiley & Sons, Ltd

APPROACHING OTHERS FOR HELP – INFLUENCING FACTORS

Having identified a concern about a child's welfare the first step for most practitioners, in both statutory and voluntary sector agencies, is to approach someone for help. Whom they approach and how will depend upon two factors. The first of these is local policies and procedures.

LOCAL POLICIES AND PROCEDURES

Local policies and procedures should clearly set out the actions that practitioners should take within their agency if they have concerns about a child. Procedures will help practitioners to identify exactly who they should approach for advice and assistance. For example, a school's procedures may specify that if a class teacher is concerned about a child's welfare they should approach the designated member of staff. Procedures will normally be located within an agency's procedures manual and/or the Local Safeguarding Children Board (LSCB) procedures. LSCB procedures also set out the actions key statutory agencies, such as children's social care and the police, will take on receiving a referral.

Each agency should ensure that practitioners have easy access to a copy of these procedures. It is the responsibility of all practitioners in contact with children and young people, whether directly or through their work with adults in a family, to ensure that they are aware of the actions they should take if they have concerns about a child's welfare and where their individual or team copy of their agency's and LSCB procedures are located. *What To Do If You're Worried a Child Is Being Abused* (HM Government, 2006d) provides practitioners with a clear guide to the actions they should take if they have concerns about a child's welfare and the actions that other child care practitioners will take.

More detailed information may be found in the government's guidance *Working Together to Safeguard Children* (HM Government, 2006a, Paragraphs 5.1–5.30).

THE NATURE OF THE CONCERN

The second factor which will influence whom a practitioner contacts to discuss a concern about a child is the nature of the concern itself. Where there are concerns that a child is at risk of suffering significant harm, practitioners should discuss these concerns immediately with the individual designated within their procedures. This will ensure that appropriate action is taken to protect the child from harm. Where concerns about a child's welfare are more general, for example if there is a change in a child's attitude or behaviour, a practitioner may want to discuss these with a colleague who also knows the child, or with their manager. In these situations, discussion will help practitioners to clarify the nature and extent of their concerns and identify what further action should be taken to safeguard and promote the child's welfare. They may decide to carry out a common assessment to help decide what to do next (HM Government, 2006c).

A further consideration for some practitioners will be their organisational context and management arrangements. While most practitioners work in settings with a management structure and/or established supervision processes, some will be independent practitioners, without a line manager or access to formal supervision, such as childminders and private foster carers. For practitioners who do not have easy access to a manager or supervisor, their local children's social care department and the NSPCC Helpline (0808 800 5000) are able to provide advice.

WHY APPROACH SOMEONE FOR HELP?

There are five main reasons why practitioners should approach someone for help when they are concerned about a child. However, these are not mutually exclusive and in most cases approaching someone for help will have several benefits for the practitioner.

TO HELP THE PRACTITIONER CLARIFY THE NATURE AND EXTENT OF THEIR CONCERNS

In some cases, as highlighted in Chapter 6, concerns about a child will develop over time; a gradual deterioration in a child's appearance or changes in their behaviour may lead to a practitioner becoming concerned about a child. In these situations, approaching someone to discuss concerns about a child will help to decide whether further action is necessary to safeguard and promote the child's welfare.

In other situations injuries to a child, or comments made by a child, may cause a practitioner to believe that the child is at risk of suffering significant harm. Approaching someone for help should assist the practitioner to determine whether immediate action is required to safeguard the child's welfare.

For further discussion of the circumstances that may make you want to ask for help with concerns about a child, see Chapter 6.

Jayne Wilson, a primary school teacher, was concerned to notice what appeared to be a large bruise on the back of one of her pupils, Alan Munro, aged 5 years. Alan had joined the class only the previous week when he and his mother moved to a nearby women's refuge.

Alan was very shy and would not say anything to Jayne about the mark on his back. Under the local procedures Jayne spoke to Geraldine Malcolm, the designated member of staff for child protection, about what she had seen. Geraldine agreed that she would look at Alan's back to see whether it required any immediate treatment. When she saw the mark on Alan's back, she recognised it as a form of birthmark known as *Mongolian blue spot.*

Geraldine said that she would speak to Alan's mother when she arrived to pick him up that evening. When asked whether Alan had any distinguishing marks, Alan's mother immediately mentioned that he had a birthmark on his back. Geraldine explained to Ms Munro what had happened and said that she would make sure that Alan's birthmark was recorded in his school notes.

Geraldine reassured Jayne that she had done the right thing by contacting her, and she ensured that the incident was written up and signed by Jayne and herself.

TO CLARIFY WHAT FURTHER ACTION SHOULD BE TAKEN

In some circumstances, a practitioner may be uncertain about what actions should be taken. Approaching someone can help the practitioner to identify exactly what further action is necessary and how this should be carried out. For example, discussing a concern with a line manager will clarify whether the child should be referred to children's social care and, if so, to which agency the referral should be made.

Mary Smith, a volunteer at a local athletic club, was approached by Sally Brown, aged 13. Sally told Mary that her uncle, who had recently moved into the family home, had come into her room the previous night and sexually abused her.

Mary knew from the club's child protection procedures that she should report the incident immediately, but was not sure whether she should contact the police or children's social care first.

Mary made sure that Sally was all right and went to speak to Brian Marshall, the senior staff member on duty. Brian confirmed that Mary should contact children's social care who would liaise with the police. Brian said that he would rearrange the club activities for the evening to allow Mary to contact children's social care and support Sally. Mary quickly wrote down exactly what Sally had told her about the incident, using Sally's words, and retrieved Sally's index card from the club files as this gave her full name, address and date of birth.

Mary explained to Sally that she was going to contact children's social care to make sure that she was safe. Sally was concerned that her parents would be angry with her, and Mary reassured her that she had done the right thing. Mary contacted children's social care and referred Sally to them.

Both the social worker and Mary kept Sally informed about what was happening. Sally was subsequently interviewed jointly by the police and children's social care and medically examined. As a result of the evidence obtained her uncle was arrested.

TO CLARIFY WHETHER A CRIMINAL OFFENCE MAY HAVE BEEN COMMITTED

In Sally's case it was immediately clear to Mary and Brian, staff at the athletics club, that the sexual assault Sally was describing amounted to a serious criminal offence and necessitated involvement of the police. Sometimes, practitioners who have worries about a child can be uncertain whether there has been an offence and whether they should report what has happened to the police. They may worry that this is an over-reaction that might escalate problems in the family, or that the parents or the child will be unhappy about police involvement and it will then be more difficult to help a child or family. The guidance in *Working Together to Safeguard Children* (HM Government, 2006a), however, is clear:

> The police should be notified as soon as possible by local authority children's social care wherever a case referred to them involves a criminal offence committed, or is suspected of having been committed, against a child. Other agencies should consider sharing such information. (See paragraphs 5.17 onwards for detailed guidance on this point.) This does not mean that in all such cases a full investigation will be required, or that there will necessarily be any further police involvement. It is important, however, that the police retain the opportunity to be informed and consulted, to ensure all relevant information can be taken into account before a final decision is made.
>
> HM Government, 2006a, Paragraph 2.103

The guidance makes it clear that a decision on the prosecution of an alleged abuser must take into account whether this is in the interest of the child, as well as questions of the quality of evidence and the public interest. The LSCB is required to develop clear protocols for the circumstances in which practitioners should contact the police and for dealing with any joint enquiries, and practitioners should check what protocols exist in their local LSCB procedures.

The most sensible course of action for a practitioner who is unsure about whether something that has happened to a child is a criminal offence is to seek the advice of the local police child abuse investigation units (CAIUs).

TO PROVIDE SPACE AND TIME FOR THE PRACTITIONER TO TAKE FURTHER ACTION

Concerns about a child often arise when practitioners feel they do not have sufficient time and space to deal with them. Approaching someone for help can ensure that they are provided with practical support and sufficient time to deal appropriately with their concerns.

It may be particularly important to have time for reflection and guidance in situations where there have been long-term chronic problems, where there is uncertainty about whether the situation is serious enough to warrant action. Practitioners can sometimes become desensitised in such situations and may accommodate to unacceptably low standards of care. Supervision, where this is available and when it is of good quality, can provide a vital opportunity to address complex situations, where the worker may have become enmeshed in the family or feel intimidated and be avoiding action because of unspoken fears about violence.

TO SUPPORT THE PRACTITIONER TO TAKE FURTHER ACTION

It is important that practitioners are aware that concerns about the safety and welfare of a child can have a psychological and emotional impact on themselves, no matter how experienced they are. In addition to the practical support and advice they may offer, approaching someone for help can provide an important psychological support to a practitioner. At a very basic level, managers and other practitioners can provide reassurance that a practitioner was right to be concerned and that action was necessary.

Practitioners often worry about broaching concerns about children with children's parents. In these situations, a manager or colleague can help the practitioner to think through how the parents can be best approached and what should be said when explaining why the agency has concerns about the child. In situations where there are worries over how parents may react, the presence of a colleague can be a support.

Clare Green, a health visitor, had been working with Gail Muldoon (aged 20) and her two children Michael (aged 3) and Sean (aged 2) for 18 months. Gail has a moderate learning disability but with the support of her partner, Connor, the children were well cared for. Three months ago, Connor had to go back to Ireland as his father was seriously ill. When Clare visited 3 weeks after Connor had left, she noted a marked deterioration in the condition of the home and the children's appearance. Clare discussed the possibility of a referral to children's social care with Gail who became very verbally abusive, shouting and screaming that she did not want children's social care involved.

> On Clare's most recent visit the family home was in a dreadful state. The kitchen was full of overflowing rubbish bags, some of which had maggots in them. The children appeared to have been unwashed for days.
>
> Clare explained to Gail that because she was concerned that Gail was not able to look after the children and manage the home alone she wanted to talk to a colleague about what help could be offered. She would call back later that day to discuss what support was available.
>
> When she got back to the office, Clare made a careful note of what she had seen during her visit. She concluded that in her opinion the conditions of the family home presented a health hazard for the children. Clare contacted Karen Trent, the named nurse for child protection, and talked through her concerns with her. Karen agreed with Clare that the children might be at risk of significant harm from neglect and that Gail required help in Connor's absence.
>
> Karen suggested that, although they could make a referral to children's social care without Gail's consent, it would be best if Gail could be persuaded to accept help from children's social care. Clare agreed but was concerned about Gail's reaction so Karen agreed to do a joint visit with Clare.
>
> Gail was initially very angry that Clare had brought Karen with her. With Karen's support, Clare was able to explain to Gail that support from children's social care would help her and the children to manage until Connor returned. Gail revealed to Clare and Karen that she was frightened that the children would be taken away from her if children's social care became involved as she had been looked after herself as a child. Clare reassured Gail that children's social care would want to keep the family together. With Gail present, Clare rang children's social care and arranged an appointment to go to the office with Gail later that day.

Occasionally, practitioners may face a situation where they are threatened by a parent or another adult, for example those facing section 47 enquiries or criminal investigations about their behaviour towards a child. In such situations, where they have fears for their own safety, it is essential that practitioners seek advice from their managers and the police about the best way to proceed. This will ensure that practitioners do not place themselves at risk of harm, whilst ensuring that action is taken to protect the child.

For further discussion of situations where practitioners may meet hostility from parents, see Chapter 2.

COMMUNICATING YOUR CONCERNS

PREPARATION

When practitioners are concerned about the welfare of a child it is natural that they want to do something straightaway. However, it is important to be prepared before approaching someone for help. Preparation includes knowing the physical location and content of agency and LSCB procedures and ensuring that records on the child are up to date. Being prepared is an integral part of taking action to safeguard and promote a child's welfare. Preparation will help both to minimise delay and ensure that the person who is contacted is able to provide the most appropriate advice and support.

KNOW YOUR PROCEDURES

Being aware of the physical location and content of agency and LSCB procedures will help practitioners remain knowledgeable about the indicators of abuse and neglect, know what to do when they have a concern about a child's welfare and therefore increase their confidence in taking the most appropriate action.

GETTING THE FACTS STRAIGHT

Before approaching someone to discuss concerns about a child, practitioners should ensure that they have at hand all the key information available about the child. This should include basic information the agency has concerning the child, such as the child's name, sex, date of birth, address(es), any language and communication issues, the names of those with parental responsibility for the child, the date the practitioner's involvement with the child and/or family commenced and the reason for that involvement, the facts that have caused the practitioner to become concerned about the child and details of any previous concerns.

CLARIFYING CONCERNS

When approaching someone for help, practitioners will have to explain what they are concerned about and how these concerns have arisen. To do this effectively, practitioners should take time to organise their thoughts and check any records they hold on the child to ensure all factual information is accurate. Understanding the conceptual framework – that is the domains and dimensions or three sides of the triangle in the *Framework for the Assessment of Children in Need and their Families* (Department of Health, Department for Education and Employment and Home Office, 2000) – can help practitioners organise their information and clarify the nature of their concerns about the child's safety or welfare.

The Assessment Framework triangle can be found in Chapter 8.

Jatinder, a health visitor, held her well-baby clinic in the general practitioner's surgery. A mother with an 18-month-old child came in for a routine check-up. Jatinder noted that there were, what appeared to be, fingertip bruises in the soft part of the child's cheeks – two on one side and one larger one on the other.

Jatinder considered carefully what she knew about the family. The child had always been a fussy feeder. Mum gave up breastfeeding after a couple of weeks because it was taking so long to feed the baby and taking so much out of her. When the child was being weaned there were more difficulties. The child's weight was just under the 2nd centile, with the height and head circumference on the 25th centile. Jatinder tried to organise her thoughts as she looked back through all the records. From the birth of the baby, reflecting back, there were mounting concerns about the quality of interaction between parent and child, attachment difficulties in the early days and, later, harsh words spoken to the child in front of health practitioners. The child was overdue her immunisations and now there was apparent bruising on the child's face which looked as if someone had tried to force open the child's mouth.

Jatinder approached the child's GP for an opinion on the bruising to the face and to discuss what to do next.

RECORDING

Recording is an essential component of any work involving children and families. However, it is an area that has been the subject of ongoing concern.

Numerous inquiries in the past have called for higher standards of case recording and the more thorough maintenance of case files by professionals from all agencies involved in the welfare of children. In view of the regularity with which deficiencies in this regard have been identified, it is disappointing to find them repeated with such regularity throughout Victoria's case (Cm 5730, 2003, p. 208).

It is important that practitioners view recording as an integral and important part of their practice rather than as a bureaucratic exercise. Contacts with children should be written up succinctly and clearly as soon as possible after they have occurred. Written information should clearly differentiate between fact and opinion, and any assessments or professional judgements should be supported by the evidence they are based on.

Where concerns have arisen as a result of an injury to the child, the nature of the injury and an account of how it happened should be clearly described. A diagram or drawing of the injury's location is also helpful. When a child has disclosed abuse to a practitioner, this should be recorded in the child's own words. All records should be signed and dated.

Accurate and up-to-date recording will assist practitioners clarify the nature and extent of their concerns and help them be clear and accurate in describing and discussing these.

For further information in relation to recording, see *What To Do If You're Worried a Child Is Being Abused* (HM Government, 2006d, p. 6, Paragraphs 10.9 and 10.10).

WHO TO APPROACH FOR HELP?

A COLLEAGUE WHO KNOWS THE CHILD

Where practitioners think that they have noticed a change in a child's behaviour or deterioration in a child's appearance, it may be useful to discuss these changes with a colleague who also knows the child well.

A SUPERVISOR OR MANAGER

Supervisors or managers can help a practitioner clarify the nature and extent of their concerns and identify what further action should be taken. As noted earlier, for practitioners who do not have easy access to a manager or supervisor, their local children's social care department and the NSPCC Helpline (0808 800 5000) are able to provide advice in relation to child protection and child welfare.

THE NAMED OR DESIGNATED PROFESSIONAL FOR YOUR AGENCY

Some agencies, such as health and education, have named or designated professionals who have additional training and/or experience in child protection matters. Their role is to provide professional support and advice to help clarify concerns and identify the actions that are required.

For further details on the responsibilities of named and designated professionals, see Chapter 5.

A COLLEAGUE FROM ANOTHER AGENCY

In some situations, approaching a colleague from another agency may help practitioners develop an understanding about the nature of their concerns. Contacting a colleague from another agency need not result in a referral; practitioners can discuss their concerns without giving the child's name.

For a discussion of confidentiality and information sharing between practitioners in inter-agency working, see Chapter 5. Chapter 8 has a more detailed account of information sharing in assessment.

Bob Collins, a community psychiatric nurse, made regular 3-weekly visits to Sunita Gulati, a young single mother with severe postnatal depression and her two children: Ahmed, 3 years, and Amit, 11 months. Mrs Gulati was making steady progress. She was receiving a lot of support from her parents who lived nearby and visited every day. She also attended a local 'family unit' for parents who experience mental health problems.

On his most recent visit, Bob noticed the curtains were drawn at 11.30 a.m. He could hear the baby crying from inside the house. After approximately 10 minutes of knocking and waiting, Ahmed pushed open the letter box to say, 'Mummy is in bed.' A further 10 minutes elapsed before Mrs Gulati came to the door. She was in her dressing gown and looked confused and dishevelled. She would not let Bob into the house, but he could see over her shoulder that the house, which was usually tidy and organised, had unwashed plates and cups on the floor, and dirty nappies on the settee. The baby continued to cry upstairs. Bob asked Mrs Gulati if she would like him to get in contact with her parents and she said that they were on holiday for another 3 weeks. Bob asked again whether he could come in, but Mrs Gulati said no and closed the door.

Bob was concerned about Mrs Gulati's ability to care for the children. On his return to the office Bob immediately spoke to his manager, following LSCB procedures, but his manager was not sure whether a referral to children's social care should be made. Bob's manager suggested that he contact children's social care and discuss the circumstances with the duty social worker. As Bob discussed the case with the duty social worker, it became clear to them both that the children could be at risk of significant harm, given their ages, Mrs Gulati's history of depression and her current lack of family support. The children's situation required immediate action. Bob then referred the two children to children's social care in accordance with the LSCB safeguarding children procedures.

A COLLEAGUE FROM A SPECIALIST SERVICE OR WITH SPECIALIST KNOWLEDGE

Sometimes, practitioners are uncertain what to do because they feel that they lack the knowledge to interpret what they see and to judge whether there are reasons for concern about a child's welfare. This can arise in many different circumstances. Cleaver, Wattam and Cawson (1998) found that social workers carrying out section 47 enquiries were often faced with situations where they felt they lacked the specialist knowledge to assess the likelihood of harm – for example, if parents were drug users, or if they were told that a disabled child's injuries were self-inflicted. They welcomed specialist advice both from within their own agency and from other agencies when it was available.

Thoburn, Chand and Procter (2004) conclude that practitioners need facilities to obtain appropriate advice when working with children and families from minority ethnic backgrounds. Practitioners in several services thought that Victoria Climbié had an unusual, exceptionally respectful, response to her 'mother' but concluded that this might be normal in the family's culture. In fact, it was a sign that Victoria was afraid of her carer and was being abused (Cm 5730, 2003). If a child's ethnicity is different from yours and you are unsure about whether something that has occurred is usual or acceptable in the family's context, talking to someone with knowledge of the child's ethnicity or culture will help you be clear about the nature of your worries.

If a child or parent is disabled, practitioners can sometimes be unsure when a particular characteristic or behaviour is a consequence of the disability or has another meaning. Speaking to a colleague with the relevant specialist knowledge will help clarify your understanding.

Children and teenagers whose behaviour is troublesome or withdrawn, or who exhibit sexualised behaviour, can also leave practitioners uncertain as to how they should interpret what they see, and whether it should be regarded as a safeguarding or disciplinary issue. Getting it wrong can leave children at risk from abusive behaviour, for example, sexual abuse by peers. If you are worried that a child's behaviour might indicate possible abuse or be placing the child or other children at risk of harm, but are unsure about what to do next, discuss it with someone in your agency or a colleague in another agency who has specialist knowledge of childhood and adolescent behaviour disorders.

When consultation is sought, it is essential to be clear about accountability for decisions and actions.

For a more detailed discussion of abusive behaviour between children, see Chapter 4.

For further information on safeguarding children from minority ethnic communities, see Dutt and Phillips (2000) and Thoburn, Chand and Procter (2004).

For a discussion of safeguarding issues relevant to disabled children, see Cross *et al.* (1993), Morris (2002) and National Working Group on Child Protection and Disability (2003).

For further reading on sexually abusive behaviour by children, see Epps (1999).

Local authorities and health bodies all have staff who are knowledgeable about childhood disability and childhood behaviour disorders, as do many specialist voluntary organisations.

Make sure you know who your local specialist contacts are. Your named or designated staff member with responsibility for safeguarding children will be able to help you. As described above, contacting a colleague from another department or agency with specialist knowledge need not result in a referral; practitioners can discuss their concerns without giving the child's name.

Use of local safeguarding children procedures will help practitioners locate the right person to approach if they are concerned about a child's welfare.

For further discussion on consulting and working with other agencies, see Chapter 5.

MAKING A REFERRAL

If, following discussions with a colleague, manager, specialist, or the named or designated professional for your agency, practitioners believe that a child may be suffering or may be at risk of suffering, significant harm then they should always refer their concerns to children's social care, the police or the NSPCC. Concerns should generally be discussed with parents and agreement sought to make a referral, unless to do so would place a child at risk of significant harm. When making a referral, the practitioner should pass on

- the child's basic details – including full name, age or date of birth, ethnicity, any language or communication issues, address(es);
- household composition – including, where known, details of other children in the family;
- details of their concerns – including how and why these have arisen – which may have been explored during a common assessment (HM Government, 2006b, 2006c);
- information on the child's needs and the parents' or carers' ability to respond to those needs within the context of their wider family and environment (HM Government, 2006d, Paragraph 10.6);
- whether parents are aware of, and agree with, the referral;
- if known, where the child is at present;
- other relevant information that may be available.

A referral that includes as much relevant information as possible will help the agency receiving the referral respond promptly and appropriately.

If the referral was made by telephone, the practitioner should confirm it in writing within 48 hours.

When practitioners have made a referral to children's social care without the parents' knowledge they should agree with the person receiving the referral what the child and family members should be told and when.

In some circumstances, a practitioner may consider that a child is not at risk of significant harm but could benefit from services to promote their welfare. In these situations, the child may be a 'child in need' under the Children Act 1989, and the practitioner should discuss with the family why they think it appropriate to make a referral to children's social care.

Some families may be reluctant to agree to this action. The practitioner should reassure the family that the purpose of the referral is to help support the child and family. In circumstances where families continue to refuse permission for a referral to be made, practitioners should, in consultation with their line manager, consider whether the absence of any services to support the child may place them at risk of significant harm. If the practitioner and manager conclude that there is a risk of significant harm to the child, then a referral should be made to children's social care in accordance with their local safeguarding children procedures.

A referral may be made verbally or in writing following the process outlined above.

For further information on making and taking a referral, see Cleaver, Wattam and Cawson (1998); Walker, Scott and Cleaver (2004); Department of Health, Department for Education and Employment and Home Office (2000) and HM Government (2006a).

For further information on the Common Assessment Framework, see Cm 5860 (2003) and HM Government (2006b, 2006c).

There is a more detailed discussion of assessment in Chapter 8.

WHEN THERE IS A NEED FOR URGENCY

If a practitioner thinks that immediate action is necessary to save a child's life or to prevent serious harm, children's social care, the police or the NSPCC can use statutory powers under the Children Act 1989 to protect a child in an emergency or remove a child to a safe place. The local authority can obtain an Emergency Protection Order (s 44) and police can use powers of protection (s 46). Practitioners in other agencies faced with the possible need for urgent action should ask for help at once from an authorised agency. For further information, see *Working Together to Safeguard Children* (HM Government, 2006a, Paragraphs 5.49–5.53 and Appendix 1, Paragraph 17). The principles of preparation and recording described above still apply.

Urgent action in the context of an initial assessment is discussed in Chapter 8.

INVOLVING THE PEOPLE CONCERNED

INVOLVING CHILDREN

In general, seek to discuss your concerns with the child, as appropriate to their age and understanding, and with parents and seek their agreement to making a referral to children's social care unless you consider such a discussion would place the child at risk of significant harm.

HM Government, 2006d, Paragraph 11.3

It is easy for children to be overlooked in all the activity that arises from concerns about their safety or welfare. Often children report that after they had raised their concerns no one listened to what they had to say.

Butler and Williamson, 1994

Children want practitioners to see them as individuals and not as a case or the subject of concerns. They value practitioners who keep them informed and are open and honest with them – even when what they have to say is difficult for them to hear. Children will talk to adults whom they trust. Therefore, it is important for children to know that the practitioner will be available if they need them.

Practitioners should communicate with children and young people in their preferred language, in a manner consistent with their age, ability and communication style. Communicating with some disabled children may require more preparation or specific materials and in some cases specialist expertise (Marchant and Jones, 2000; Jones, 2003).

If the information that a child or young person gives to the practitioner suggests the child is at risk of significant harm, practitioners should reassure the child or young person and explain to them what action they will be taking.

When talking with children and young people, it is important that practitioners do not promise confidentiality in the early stages of discussions as it may not be possible to maintain it. Practitioners must remember that in some cases a disclosure made by a child may result in a criminal investigation. Once children have given information that indicates they may have been abused, the practitioner should not ask any further questions about the incident as this may jeopardise further investigative action by the police.

Whilst the class was changing for PE, Anna McAllister, the PE teacher, noticed two bruises that went right across the shoulders of one of the class members, Teri Roberts. Ms McAllister waited until the rest of the class had left and then asked Teri what had happened to her back. Teri became upset and said that she and her mother had an argument the previous evening. During the argument, Teri said she had sworn at her mother and her father had heard her. He had rushed into the kitchen and told her to go to her room. Teri had refused to go and her father had pulled her by the arm, telling her to go to her room. She had slipped and fallen backwards against the kitchen table, hitting her back.

Ms McAllister said that she thought that it was important that Teri and her family got some help to resolve their difficulties. She explained to Teri that in these circumstances she needed to get some advice to make sure that she did the right thing and that she would have to talk to Mrs Patel, the designated teacher. Ms McAllister reassured Teri that she would tell her what Mrs Patel advised before she took any further action. Mrs Patel recommended that a referral be made to children's social care. She provided Ms McAllister with the number and checked that she was happy to contact them. Ms McAllister confirmed that she was and Mrs Patel agreed to arrange cover for Ms McAllister's classes for the afternoon.

Ms McAllister explained Mrs Patel's advice to Teri. Initially, she was very upset and anxious. Ms McAllister reassured her that the most important thing was that she and her family got some help. Ms McAllister said to Teri that she could be with her when she made the referral, and if she had any questions she could either ask her to ask the social worker or she could speak to the social worker herself.

Teri was then happy for Ms McAllister to inform her parents of her planned action and to make a referral to children's social care.

For further discussion of involving children and communicating with children, see Chapter 1. See also Butler and Williamson (1994); Modi, Marks and Wattley (1995); Scutt (1995); Marchant and Jones (2000) and Jones (2003).

INVOLVING FAMILIES

Research carried out in the 1990s found that many parents were unaware that a referral had been made to children's social care (Cleaver and Freeman, 1995; Farmer and Owen 1995; Sharland *et al.,* 1995). Often their first contact with professionals about the concern was when the social worker and/or police officer called at their home. These initial contacts, characterised by Cleaver and Freeman (1995) as 'confrontations', set the tone for the families' ongoing involvement with professionals. No matter how constructive the support that was offered, it was difficult for families to forget the feelings of powerlessness and suspicion that they experienced during the initial phases of the section 47 enquiry.

Unless to do so would place a child at risk of significant harm, discussing concerns with a parent can help the parent understand why practitioners are concerned and prepare the parent for contact with children's social care. Recent research (Cleaver, Walker and Meadows, 2004) found that in almost three quarters of cases concerns were discussed with parents before a referral was made, suggesting a significant improvement in practice in this area.

Some practitioners may be concerned that raising issues, particularly concerns about significant harm, may jeopardise their professional or working relationship with family members. However, any effective relationship should be built on the basis of honesty and trust. If practitioners are open with children and families and explain why they are concerned, they are likely to retain their respect.

Research (Cleaver and Freeman, 1995; Thoburn, Lewis and Shemmings, 1995; Cleaver, Walker and Meadows, 2004) suggests that parents value professionals who explain things to them, involve them in the process, keep them informed, treat them with respect, and understand the family's difficulties.

For a detailed discussion of working with parents, see Chapter 2.

For further information on involving families, see Cleaver and Freeman (1995); Freeman and Hunt (1998); Thoburn, Wilding and Watson (2000) and Cleaver, Walker and Meadows (2004).

For information on working with fathers, see Ryan (2000).

Explain things to families

Unless to do so would place the child at risk of significant harm, explain to the child and family what your concerns are, why you think a referral is necessary and how it will help them. Remember, if you are concerned that a child has suffered or may suffer significant harm, you are not seeking the family's agreement to refer, you are simply explaining why you will be making a referral. If you think that telling the family could result in an unacceptable delay in the child receiving emergency services – for example, if medical treatment is urgently required – make the referral and then explain to the family why you have made the referral.

Involve families in the process

Once a referral has been made, families report that they often feel powerless and that the situation is out of their control. As far as possible, families should be involved in the process. For example, they could be encouraged to make the referral themselves with the support of the practitioner, or the practitioner could make the referral in the presence of family members so that they know exactly what has been said.

Keep families informed

Another way of supporting families is to keep them informed of what is happening or will be happening. Often the practitioner making a referral may not know the exact timetable for actions. The LSCB procedures outline the process that will be followed and the possible decisions, and can therefore be used as a guide to what is likely to happen.

Treat families with respect

Both the attitude and approach of the practitioner should convey respect for family members. This requires both attention to detail and approaching families in a manner that is honest, polite and shows an awareness of their needs and circumstances. For example, if you do not know the adult in the family, ask them how they would like to be addressed (by their first name or as Mr, Mrs or Ms). Consult the family over appointment times to make sure these do not conflict with mealtimes or other appointments. Ensure that where a family requires an interpreter one is available, and pass this information on to other agencies so that family members do not have to ask for one repeatedly.

Understand the family's difficulties

In most situations where concerns arise about a child's health and development, families usually face a number of difficulties. Show the family that you are aware of the pressure they may be under and that a referral to another agency – even when it relates to concerns about a child's safety – is intended to help them address these difficulties. This can help to reassure families.

CONCLUSION

Whenever practitioners have concerns about a child, no matter how vague, they should approach someone for help in considering what to do in response to these concerns. Personal anxiety about appearing foolish or inexperienced should never prevent practitioners from raising their concerns. The information that an individual practitioner has is often unique and will add to the overall understanding of the child's needs, the parenting he or she is receiving and the family and environment in which he or she lives.

Practitioners may be reluctant to discuss concerns because they are worried that they will unleash an army of professionals who will then descend on the family. This is an unwarranted concern. Strategy discussions and other types of planning fora ensure that professional action is coordinated. Remember, if concerned about a child's welfare, practitioners can approach colleagues from another agency to discuss these concerns without naming the child.

Sometimes, having approached someone for help, practitioners may not be satisfied with the response they receive. It is important that when practitioners still feel concerned about a child they do not simply ignore these concerns. Pursuing concerns can sometimes feel uncomfortable for practitioners, for example, when the person they have spoken to is more experienced or occupies a more senior position in the organisation. Practitioners should always remember that the welfare of the child should be their first consideration. Practitioners will have to consider whether they have properly and fully explained their concerns and whether they approach the same colleague again to reiterate their worries or, alternatively, approach another more experienced colleague within their agency or in another agency.

Approaching someone for help and advice about what to do can feel daunting. However, it is a crucial part of practitioners' responsibilities to safeguard and promote children's welfare.

REFERENCES

Butler, I. and Williamson, H. (1994) *Children Speak*, Longman, London.

Children Act 1989, Chapter 41, The Stationery Office, London, http://www.opsi.gov.uk/acts/acts1989/Ukpga_19890041_en_1.htm (accessed 22 August 2008).

Children Act 2004, Chapter 31, The Stationery Office, London, http://www.opsi.gov.uk/acts/acts2004/20040031.htm (accessed 22 August 2008).

Cleaver, H. and Freeman, P. (1995) *Parental Perspectives in Cases of Suspected Child Abuse*, HMSO, London.

Cleaver, H. and Walker, S. and Meadows, P. (2004) *Assessing Children's Needs and Circumstances: The Impact of the Assessment Framework*, Jessica Kingsley, London.

Cleaver, H., Wattam, C. and Cawson, P. (1998) *Assessing Risk in Child Protection*, NSPCC, London.

Cm 5730 (2003) *The Victoria Climbié Inquiry Report*, The Stationery Office, London, http://www.victoria-climbie-inquiry.org.uk/finreport/finreport.htm (accessed 22 August 2008).

Cm 5860 (2003) *Every Child Matters*, The Stationery Office, London.

Cross, M., Gardner, R., Kennedy, M. and Marchant, R. (1993) *Abuse and Children Who Are Disabled: A Resource and Training Pack*, NSPCC, Leicester.

Department of Health, Department for Education and Employment and Home Office (2000) *Framework for the Assessment of Children in Need and Their Families*, The Stationery Office, London, http://www.dh.gov.uk/PublicationsAndStatistics/Publications/PublicationsPolicyAndGuidance/PublicationsPolicyAndGuidance Article/fs/en?CONTENT_ID=4003256&chk=Fss1ka (accessed 22 August 2008).

Dutt, R. and Phillips, M. (Department of Health) (2000) Assessing black children in need and their families, in *Assessing Children in Need and Their Families: Practice Guidance*, The Stationery Office, London.

Epps, K. (1999) Looking after young sexual abusers: child protection, risk management and risk reduction, in *Children and Young People Who Sexually Abuse Others* (eds M. Erooga and H. Masson), Routledge, London.

Farmer, E. and Owen, M. (1995) *Child Protection Practice: Private Risks and Public Remedies*, HMSO, London.

Freeman, P. and Hunt, J. (1998) *Parental Perspectives on Care Proceedings*, The Stationery Office, London.

HM Government (2006a) *Working Together to Safeguard Children*, The Stationery Office, London, http://www.everychildmatters.gov.uk/safeguarding (accessed 22 August 2008).

HM Government (2006b) *Common Assessment Framework for Children and Young People: Managers' Guide*, The Stationery Office, London, http://www.everychild matters.gov.uk/caf (accessed 22 August 2008).

HM Government (2006c) *Common Assessment Framework for Children and Young People: Practitioners' Guide*, The Stationery Office, London, http://www.everychild matters.gov.uk/caf (accessed 22 August 2008).

HM Government (2006d) *What To Do If You're Worried a Child Is Being Abused*, Department for Education and Skills, London, http://www.everychildmatters.gov. uk/safeguarding (accessed 22 August 2008).

Jones, D. (2003) *Communicating with Vulnerable Children: A Guide for Practitioners*, Gaskell, London.

Marchant, R. and Jones, M. (Department of Health) (2000) Assessing the needs of disabled children and their families, in *Assessing Children in Need and Their Families: Practice Guidance*, The Stationery Office, London.

Modi, P., Marks, C. and Wattley, R. (1995) From the margin to the centre: empowering the black child, in *Participation and Empowerment in Child Protection* (eds C. Cloke and M. Davies), Pitman, London.

Morris, J. (2002) *A Lot to Say! A Guide for Social Workers, Personal Advisors and Others Working with Disabled Children and Young People with Communication Impairments*, Scope, London, www.scope.org.uk (accessed 22 August 2008).

National Working Group on Child Protection and Disability (2003) *'It Doesn't Happen to Disabled Children': Child Protection and Disabled Children*, NSPCC, London, http://www.nspcc.org.uk/inform (accessed 22 August 2008).

Ryan, M. (2000) *Working with Fathers*, Radcliff Medical Press, Abingdon.

Scutt, N. (1995) Child advocacy – getting the child's voice heard, in *Participation and Empowerment in Child Protection* (eds C. Cloke and M. Davies), Pitman, London.

Sharland, E., Jones, D., Aldgate, J. *et al.* (1995) *Professional Intervention in Child Sexual Abuse*, HMSO, London.

Thoburn, J., Chand, A. and Procter, J. (2004) *Child Welfare Services for Minority Ethnic Families: The Research Review*, Jessica Kingsley, London.

Thoburn, J., Lewis, A. and Shemmings, D. (1995) *Paternalism or Partnership? Family Involvement in the Child Protection Process*, HMSO, London.

Thoburn, J., Wilding, J. and Watson, J. (2000) *Family Support in Cases of Emotional Maltreatment and Neglect*, The Stationery Office, London.

Walker, S., Scott, J. and Cleaver, H. (2004) *Implementing the Integrated Children's System: A Training and Resource Pack*, Department of Health, London, http://www.everychildmatters.gov.uk/socialcare/ics/ (accessed 22 August 2008).

8 Carrying Out or Contributing to an Assessment

HEDY CLEAVER

This chapter details the process of assessment when there are concerns about children's welfare such that their health or development may be impaired. The *Common Assessment Framework* (HM Government, 2006a, 2006b) and the Assessment Framework (Department of Health *et al.*, 2000), which underpins the Integrated Children's System (http://www.everychildmatters.gov.uk/socialcare/ics), are described and important issues to consider when carrying out an assessment are highlighted. The process of assessment is explored, including planning the assessment, information gathering, analysis, judgements and decision making. Involving children and families is essential and possible pitfalls and how to overcome these are discussed. Finally, the chapter discusses the importance of inter-agency collaboration and considers the legal basis for information sharing.

CORE KNOWLEDGE

- An assessment is the process of gathering relevant information in order to understand children's developmental needs and their parent's/carer's capacity to respond to these needs in the context of their wider family and community environment. The outcome of the assessment should be informed by a careful analysis of all the information gathered during the assessment.
- Careful planning will help ensure the aims of the assessment are met, the most appropriate approach to the child and family is taken and the most appropriate tools, tests or questionnaires are used.
- Communication with the child and involving the family in the assessment process are essential to understand what is happening within the family.
- To gain a full picture of the child's needs and circumstances within their family context, agencies should collaborate during the assessment which, for children in need, is led by children's social care.

Safeguarding Children   Edited by Hedy Cleaver, Pat Cawson, Sarah Gorin and Steve Walker
Copyright © 2009 by John Wiley & Sons, Ltd

WHAT IS AN ASSESSMENT?

Undertaking an assessment can seem a daunting task. However, it is a process we frequently go through to inform our decision making. For example, in deciding where to go on holiday we may consider a range of issues such as the interests and capacities of those going on the holiday, the facilities that the selected holiday destination can offer, the weather at the time we plan to go, the mode of travel and its cost and the type of accommodation. The assessment of this information – which entails drawing together the different strands, gauging the importance of particular issues and seeing how they have an impact on each other – enables us to gain a full understanding of the situation and informs our judgements and subsequent decision making.

When concerned that a child has additional needs, practitioners should take a holistic approach to assessment and consider all the issues that may be having an impact on the child's health and development. For example, when teachers are worried about recent changes in a child's behaviour, the focus of their assessment should not be confined to a single issue such as the child's schoolwork, but take into consideration all aspects of their behaviour as well as information known about the child's home life. Any assessment should identify the strengths within the child and family as well as the difficulties. To ensure early intervention for children with additional needs the government announced, in the Green Paper *Every Child Matters* (Cm 5860), the development of a Common Assessment Framework (CAF) for use across all agencies.

THE COMMON ASSESSMENT FRAMEWORK

Non-statutory guidance to assist implementation of the CAF (HM Government, 2006a, 2006b) was issued to local authorities in April 2006. The CAF is intended to enable practitioners to assess children's additional needs for services earlier and more effectively. It introduces a nationally standardised approach to be used with unborn babies, infants or children and young people and their families across all children's services. It aims to help early identification of needs, leading to coordinated provision of services, involving a lead professional where appropriate and sharing information to avoid duplication of assessments (HM Government 2006b, Paragraph 2.1).

The CAF has drawn on the conceptual *Framework for the Assessment of Children in Need and Their Families* (Department of Health *et al.*, 2000) as well as other assessment systems for children, including the APIR (assess/plan/implement/review) framework (it is a comprehensive framework for one-to-one interaction with young people used by those working with the Connexions service).

A CAF is a generic assessment. It has been designed to enable practitioners to undertake an early assessment of a child's needs that can act as a basis for early intervention before problems reach crisis point. Where a referral to a more specialised practitioner is required, the CAF should ensure that the referral is supported by accurate, up-to-date information. The Assessment Framework (Department of Health *et al.*, 2000) guidance should be followed where a practitioner considers that a child is a child in need under the Children Act 1989, and where there are concerns about a child being at risk of significant harm.

THE ASSESSMENT FRAMEWORK

The Assessment Framework (see Figure 8.1) is used by practitioners when assessing children in need under the Children Act 1989. The Assessment Framework is a map that practitioners use for thinking about children and their health and development, and provides a structure to the way in which information is gathered and recorded. Practitioners are required to adopt a systematic approach to gathering and analysing information about children and their families to inform their decision making. These decisions will provide the basis for the child's plan. The use of the Integrated Children's System (http://www.everychildmatters.gov.uk/socialcare/ics/) means that the domains and dimensions used in the assessment will structure the subsequent planning, intervention and reviewing processes (Department of Health, 2002a).

See Chapter 9 on planning, Chapter 10 on intervention and Chapter 11 on reviewing.

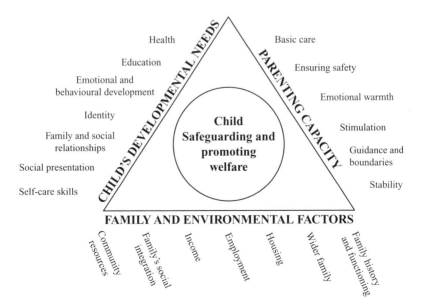

Figure 8.1 The Assessment Framework

When carrying out an assessment to understand what is happening to a child and why, professionals should take account of the child's developmental needs and the parenting capacity to respond to these needs. The assessment should include identifying the child's and the family's strengths and difficulties, as well as the impact of the wider family and environmental factors. These are the three interrelated domains of the Assessment Framework (see Figure 8.1). Within each domain there are a number of critical dimensions. It is the understanding of how these dimensions interact and influence each other in relation to the duty to safeguard and promote the welfare of the child that is the focus of careful exploration during an assessment. Assessments should, whenever possible, be carried out in partnership with the child and the family, and will require working closely with colleagues in the statutory or voluntary sectors who are also involved with them to ensure a full understanding of what is happening. Professionals who adopt such an approach to assessments report that it has improved their understanding of the child's needs and circumstances, and their ability to make decisions about children for whom they have concerns:

> I am now able to identify children who are vulnerable but who have not necessarily suffered significant harm. Hence, I can begin to try and access help in a preventative framework/model rather than purely reactive.
>> Health visitor describing the impact of the Assessment Framework on her work, quoted in Cleaver, Walker and Meadows (2004, p. 139)

> A more thorough assessment is done by myself. This is good as it gives me more information to work with.
>> Educational welfare officer describing the change to his work since using the Assessment Framework, quoted in Cleaver, Walker and Meadows (2004, p. 144)

CHILDREN'S DEVELOPMENTAL NEEDS

The Assessment Framework is based on the principle that all assessments should be child centred and they therefore require direct observation and communication with the child. To understand what is happening to a child or young person, professionals should have a sound knowledge of child development. For example, the main developmental tasks for infants are to establish secure attachments to caregivers, to develop gross and fine motor coordination and to start to communicate. Middle childhood is taken up with achieving more complex physical skills and coordination; developing empathy; understanding notions of right and wrong, of truth and fairness; becoming numerate and literate and developing peer relationships. Adolescence heralds the onset of puberty and sexual maturation. Young people frequently question the belief system with which they were brought up, and have an increasing ability to reason about hypothetical events. It is a time when a cohesive self-identity is established and close friendships with both sexes are formed.

The assessment will explore whether children's health and development are at the level that would be expected for their age, taking into account individual differences such as physical disabilities, learning disabilities, language and methods of communication.

For detailed information on child development, see Daniel, Wassell and Gilligan (1999), Bee (2000); Meggitt and Sunderland (2000) and Aldgate *et al.* (2006).

PARENTING CAPACITY

> Critically important to a child's health and development is the ability of parents or caregivers to ensure that the child's developmental needs are being appropriately and adequately responded to, and to adapt to his or her changing needs over time.
>
> Department of Health *et al.*, 2000, p. 20, 2.9

There is much research which suggests that when parenting capacity is affected by issues such as domestic violence, alcohol or drug misuse, mental illness or learning disability, there is less risk of significant harm to children when issues exist in isolation and when families remain cohesive and harmonious. Children are more vulnerable when problems coexist, when a lone parent is unsupported or when both parents are experiencing difficulties:

> I stopped loving my kids ... my drugs were more important than my kids ... I wasn't hitting them ... I was just neglecting them. I wasn't feeding them regular. I wasn't washing them regular.
>
> A quotation used in Kroll and Taylor (2003, p. 122), taken from Klee and Jackson (1998)

Although there is considerable evidence to suggest that children can be protected from the adverse effects of parental mental illness, substance misuse or learning disability, there is little or no evidence for this in the case of domestic violence.

Although research identifies some aspects of parental behaviour that place all children at risk of suffering significant harm, the impact on a child will vary depending on his or her age and stage of development, the child's own personality and coping strategies and the supportive factors within the family and environment:

> We all coped differently ... I coped by believing everything my mother said was right ... my dad was bad. My brother coped by rebelling but he might have rebelled anyway ... My sister just kept herself to herself and studied incessantly.
>
> A quotation used in Kroll and Taylor (2003, p. 172), in reference to parental substance misuse, taken from Laybourn, Brown and Hill (1996)

The assessment should explore the strengths and difficulties within the immediate family and how these directly affect the child and the parents' or carers' capacity to meet the needs of their child.

For more detailed information on the impact of parental issues on children's development, see Quinton and Rutter (1985), Velleman and Orford (1993), Mullender and Morley (1994), Booth and Booth (1996), Velleman (1996) Cleaver, Aldgate and Unell (1999), Falkov (2002), Klee, Jackson and Lewis (2002), McConnell and Llewellyn (2002), Fowler (2003), Reder, Duncan and Lucey (2003) and Kroll and Taylor (2003).

FAMILY AND ENVIRONMENTAL FACTORS

Assessments should also take account of wider family and environmental factors and how these affect the child and family. Families may offer both support and/or additional stress. A grandparent living nearby may provide substantial support and day-to-day comfort and care. In these circumstances, the negative impact of parental issues on children's health and development can be reduced. In other cases, the impact of parental issues on children may be exacerbated if accompanied by ongoing family feuding, rejection and family violence.

In assessing children's needs and circumstances, practitioners should also consider the impact of the environment and community on the family, not forgetting that children and young people may experience some aspects in very different ways from their parents or carers. Equally important is a consideration of the experiences of individual children. For some vulnerable children, school can provide a haven from the worries and anxiety of home life. For others, however, the difficulties they are experiencing at home may result in peer rejection, bullying and the criticism of school staff. For some vulnerable young people, neighbourhood resources such as health centres, Connexions or youth clubs may offer valuable confidential advice and support, enabling problems to be shared and preventing difficulties from escalating.

Moreover, the environment and community in which the child and family live will have a very different impact on individual children. The same environment may appear threatening and alienating to some children while for others it may be an exciting and accepting milieu.

The challenge facing practitioners is to assess the impact of parental issues and family and environmental factors on the health and development of individual children. Taking time to plan the assessment is the first stage of the process.

For further information about the impact of family and the environment on children and families, see Chapter 3. See also Quinton (1994), Jack (2001), Ghate and Hazel (2002) and Jack and Gill (2003).

PLANNING THE ASSESSMENT

Undertaking an assessment requires careful planning: practitioners have to keep a clear focus both on the reason for the assessment, their own role and responsibilities and those of caregivers and other practitioners, and on how the assessment itself may have an impact on the child and other family members. The child and family need to understand why the assessment is taking place, what it will involve, the timescale and the possible consequences. Where necessary, families need reassurance that 'child in need' assessments rarely result in children being 'taken away' from their care. Planning should include how this process and its subsequent decisions will be communicated to other professionals and caregivers, as well as to the child and family.

The aim of the assessment should be to identify and clarify the developmental needs of the child, while the process should be helpful and intrude in the life of the family as little as possible without ever compromising the safety of the child. It is essential that assessments keep the child in focus and that workers are not distracted by parental problems, which in some families can be overwhelming for staff and families alike.

Key questions to be addressed at the planning stage include the following:

- Who is the best person to undertake the assessment?
- What other agencies or practitioners should be involved in the assessment?
- What resources are required?
- What is the child and family's previous experience of professional interventions?
- How will the child's wishes and feelings be ascertained, having regard to his or her age and understanding?
- Does the child or his or her parent(s) want a friend, relative or advocate present during interviews?
- Where will the assessment be done?

The plan for the assessment should be discussed with the child and family and reviewed in the light of their comments, whilst at the same time ensuring the child's safety.

It is important to consider which family members to include in the assessment and whether there are specific communication issues to be addressed or taken account of. Interviews with the child and family members should be conducted separately and together as appropriate. These should be undertaken in the preferred language of the child and each family member. For some disabled children and family members expertise in non-verbal communication will be necessary. Finally, planning the assessment should be informed by what information is already available in agency records and consider how further information will be collected, recorded and analysed, and over what timescale.

Unfortunately, when the assessment process is not planned, and there is a lack of adequate preparation and no clear sense of purpose, things can go badly wrong.

Margaret [a social work student in her first practice placement] was eager to begin practice. She telephoned Carol and organised a convenient time and date to visit. The day of the visit arrived. Margaret made her way to the house, rang the bell and introduced herself when Carol answered. It was at this point that she realised she had no plan, did not know what information to collect, how to collect it and to what ends she was making an assessment. Carol asked Margaret what she was going to do to help her with her children. Margaret did not know how to answer. The visit became tense and after 15 min ended with no further plans. Carol telephoned her health visitor the following day to say the social worker was 'useless'.

Case study used in Parker and Bradley (2003, p. 9)

The nature of the concerns will influence the process of the assessment and the depth at which issues are explored. In order to understand a child's developmental needs, multiple sources of information should be used. These may include

- direct work with the child, parents/current caregivers and the wider family;
- observation of the child;
- involving or working with other practitioners who have known the child and family;
- checking files and records for information already held about the child and family;
- the application of questionnaires, tests or scales or commissioning a specialist assessment.

For detailed information about the use of questionnaires and scales to evidence assessment and decision making, see Appendix 3 of HM Government (2006c).

For further reading on planning an assessment, see Cleaver, Wattam and Cawson (1998), Department of Health *et al.* (2000), Adcock (2001) and Kennedy and Wonnacott (2003).

COMMUNICATING WITH CHILDREN

When assessing children's developmental needs and circumstances, it is essential always to see the children, however young and whatever their circumstances:

Communicating with children is an essential part of the assessment, as well as recognising their rights to be involved and consulted about matters which affect their lives.

Department of Health *et al.*, 2000, p. 43, 3.41

In carrying out an assessment the child's behaviour and interactions with family members and peers should be observed, and the child's thoughts and concerns ascertained through direct work. It is a statutory requirement under section 17 of the Children Act 1989 as amended by section 53 of the Children Act 2004 to ascertain the child's wishes and feelings, having regard to their age and understanding, when considering how best to meet their needs following an assessment and the services they may require.

Communicating with children can be a challenge. Communicating with disabled children may require more preparation, take more time and on occasions require the expertise of someone who is familiar with the child's mode of communication. Similarly, if English is not the child's preferred language, children should have the opportunity to communicate in the language of their choice. When there are concerns that a child's health or development is being impaired or the child may be suffering harm, someone outside the family should be used to facilitate communication with the child. Finally, many vulnerable children have learnt to mistrust adults in positions of authority, and much work may be required to rebuild that trust:

> Social workers are all horrible ... I don't trust them at all ... Like I said, she's nasty, really nasty ... First off she was going to keep it to herself; she was supposed to do that, but she didn't.
>
> A 9-year-old girl talking about her experience of social workers, quoted in Cleaver (2000, p. 214)

Research has shown that children and young people value practitioners who

- listen to what they say;
- are available and accessible;
- have a sense of humour;
- are straight talking;
- can be trusted.

For a detailed discussion about communicating with children, see NSPCC/Chailey Heritage (1998), Department of Health (2000), Department of Health *et al.* (2000), Aldgate and Statham (2001), Jones (2003, 2006a) and Lancaster (2003); Integrated Children's System web site: http://www.dfes. gov.uk/integratedchildrenssystem.

INVOLVING THE FAMILY IN THE ASSESSMENT PROCESS

When a child's welfare or behaviour is causing concern, while most parents are likely to be worried and welcoming of help, they also fear practitioners will judge them as inadequate and take away their children. How professionals first approach families when concerned about a child's welfare can influence parents' and carers' perspectives of what is happening and affect all further interactions. Professionals should be aware that preconceptions and stereo-types may affect their behaviour towards family members, setting up patterns of interaction that are difficult to change.

Parents and carers value practitioners who give clear explanations, are open and honest, and treat them with respect and dignity. They do not want to be kept in the dark, nor have practitioners talk about them without their knowl-edge and in a patronising manner. In arranging interviews and carrying out assessments, practitioners should take into account family life and day-to-day routines – for example explaining how many times they expect to visit the family and how long each visit will take, not calling at mealtimes or bedtimes unless necessary, respecting the family's space and customs as far as possible and being careful to ask or inform them before talking to relatives or other professionals.

When carrying out an assessment, professionals need to explain to family members including, when relevant, the child

- what an assessment is;
- why an assessment is being carried out;
- what will happen;
- what will be expected of the family;
- what the family can expect from practitioners.

> We were happy at the way the assessment was done. It was much longer than we expected but we did not mind that. There were certainly a lot of questions but they needed to ask them. The social worker did explain everything so we are happy with the assessment.
>
> Mother of a learning disabled child, quoted in Cleaver, Walker and Meadows (2004, p. 84)

Where communication methods require particular thought and planning, for example when English is not the family's preferred language or when par-ents have literacy problems or are learning disabled, practitioners need to spend more time explaining their actions and consider when the help of those with special communication skills is necessary. Even when parents with learn-ing disabilities appear quite fluent they may not grasp subtle points:

> The pace of working with a learning disabled mum and going through the reasons for involvement and the process was very time consuming. Also during interviews it took a lot longer than normal to get answers to questions. I had to be more creative in the way I put the questions ... However, I do think that spending time was well worth it in the end...
>
> Social worker describing her approach to a learning disabled mother, quoted in Cleaver and Nicholson (2007, p. 56)

In order for practitioners to undertake an assessment of the child's needs and circumstances they will need to engage with the child and the child's fam-ily to identify their strengths as well as the difficulties they are experiencing.

For example, when children and families are referred to or seek help from children's social care, a social worker should carry out an initial assessment in order to decide if the child is a child in need and what services may be required. This will involve seeing the child and other family members, either together or separately as appropriate, as well as seeking information from other agencies (with the consent of parents and older children) that have worked with or are currently working with the child and family. Research findings show that most professional assessments and interventions focus on the mother (Ryan, 2000). Whenever appropriate, fathers should be involved in discussions about the child's welfare, and assessments should include an exploration of the father's parenting capacity.

For more detailed discussion of communicating with parents, see Chapter 2.

For further information on involving families in the assessment process, see Cleaver and Freeman (1995), Freeman and Hunt (1998) Thoburn, Wilding and Watson (2000), Aldgate and Statham (2001) and Cleaver, Walker and Meadows (2004). For working with fathers, see Ryan (2000).

THE INITIAL ASSESSMENT

An initial assessment, led by children's social care, should be completed within seven working days. Decisions and plans for the child and family should be based on an analysis of the information gathered during the assessment, and undertaken in collaboration with the child and family and other relevant agencies. The possible decisions following an initial assessment include no further action, a referral to another agency, the provision of services, a core assessment or a combination of these. The information that is recorded should be consistent with the information set out in the Initial Assessment Record (Department of Health, 2002a, 2002b):

> Record the assessment findings and your initial analysis and decisions following the initial assessment, including the reasons for any decisions made and further action to be taken in the Initial Assessment Record.
>
> HM Government, 2006d, Paragraph 16.6

When the initial assessment identifies that a child is suffering or likely to suffer significant harm, children's social care should initiate a strategy discussion. When there is a risk to the child's life or a likelihood of serious injury, children's social care, the police or the NSPCC should act quickly to ensure the child is safe.

See Appendix 1 in *Working Together to Safeguard Children* (HM Government, 2006d) for a summary of statutory orders that may be used to protect a child from harm.

THE CORE ASSESSMENT

A core assessment is undertaken when

- the child and family have complex needs and the initial assessment does not provide the depth of information required to develop an appropriate plan for the provision of services;
- suspected actual or likely significant harm has resulted in children's social care together with other agencies deciding to initiate enquiries under section 47 of the Children Act 1989;
- a child becomes looked after and a previous core assessment is not up to date. The core assessment is used to inform the child's first care plan (Department of Health, 2002a).

A core assessment is an in-depth assessment led by children's social care which, like the initial assessment, follows the structure provided by the Assessment Framework domains and dimensions, and is carried out whenever possible in conjunction with the child and family, drawing on the knowledge and expertise of all relevant statutory and voluntary agencies. When there has been a decision to initiate enquires under section 47 of the Children Act 1989, children's social care is responsible for taking the lead on the assessment and planning processes. The police should investigate any allegations of crime or suspected crime and the criminal antecedents of any known or suspected offender, and use the information gained appropriately to assist other agencies in understanding the child's circumstances, in the best interests of the child.

In some cases, social workers may use specific tests, questionnaires, tools and diagrammatic aids to explore particular aspects of a child's development and family life or request a specialist assessment – for example of a parent's current mental state and its impact on a particular child's developmental progress. When undertaking a core assessment, social workers have lead responsibility and should keep detailed records which are shared with the child and family members.

Good case recording is essential because, together with reports from other professionals, it provides the basis for analysis, judgements, decision making and developing plans. Recording should include both the details of when and how the assessment was carried out, such as dates and details of meetings with the child and family members, as well as the information gathered about the child's developmental needs, parenting capacity, and family and environmental factors. The information recorded should be consistent with the information set out in the Core Assessment Record (Department of Health, 2002a, 2002b).

For further information on section 47 enquiries, see HM Government (2006d), Department of Health *et al.* (2000).

For further information on tools to assist assessments, see McGoldrick, Gerson and Shellenberger (1999); Calam *et al.* (2000, 2005), Department of Health *et al.* (2000), Department of Health, Cox and Bentovim (2000), Bentovim and Bingley Miller (2001), Department for Education and Skills (2001), Cox and Walker (2002), Parker and Bradley (2003) and Carter, Briggs-Gowan and Ornstein Davis (2004); Integrated Children's System web site: http://www.everychildmatters.gov.uk/socialcare/ics.

THE ANALYSIS

To ensure that plans for the child and family meet their needs, professionals have to analyse the information gathered during the assessment (HM Government, 2006c, Paragraph 51.3).

The analysis will entail

- summarising the data gathered about the child's developmental needs, parenting capacity and family and environmental factors;
- identifying the strengths and difficulties in each of these areas;
- understanding the interaction between the three areas and weighing up the impact on the child's health and development;
- understanding the parent's or carer's capacity for change.

In conjunction with the information gained from the analysis, professionals should draw on their respective knowledge bases to inform their judgements about a child's circumstances, whether the child is in need and whether the child's health and development are likely to be impaired without the provision of services. For some children, practitioners will need to make the judgement as to whether the child is suffering or is likely to suffer significant harm.

Once this has been done the range of interventions that could address the identified needs, building on the family's strengths, is considered. The decision about what action to take is made collaboratively with other professionals and with the child and family members. The research evidence on the success of different types of interventions, the resources available and the family's likelihood of cooperating with particular aspects of the plan, should inform these decisions.

The core assessment should be completed within 35 working days and include a plan for the child and family on the basis of the analysis of all the information gathered during the assessment, and made in conjunction with the child and family and the other relevant agencies.

For more information on analysis, see Chapters 9 and 10.

See also Bentovim (1998), Cleaver (2001), Jones (2001), Jones (2006b) and Fowler (2003).

For further information on the efficacy of different types of interventions, see Kluger, Alexander and Curtis (2000), Macdonald (2001), McAuley, Pecora and Rose (2006) and Scott and Ward (2005).

THE NEED FOR URGENT ACTION

> Where there is a risk to the life of a child or a likelihood of serious immediate harm, an agency with statutory child protection powers, i.e. children's social care, police or NSPCC, should act quickly to secure the immediate safety of the child.
>
> HM Government, 2006c, p. 24, Paragraph 22

When considering whether emergency action is necessary, practitioners should always consider whether action is required to safeguard other children in the same household, in the household of an alleged perpetrator or elsewhere. The reasons why action is needed to secure the immediate safety of each child should be recorded. At this stage the information available may mean the recording is very brief. This will, in part, depend on how well the child and family are known to children's or adults' social care and other agencies.

In cases where urgent action is necessary to protect a child, an application for an Emergency Protection Order can be made by the local authority under section 44 of the Children Act 1989 or the police may use their powers of protection under section 46 of the same Act. For some children, the circumstances may be such that action is taken without prior consultation with the child and family:

> An emergency protection order gives authority to remove a child, and places the child under the protection of the applicant for a maximum of eight days (with a possible extension of up to seven days).
>
> HM Government, 2006d, Appendix 1, Paragraph 17

Once the child is safe, children's social care will convene a strategy discussion. The discussion should be used to

- share available information;
- agree on the conduct and timing of any criminal investigation;
- decide whether a core assessment under section 47 of the Children Act 1989 (section 47 enquiries) should be initiated, or continued if it has already begun;
- plan how the section 47 enquiry should be undertaken (if one is to be initiated), including the need for medical treatment, and who will carry out what actions, by when and for what purpose;
- agree what action is required immediately to safeguard and promote the welfare of the child, and/or provide interim services and support. If the child

is in hospital, decisions should also be made about how to secure the safe discharge of the child;

- determine what information from the strategy discussion will be shared with the family, unless such information sharing may place a child at increased risk of significant harm or jeopardise police investigations into any alleged offence(s);
- determine if legal action is required.

HM Government, 2006d, Paragraph 5.55

A core assessment should be started when the strategy discussion results in a decision to initiate enquiries under section 47. Even in these cases, professionals who work sensitively with families may overcome the resistance, fear and hostility engendered by the child protection enquiry in order to work in conjunction with families to safeguard and promote the welfare of their child(ren).

For further information on significant harm, see Adcock and White (1998), HM Government (2006d), Paragraphs 5.49–5.53.

A key principle of the Assessment Framework is that children's needs and their families' circumstances will require inter-agency collaboration to ensure full understanding of what is happening and to ensure an effective service response.

Department of Health *et al.*, 2000, p. 63, 5.1

INTER-AGENCY COLLABORATION IN ASSESSMENTS

This principle of inter-agency collaboration when working with children in need underpins the Children Act 1989 (s 27 and s 47(9)), which sets out a legal duty to collaborate where children's social care are undertaking their duty to safeguard and promote a child's welfare. Professionals should work together not only to avoid duplicating or unnecessarily repeating assessments, but also to make sure the assessment benefits from the expertise and knowledge of others. The Children Act 2004 also places a duty on statutory agencies to cooperate to improve the well-being of children in their area.

Statutory and voluntary agencies and organisations may be involved at any and every stage in an assessment. For example, the work of general practitioners, nurses and health visitors frequently brings them into direct contact with vulnerable children and their families. Indeed, they are uniquely placed to identify parenting issues, such as mental ill health or substance misuse, and observe the impact they are having on the health and development of children within the family. When their own assessment suggests that the welfare of the child is being affected, agencies are responsible for talking to the child and family about their concerns and, when necessary, making a referral to children's social care.

At this point, providing as much written information as possible in relation to the child's developmental needs, parenting capacity and family and environmental factors will support the referral and contribute to the social worker's initial or core assessment. In carrying out an assessment, social workers will be seeking additional information and involving staff from other agencies. Inter-agency collaboration in relation to the case is likely to continue with the development of plans for the child and family, service provision and reviews.

For a discussion of multi-agency work in safeguarding, see Chapter 5.

For more information about a multi-agency approach to assessment, see Hallett (1995), Glisson and Hemmelgarn (1998), Department of Health *et al.* (2000), Hudson (2001), Sturge (2001) and HM Government (2006a and 2006b) (CAF Guidance).

INFORMATION SHARING

In all cases, the disclosure of information is governed by

- a common law duty of confidence;
- the Human Rights Act 1998;
- the Data Protection Act 1989.

In general, information can be shared with other practitioners for the purposes of promoting and safeguarding the welfare of children when

- those likely to be affected consent; or
- the public interest in safeguarding the child's welfare overrides the need to keep the information confidential; or
- disclosure is required under a court order or other legal obligation.

HM Government, 2006c, Paragraph 5

In the course of their work with children and families practitioners must exercise judgement about what they disclose and to whom. There is no breach of confidence if the relevant person consents to the information being shared. This consent can be inferred from the circumstances in which the information was given (implied consent) or expressed orally or in writing. When consent is refused, the law is not a barrier to sharing information to protect a child from harm:

> The key factor in deciding whether or not to disclose confidential information is proportionality: is the proposed disclosure a proportionate response to the need to protect the welfare of the child?
>
> HM Government, 2006c, Paragraph 11

For more information about information sharing, see HM Government (2006e, 2006f).

CONCLUSION

The assessment should not be a discrete event but part of a continuing process that includes assessment, planning, intervention and review. In many situations there is inevitably overlap between the different activities. Undertaking the assessment, that is talking to the child and family members and listening to what they have to say, may be therapeutic in itself. Providing timely advice and information can be beneficial. Indeed, the assessment process 'does not preclude taking timely action either to provide immediate services or to take steps to protect a child who is suffering or is likely to suffer significant harm' (Department of Health *et al.*, 2000, p. 16).

Research, however, continues to show that assessments are frequently seen as an end in themselves. There may be little relationship between the needs identified during the assessment and the subsequent plans for the child and family (Cleaver, Walker and Meadows, 2004). To ensure that the services provided are relevant, plans for children should be based on the assessment of an individual child's developmental needs, the parents' capacity to meet those needs and the impact of wider family and environmental factors. Planning an assessment is explored in detail in the following chapter.

REFERENCES

Adcock, M. (2001) The core assessment: how to synthesise information and make judgements, in *The Child's World: Assessing Children in Need* (ed. J. Horwath), Jessica Kingsley, London.

Adcock, M. and White, R. (eds) (1998) *Significant Harm: Its Management and Outcome*, Significant Publications, Surrey.

Aldgate, J., Jones, D.P.H., Rose, W. and Jeffery, C. (eds) (2006) *The Developing World of the Child*, Jessica Kingsley, London.

Aldgate, J. and Statham, J. (2001) *The Children Act Now: Messages from Research*, The Stationery Office, London.

Bee, H. (2000) *The Developing Child*, 9th edn, Allyn and Bacon, London.

Bentovim, A. (1998) Significant harm in context, in *Significant Harm: Its Management and Outcome*, 2nd edn (eds M. Adcock and R. White), Significant Publications, Surrey.

Bentovim, A. and Bingley Miller, L. (2001) *The Family Assessment: Assessment of Family Competence, Strengths and Difficulties*, Child and Family Training, London.

Booth, T. and Booth, W. (1996) Parental competence and parents with learning difficulties. *Child and Family Social Work*, **1** (2), 81–86.

Calam, R.M., Cox, A., Glasgow, D.V. *et al.* (2000) Assessment and therapy with children. Can confidence help? *Child Clinical Psychology and Psychiatry*, **5** (3), 329–43.

Calam, R.M., Cox, A., Glasgow, D.V. *et al.* (2005) *In My Shoes: A Computer Assisted Interview for Communicating with Children and Vulnerable Adults*, University of Manchester, Department of Psychology, Manchester, www.inmyshoes.org.uk (accessed 22 August 2008).

Carter, A., Briggs-Gowan, M. and Ornstein Davis, N. (2004) Assessment of young children's social-emotional development and psychopathology: recent advances and recommendations for practice. *Journal of Child Psychology and Psychiatry*, **45** (1), 109–34.

Children Act 1989, Chapter 41, The Stationery Office, London, http://www.opsi.gov.uk/acts/acts1989/Ukpga_19890041_en_1.htm (accessed 22 August 2008).

Children Act 2004, Chapter 31, The Stationery Office, London, http://www.opsi.gov.uk/acts/acts2004/20040031.htm (accessed 22 August 2008).

Cleaver, H. (2000) *Fostering Family Contact*, The Stationery Office, London.

Cleaver, H. (2001) When parents' issues influence their ability to respond to children's needs, in *The Child's World: Assessing Children in Need* (ed. J. Horwath), Jessica Kingsley, London.

Cleaver, H., Aldgate, J. and Unell, I. (1999) *Children's Needs – Parenting Capacity: The Impact of Parental Mental Illness, Problem Alcohol and Drug Use, and Domestic Violence on Children's Development*, The Stationery Office, London.

Cleaver, H. and Freeman, P. (1995) *Parental Perspectives in Cases of Suspected Child Abuse*, HMSO, London.

Cleaver, H. and Nicholson, D. (2007) *Parental Learning Disability and Children's Needs: Family Experiences and Effective Practice*, Jessica Kingsley, London.

Cleaver, H. and Walker, S. and Meadows, P. (2004) *Assessing Children's Needs and Circumstances: The Impact of the Assessment Framework*, Jessica Kingsley, London.

Cleaver, H., Wattam, C. and Cawson, P. (1998) *Assessing Risk in Child Protection*, NSPCC, London.

Cm 5860 (2003) *Every Child Matters*, The Stationery Office, London, www.everychildmatters.gov.uk (accessed 22 August 2008).

Cox, A. and Walker, S. (2002) *The Home Inventory – Home Observation and Measurement of the Environment*, Child and Family Training, London.

Daniel, B., Wassell, S. and Gilligan, R. (1999) *Child Development for Child Care and Protection Workers*, Jessica Kingsley, London.

Department for Education and Skills (2001) *SEN Toolkit*, Department for Education and Skills, London, http://publications.teachernet.gov.uk/default.aspx?PageFunction=productdetails&PageMode=publications&ProductId=DfES+0558+2001 (accessed 22 August 2008).

Department of Health (2000) *Assessing Children in Need and Their Families: Practice Guide*, The Stationery Office, London, http://www.dh.gov.uk/assetRoot/04/07/93/83/04079383.pdf (accessed 22 August 2008).

Department of Health (2002a) *Introduction to the Records Used within the Integrated Children's System. Consultation Document*, Department of Health, London, http://www.everychildmatters.gov.uk/socialcare/ics (accessed 22 August 2008).

Department of Health (2002b) *The Exemplar Records for the Integrated Children's System*, Department of Health, London, http://www.everychildmatters.gov.uk/socialcare/ics (accessed 22 August 2008).

Department of Health, Cox, A. and Bentovim, A. (2000) *The Family Pack of Questionnaires and Scales*, The Stationery Office, London, http://www.dh.gov.uk/PublicationsAndStatistics/Publications/PublicationsPolicyAndGuidance/PublicationsPolicyAndGuidanceArticle/fs/en?CONTENT_ID=4008144&chk=CwTP%2Bc (accessed 22 August 2008).

Department of Health, Department for Education and Employment, and Home Office (2000) *Framework for the Assessment of Children in Need and Their Families*, The Stationery Office, London, http://www.dh.gov.uk/Publications AndStatistics/Publications/PublicationsPolicyAndGuidance/PublicationsPolicyAnd GuidanceArticle/fs/en?CONTENT_ID=4008144&chk=CwTP%2Bc (accessed 22 August 2008).

Falkov, A. (2002) Assessing family needs when a parent is mentally ill, in *Approaches to Needs Assessment in Children's Services* (eds H. Ward and W. Rose), Jessica Kingsley, London.

Fowler, J. (2003) *A Practitioners' Tool for Child Protection and the Assessment of Parents*, Jessica Kingsley, London.

Freeman, P. and Hunt, J. (1998) *Parental Perspectives on Care Proceedings*, The Stationery Office, London.

Ghate, D. and Hazel, N. (2002) *Parenting in Poor Environments*, Jessica Kingsley, London.

Glisson, C. and Hemmelgarn, A. (1998) The effects of organizational climate and interorganizational coordination on the quality and outcomes of children's service systems. *Child Abuse and Neglect*, **22** (5), 401–21.

Hallett, C. (1995) *Interagency Coordination in Child Protection*, HMSO, London.

Hudson, B. (2001) Inter-agency collaboration – a sceptical view, in *Critical Practice in Health and Social Care* (eds A. Brechin, H. Brown and M.A. Eby), Sage, London.

HM Government (2006a) *Common Assessment Framework for Children and Young People: Managers' Guide*, The Stationery Office, London, http://www.everychild matters.gov.uk/caf (accessed 22 August 2008).

HM Government (2006b) *Common Assessment Framework for Children and Young People: Practitioners' Guide*, The Stationery Office, London, http://www.everychild matters.gov.uk/caf (accessed 22 August 2008).

HM Government (2006c) *What To Do If You're Worried a Child Is Being Abused*, Department for Education and Skills, London, http://www.everychildmatters. gov.uk/safeguarding (accessed 22 August 2008).

HM Government (2006d) *Working Together to Safeguard Children*, The Stationery Office, London, http://www.everychildmatters.gov.uk/safeguarding (accessed 22 August 2008).

HM Government (2006e) *Information Sharing: Practitioners' Guide. Integrated Working to Improve Outcomes for Children and Young People*, The Stationery Office, London, http://www.everychildmatters.gov.uk/informationsharing (accessed 22 August 2008).

HM Government (2006f) *Information Sharing: Further Guidance on Legal Issues. Integrated Working to Improve Outcomes for Children and Young People*, The Stationery Office, London, http://www.everychildmatters.gov.uk/resources-and-practice/IG00065 (accessed 22 August 2008).

Jack, G. (2001) Ecological perspectives in assessing children and families, in *The Child's World: Assessing Children in Need* (ed. J. Horwath), Jessica Kingsley, London.

Jack, G. and Gill, O. (2003) *The Missing Side of the Triangle*, Barnardo's, Ilford.

Jones, D.P.H. (2001) The assessment of parental capacity, in *The Child's World: Assessing Children in Need* (ed. J. Horwath), Jessica Kingsley, London.

Jones, D.P.H. (2003) *Communicating with Vulnerable Children: A Guide for Practitioners*, Gaskell, London.

Jones, D.P.H. (2006a) Communicating with children about adverse experiences, in *The Developing World of the Child* (eds J. Aldgate, D.P.H. Jones, W. Rose and C. Jeffery), Jessica Kingsley, London.

Jones, D.P.H. (2006b) Making plans: assessment, intervention and evaluating outcomes, in *The Developing World of the Child* (eds J. Aldgate, D.P.H. Jones, W. Rose and C. Jeffery), Jessica Kingsley, London.

Kennedy, M. and Wonnacott, J. (2003) Disabled children and the assessment framework, in *Assessment in Child Care* (eds M.C. Calder and S. Hackett), Russell House, Dorset.

Klee, H. and Jackson, M. (1998) *Illicit Drug Use, Pregnancy and Early Motherhood: An Analysis of Impediments to Effective Service Delivery*, Report to the Department of Health Task Force to Review Services for Drug Misusers, Manchester Metropolitan University, Manchester.

Klee, H., Jackson, M. and Lewis, S. (2002) *Drug Misuse and Motherhood*, Routledge, London.

Kluger, M., Alexander, G. and Curtis, P. (2000) *What Works in Child Welfare*, Child Welfare League of America, Washington, DC.

Kroll, B. and Taylor, A. (2003) *Parental Substance Misuse and Child Welfare*, Jessica Kingsley, London.

Lancaster, Y.P. (2003) *Listening to Young Children: A Resource Pack*, Open University Press, Maidenhead.

Laybourn, A., Brown, J. and Hill, M. (1996) *Hurting on the Inside*, Avebury, Aldershot.

Macdonald, G. (2001) *Effective Interventions for Child Abuse and Neglect*, John Wiley & Sons, Ltd, Chichester.

McAuley, C., Pecora, P.J. and Rose, W. (2006) *Enhancing the Well-being of Children and Families through Effective Interventions: International Evidence for Practice*, Jessica Kingsley, London.

McConnell, D. and Llewellyn, G. (2002) Stereotypes, parents with intellectual disability and child protection. *Journal of Social Welfare and Family Law*, **24** (3), 296–317.

McGoldrick, M., Gerson, P. and Shellenberger, S. (1999) *Genograms: Assessment and Intervention*, 2nd edn, Norton, New York.

Meggitt, C. and Sunderland, G. (2000) *Child Development: An Illustrated Guide*, Heinemann Educational Publishers, Oxford.

Mullender, A. and Morley, R. (eds) (1994) *Children Living with Domestic Violence: Putting Men's Abuse of Women on the Child Care Agenda*, Whiting & Birch, Ltd, London.

NSPCC/Chailey Heritage (1998) *Turning Points: A Resource Pack for Communicating with Children*, NSPCC, London.

Parker, J. and Bradley, G. (2003) *Social Work Practice: Assessment, Planning, Intervention and Review*, Learning Matters, Exeter.

Quinton, D. (1994) Cultural and community influences, in *Development through Life: A Handbook for Clinicians* (eds M. Rutter and D. Hay), Blackwell Science, Oxford.

Quinton, D. and Rutter, M. (1985) Family pathology and child psychiatric disorder: a four-year prospective study, in *Longitudinal Studies in Child Psychology and Psychiatry* (ed. A. Nicol), John Wiley & Sons, Ltd, Chichester.

Reder, P., Duncan, S. and Lucey, C. (eds) (2003) *Studies in the Assessment of Parenting*, Brunner-Routledge, Hove.

Ryan, M. (2000) *Working with Fathers*, Radcliff Medical Press, Oxford.

Scott, J. and Ward, H. (eds) (2005) *Safeguarding and Promoting the Well-Being of Children, Families and Communities*, Jessica Kingsley, London.

Sturge, C. (2001) A multi-agency approach to assessment. *Child Psychology & Psychiatry Review*, **6** (1), 16–20.

Thoburn, J., Wilding, J. and Watson, J. (2000) *Family Support in Cases of Emotional Maltreatment and Neglect*, The Stationery Office, London.

Velleman, R. (1996) Alcohol and drug problems in parents: an over-view of the impact on children and the implications for practice, in *Parental Psychiatric Disorder: Distressed Parents and Their Families* (eds M. Gopfert, J. Webster and M.V. Seeman), Cambridge University Press, Cambridge.

Velleman, R. and Orford, J. (1993) The importance of family discord in explaining childhood problems. *Addiction Research*, **1** (1), 39–57.

FURTHER READING

Department for Constitutional Affairs (2004) *A Toolkit for Data Sharing*, Department for Constitutional Affairs, London, http://www.dca.gov.uk/foi/sharing/toolkit/index.htm (accessed 22 August 2008).

Department of Health (2003) *Children's Social Services Core Information Requirements Version 3.1*, Department for Education and Skills, London, http://www.everychildmatters.gov.uk/socialcare/ics (accessed 22 August 2008).

Department of Health, Children and Young People's Unit and Connexions (2002) *Integrated Children's System. Working with Children in Need and Their Families: Consultation Document*, Department of Health, London, http://www.everychildmatters.gov.uk/socialcare/ics (accessed 22 August 2008).

Hutton, A. and Partridge, K. (2006) *'Say it Your Own Way.' Children's Participation in Assessment: A Guide and Resources*, Barnardo's, London.

9 Judgements, Decisions and Plans

STEVE WALKER

A goal without a plan is just a wish.

Antoine de Saint-Exupery (1900–1944)

This chapter reviews the role of planning in developing effective interventions with children in need and families. The links between assessment, planning, intervention and review are discussed, and the principles that should underpin decision making and planning explored. The processes for planning are described including analysis, judgements, decision making and the development of plans. Finally, the potential pitfalls for planning are identified and strategies to avoid them, drawn from research and good practice, explored.

CORE KNOWLEDGE

- Judgements, decisions and plans should be based on an accurate and up-to-date assessment of the child's needs, parental capacity and the wider family and environment.
- Involving children and families in the decision making and planning processes strengthens the basis for decisions and the effectiveness of plans.
- Judgements, decision making and planning require knowledge of research, local resources, and the specific needs and circumstances of the child.
- The basis for judgements and decisions should be explicit and in writing.
- The plan should be focused on the identified developmental needs of the child and all actions and services, even those directed at adults in the family, should be aimed at safeguarding and promoting the child's welfare.
- Plans should specify the child's needs, the actions and services to meet these needs, when these will start and end, and the anticipated outcomes for the child.

THE LINKS BETWEEN ASSESSMENT AND PLANS

Assessment and planning are inextricably linked. Assessment is the foundation for the plan and any subsequent interventions. The assessment provides

Safeguarding Children Edited by Hedy Cleaver, Pat Cawson, Sarah Gorin and Steve Walker
Copyright © 2009 by John Wiley & Sons, Ltd

practitioners with a clear understanding of the child's developmental history and current needs, the capacity of parents/carers to meet these needs within the context of the wider family and community, and of how the factors in each of these domains have an impact on one another. The assessment should have enabled the practitioner(s) to identify *what* is happening in the child's world and *why* it is occurring. In this respect, the assessment is concerned with both the past (what has happened) and present (what is happening now). The plan is concerned with the future (what should happen and how to ensure that it happens). Therefore, although a good assessment may not always be followed by a good plan, it is impossible to develop a good plan from a poor assessment.

For information on assessment, see Chapter 8.

Often, during an assessment, it is necessary to take action, sometimes urgently, to promote the child's welfare or to ensure his or her safety. A practitioner should be clear why such action is necessary and what they intend to achieve by it. For example, during an assessment, a practitioner may be concerned that a young person is suffering from depression and, with his or her agreement, refer the person to his or her GP (general practitioner). However, such actions are reactive, responses to a situation or event, and should not be confused with plans. Planning is proactive. It anticipates situations or events and seeks to make things happen.

In the context of working with children who have unmet needs, the plan should be based upon a current assessment of the child's developmental needs and circumstances. The plan should identify clear and measurable objectives for work with the child and family, which will act as 'benchmarks against which the progress of the family and the commitment of workers are measured' (Department of Health, 2000, p. 60). The plan, therefore, provides a map for the child, family and practitioners to guide them and to monitor the child's developmental progress. Without a plan, actions and services can become uncoordinated and work with the family will have no clear direction. In the cases where children's needs and circumstances are complex, for example where there are concerns that a child may be suffering significant harm, it is essential that agencies work together to safeguard the child and promote the child's welfare.

INTER-AGENCY COLLABORATION IN JUDGEMENTS, DECISIONS AND PLANS

To support agencies to work together where there are concerns that a child is suffering or is likely to suffer significant harm, the government published *Working Together to Safeguard Children* (HM Government, 2006a). This guidance requires agencies to work together through a series of formal processes to make judgements, decisions and plans. Practitioners are most likely to be involved in planning at strategy discussions, initial and review child protection conferences or core group meetings.

STRATEGY DISCUSSION

The main purpose of a strategy discussion is to 'agree whether to initiate section 47 (child protection) enquiries and as a consequence to commence or, where one is already in progress, to complete a core assessment under this section of the Children Act 1989' (HM Government, 2006a, p. 18).

Depending on the needs of the child and the urgency of the situation, a strategy discussion may be carried out by telephone or as a face-to-face meeting. Strategy discussions should involve 'local authority children's social care and the police, and other agencies as appropriate (e.g. children's centre/school and health), in particular any referring agency' (HM Government, 2006a, Paragraph 5.54).

A strategy discussion provides a forum to share information about the child and family and to agree what further actions, including section 47 enquiries, should be taken to safeguard and promote the child's welfare.

For further discussion of multi-agency working, see Chapter 5.

For further information on strategy discussions, see HM Government (2006a, Paragraphs 5.54–5.5; 2006b, pp. 25–27).

For a copy of the Record of Strategy Discussion and Outcome of section 47 Enquiries Record from the Integrated Children's System, visit http://www.everychildmatters.gov.uk/socialcare/ics (Department of Health, 2002b).

INITIAL CHILD PROTECTION CONFERENCE

If, at the end of the section 47 enquiries, agencies 'judge that a child may continue to suffer, or to be at risk of suffering significant harm, local authority children's social care should convene a child protection conference' (HM Government, 2006a, Paragraph 5.79). The conference should be attended by family members, the child where appropriate and those professionals who are most involved with the child and family. The purpose of an initial child protection conference is

- to bring together and analyse in an inter-agency setting; the information which has been obtained about the child's developmental needs, and the parents' or carers' capacity to respond to these needs to ensure the child's safety and promote the child's health and development within the context of their wider family and environment;
- to consider the evidence presented to the conference, make judgements about the likelihood of a child suffering significant harm in future and decide whether the child is at continuing risk of significant harm; and

- to decide what future action is required to safeguard and promote the welfare of the child, how that action will be taken forward and with what intended outcomes.

HM Government, 2006a, Paragraph 5.80

If the decision of the conference is that a child is at continuing risk of significant harm, the child's welfare will need to be safeguarded by an inter-agency *child protection plan*. The conference will draw up an outline child protection plan. This identifies the objectives: what needs to change to ensure the child's safety; the actions and services to safeguard and promote the child's welfare; who will be responsible for carrying them out, including family members; and the timescale for each action. The conference will also identify a *key worker* who is from children's social care and is responsible for leading and coordinating inter-agency work, and the members of the *core group*. Members of the core group should include family members and practitioners who have direct contact with the child or family.

For further information on initial child protection conferences, see HM Government (2006a, Paragraphs 5.80–5.114).

For a copy of the Initial Child Protection Conference Report from the Integrated Children's System, visit http://www.everychildmatters.gov.uk/socialcare/ics (Department of Health, 2002b).

CORE GROUP MEETING

The core group is responsible for developing the outline child protection plan into a detailed working tool. It is responsible for ensuring that the plan is implemented, including the completion of the core assessment and any other specialist assessments, and monitoring its effectiveness. For further information on core groups, see HM Government (2006a, 5.118–5.121; pp. 29–30).

PARTICIPATING IN INTER-AGENCY JUDGEMENTS, DECISION MAKING AND PLANNING

When a practitioner is asked to participate in a strategy discussion, initial child protection conference or core group, it is essential that the practitioner is properly prepared. This is likely to result in his or her contribution being more effective.

Practitioners can do this by ensuring that they

- know the purpose of the forum;
- know the nature and extent of decisions that can be made at the forum;
- have reviewed the knowledge they, and their section of their agency, hold on the child and family, including the conclusion of any assessments;
- should, if required, prepare a written report for the meeting, and share it with the family, prior to the meeting;

- be clear about the services they and their agency can provide to the child and family, including the timescales within which services can be provided;
- contribute to the forum;
- maintain a focus on the needs of the child.

The outcome of the planning process should be a written plan based on the identified developmental needs of the child. The plans should support the involvement of children and families and strengthen inter-agency working by setting out explicitly the actions to be taken and services that each individual and agency will provide. The contribution of individuals and agencies can be monitored against the commitment given in the plan. Clear objectives, based on the child's developmental needs and coordinated services, are essential when plans are concerned with safeguarding and promoting a child's welfare. The plan should form the basis for reviewing progress.

For further information on the role and function of strategy meetings, child protection conferences and core group meetings, see HM Government (2006a).

For further information on planning for looked after children, see Department of Health (1991a).

For further information on child in need planning meetings, see Department of Health (2000) and HM Government (2006b).

THE COMPONENTS OF PLANNING

In planning to safeguard and promote the welfare of a child, practitioners are required to make judgements about safety and welfare, decide the most appropriate actions, work out how best to do this (formulating the plan), and finally ensure that contingencies are in place to deal with unexpected changes.

JUDGEMENTS

On the basis of an analysis of the information gathered during their assessment of the child's needs and any additional details practitioners may have about the child and family, practitioners should then draw 'on their respective knowledge bases to inform the judgements they come to about a child's circumstances', whether they are suffering or are likely to suffer significant harm, 'whether the child is in need and whether their health and development is likely to be impaired without the provision of services' (Department of Health *et al.*, 2000, p. 55).

Making judgements concerning the welfare of children is not a simple task. It is both intellectually and emotionally difficult (Munro, 1998). Practitioners can become overwhelmed by the possible consequences of making a mistake. This can result in what Reder and Duncan (1999) call 'assessment paralysis'. When this occurs, the assessment becomes stuck on a particular issue – for example, whether a parent has a psychiatric diagnosis – and decisions to safeguard and promote the child's welfare are not made. Another form which 'assessment paralysis' may take is the 'never ending assessment'. This occurs when a practitioner is unable to make a judgement because they never believe that they have sufficient information. In these circumstances, it is important that practitioners use supervision and, where appropriate, consultation to enable them to conclude the assessment.

For more information on analysis, see Bentovim (1998), Department of Health (2000), Cleaver (2001), Jones (2001) and Fowler (2003).

For further information on the efficacy of different types of interventions, see Kluger, Alexander and Curtis (2000), Macdonald (2001), Scott and Ward (2005) and McAuley, Pecora and Rose (2006).

DECISION MAKING

Having made a judgement about the child's welfare, including any need for protection, practitioners and their managers have to make decisions about the actions and services that are most appropriate to the specific needs and circumstances of the child (Department of Health, 2000, p. 57). In doing so, practitioners should use their practice experience, knowledge of different theories and methods of intervention, findings from research on the effectiveness of different types of interventions and what they know of local resources. The actions and services identified must be appropriate to the identified needs and capacities of the child and family and, whenever possible, be available locally.

Making a decision about interventions is a complex process. A decision-making framework, such as that outlined by Munro (2002), provides a tool that practitioners can use to help them identify the most appropriate option. Munro's model has seven steps.

---

1. Identify the decision that needs to be made, how quickly it needs to be made and who needs to be involved.

   Munro (2002) emphasises the importance of framing any decision in child-focused terms. The decision, therefore, is not whether or not a child's name should be placed on the child protection register, but what actions are necessary to safeguard and promote the child's welfare.
2. Consider the options.

   All possible options, not just those immediately available, should be identified.
3. Decide what information is required to help select the best option.

   The practitioners should ensure that they have sufficient information about each option identified, to enable them to determine how suitable it is for the individual child and his or her specific circumstances.
4. Weigh up the likely/possible consequences of each option.

   The practitioners should use their knowledge of research and practice experience as well as their knowledge of the individual child and the family to identify what may happen if the option is selected. There will normally be more than one consequence for each action.

5. Consider the probability of each consequence.

   The practitioners, using their knowledge, should then evaluate how probable it is that a consequence will occur.

6. Evaluate the pros and cons of each consequence.

   At this stage, the practitioner should make a judgement about the value that should be given to each possible outcome, based on the benefit to the child.

7. Make the final decision.

   The practitioner then identifies the option that combines the greatest likelihood of success with the highest benefit to a child. For example, an option that offers a high possibility of a reasonable outcome would be selected over an option that offered a low possibility of an excellent outcome.

The use of a decision-making model encourages practitioners to consider all possible options, and not just those that offer an immediate or short-term solution. It can also help decision makers to identify alternative services and interventions to meet an identified need when their preferred option is unavailable. A decision-making framework can also open up the decision-making process to families and other professionals. 'The typical evaluation process is largely hidden, intuitive and approximate' (Monnickendam, Yaniv and Geva, 1984). Indeed, recent research (Cleaver, Walker and Meadows, 2004) found that some parents were unaware that a plan had been made. Practitioners can use the framework with the child, family members and other professionals as a way of reaching agreed decisions or at least ensuring that everyone is clear about the basis for these decisions. A framework requires practitioners to be explicit about the reasons for particular decisions being made, and it therefore enables decisions to be reviewed in supervision prior to actions being initiated.

It will not always be possible, or appropriate, to use a decision-making framework for every decision in relation to a child, but it is particularly valuable when considering complex issues. In some situations it may be necessary to move quickly through some steps. Nonetheless, the conclusion of the process should be a clear, explicit reason, recorded in writing, for each decision.

For further information on decision-making models, see MacDonald (2001) and Munro (2002).

FORMULATING THE PLAN

The first step in formulating a plan is to establish the overall aim or goal, that is, the desired outcome of the plan for the child. This establishes the general direction of travel and the destination to be reached. The aim or goal of the plan must be derived from the child's developmental needs identified in the assessment:

> In this way, goal statements, although somewhat abstract, are still rooted in the circumstances (person/situation/dynamic) that bring the [practitioner] and service user together.
>
> Butler and Roberts, 1997, p. 194

The case of Karen Hawthorne, the subject of a child protection plan, aged 3 years, provides an example of formulating plans in practice. Karen's name was under the category of neglect. Her weight had fallen below the third centile, with no medical cause, and there were concerns that the home environment posed a risk to her health and safety. Following the child protection conference, where an outline child protection plan had been formulated, the core group developed a child protection plan for Karen. This plan elaborated on the outline plan, drawing on the findings from the initial and core assessments.

The overall aim of the plan for Karen was to attain and maintain satisfactory progress in her weight gain within a safe family and home environment by the date of the second review conference.

The overall goal for the plan should be discussed with family members, including the child. This can help to identify shared areas of concern, establish a common purpose and enable family members to be clear what outcomes are intended as a result of the planned work with the child and family.

The aim or goal of the plan should not be confused with its objectives. If the goal specifies the destination, objectives set out the route that will be followed and identify key milestones that can be used by practitioners and family members to monitor progress towards the final destination.

For example, the objectives for Karen could include the following:

- Karen to gain weight by next review.
- Karen to be provided with a safe and hygienic home environment: home to be kept clean; kitchen to be cleaned daily; bedding to be clean and changed weekly; rubbish to be taken out from home to bin daily.
- Karen to be taken for outstanding medical checks and immunisations at a time agreed with GP.

Objectives should be specific and measurable and directly related to the needs of the child, even when the services provided are directed to adults in the family. Services to adult family members should have a real and measurable benefit for the child (Department of Health, 2000). This is not to suggest that the needs of parents should be ignored. Failing to meet the needs of parents can severely limit the impact of interventions (Farmer and Owen, 1995).

'In most situations, meeting the child's needs will almost always involve responding to the needs of family members' (Department of Health, 2000, p. 54). However, using the child's developmental needs as the framework to assess the impact of all interventions locates the child at the heart of the plan. The focus of the plan must be on the child and his or her needs. Without this focus,

> there is a danger that professionals may begin to focus more on the needs of the adult carers than those of the child. This shift may occur because the worker finds it easier to relate to adults than to children; or it may occur because the adults caring for the child begin to demonstrate legitimate needs of their own.
>
> Department of Health, 1995, p. 85

Using objectives that are based on the identified needs of the child will also ensure that plans do not become 'resource led'. Resource-led planning may occur when professionals believe that the resources required to meet all the child's needs are not available. As a result the focus of the plan, and sometimes the findings from the assessment, shifts to the resources that are available. Resource-led plans have a number of weaknesses:

- Key developmental needs of the child may be neglected.
- As the plan is not based on an up-to-date assessment of the child's needs and circumstances, it may ignore the resources and strengths within the family.
- All the options available to meet the child's needs are not considered, simply those that are immediately available or known to the practitioner.
- The objectives of the plan focus on the provision of services. Therefore, the plan lacks specified outcomes for the child. This, in turn, makes it difficult to establish whether any progress is being made in relation to the child's identified developmental needs.
- The focus on services may act as a disincentive for families to report on progress, as this may result in a loss of services.

Using the needs of the child to determine the objectives of interventions overcomes these weaknesses. Need-based plans recognise the variety and complexity of children's needs and circumstances, and draw upon the most appropriate resources from all of those available, including those within the family. Plans that focus on the individual needs of a child encourage practitioners to develop a plan specific to the particular child rather than providing an off-the-peg response. When it comes to children's needs one size does not fit all.

When formulating the plan, practitioners should remember that they are in a position of power in relation to the family. Some families may wish to be seen as cooperative or believe that they have to agree to an objective or timescale that they know is unrealistic. Practitioners should use their understanding of the family to help them set objectives, and use their skills to ensure that family members are involved in the planning process. Where an objective and/or timescale is not negotiable the reason(s) should always be explained to the parents in a way that makes sense in relation to the needs of the child.

PLANNING FOR CONTINGENCIES

Children's needs and circumstances are not static. Changes in the child's needs (or the ability of parents or carers to meet the child's needs) or in the child's wider family and environment can make a plan, no matter how carefully constructed, unworkable or irrelevant. When making a plan, practitioners should consider the possibility of significant changes occurring and plan for these developments. This is known as *contingency planning*. Contingency planning is important because changes that may have a major impact on the plan for a child can occur suddenly, giving little or no opportunity for meetings or discussions. The contingency plan should be clearly identified and its contents and rationale explained to the child and parents.

WHY PLANS ARE NOT ALWAYS MADE

Given the value of plans for practitioners and families, it is perhaps surprising to find that plans are not always put in place even where a child's needs or circumstances are complex. There is a considerable body of research highlighting deficiencies in planning for children looked after (Department of Health and Social Security, 1985; Department of Health, 1991a; Grimshaw and Sinclair, 1997). More recent research, which considered children in need, including those in need of protection, reported that similar issues exist for children living at home (Farmer and Owen, 1995; Social Services Inspectorate, 1999). Cleaver, Walker and Meadows (2004, p. 218) found that where a core assessment had been completed, 'In only a third of cases ($n = 23$) was a plan completed to meet the child's developmental needs.'

This problem is not confined to children's social care. A recent audit of National Health Service organisations in England found an absence of plans for children:

> A number of organisations acknowledge the need for action on care planning, for example, to develop dedicated care plans for children admitted (to hospital) with a history of abuse.
>
> Commission for Health Improvement, 2003, p. 28

The absence of effective inter-agency plans has been a common feature of inquiry reports (Department of Health, 1991b). For example, the inquiry report into the death of Victoria Climbié highlighted the failure of key agencies to develop a clear and effective plan:

> The 18 action points identified during the course of the meeting were, for the most part, sound. However, the lack of clarity as to who precisely was responsible for what, the absence of timescales for the completion of the various actions identified and the failure to circulate copies of the minutes . . . to those with responsibility for taking the strategy forward meant that the practical impact of those action points was seriously diminished.
>
> Cm 5730, 2003, p. 146

The consequences of these failures for Victoria were fatal.

Several factors may result in planning being neglected. Firstly, planning is a complex activity. To be done well, the practitioner and manager must feel confident that they have the necessary professional knowledge to identify the intervention that is most appropriate to meet the specific needs of the child living in a particular family and environmental context.

Secondly, planning requires space and time to reflect on the range of interventions available. When practitioners and their managers are under pressure due to high workloads or agency expectations, they may feel that they do not have sufficient time for planning. The plan, however, provides the focus and direction to work with children and families and allows practitioners and their managers to identify progress and to decide when it is appropriate, and in some cases safe, to close a case. It is, therefore, a false, and in some instances dangerous, economy not to plan.

Thirdly, some practitioners and their managers may fall into a cycle of simply responding to changes in a child's developmental needs and family circumstances. A good plan, based on a good assessment, will have anticipated some changes and will be flexible enough to respond to others. Working in a reactive manner, however, has its attractions. Rather than trying to predict and shape events and behaviour, the practitioner has only to react to a situation or event. The danger of practising in this way is that the practitioner is not in control of the situation and interventions have no clear objective or focus.

A final factor that can lead to poor planning is the low priority some practitioners give to areas of practice that do not involve direct contact with the child and family. Professionals working in the caring professions have a strong motivation and desire to be actively working with children and families. For some professionals anything that takes them away from direct work with children and families (e.g. recording) even when it supports their work is undesirable (Walker, Shemmings and Cleaver, 2003). This attitude may result in some practitioners moving directly from assessment to action. However, without a plan the practitioner has no way of knowing whether the actions they are taking or have arranged are the most appropriate or effective for safeguarding and promoting the welfare of the child. To support practitioners to develop appropriate and effective plans for children in need and to carry out other key practice processes the government has developed the Integrated Children's System (Department of Health, 2002a).

USE OF THE INTEGRATED CHILDREN'S SYSTEM
WHEN MAKING PLANS

The Integrated Children's System 'is designed to help social services managers and practitioners working with colleagues from other agencies to improve outcomes for children in need and their families' (Department of Health, 2002a, p. 2). To assist practitioners with assessment, intervention, planning and review, the Integrated Children's System includes a range of exemplar recording formats.

Planning formats within the Integrated Children's System include child protection plans, care plans (for children looked after) and child in need plans. These plans were designed to have a common framework that is intended to support practitioners to establish plans that set out SMART outcomes for children; outcomes that are Specific, Measurable, Achievable, Related to the assessment and have a clear Timescale for completion.

Each plan is organised according to the three domains in the Assessment Framework: the child's developmental needs, parenting capacity, and family and environmental factors. Within each of these areas the plan asks practitioners to record

- identified developmental needs of the child and needs of family members (from the assessment);
- actions and services to meet these needs;
- frequency and length of service (how often the service or action will be provided and for how long);
- the date services commenced/will commence;
- the planned outcome (what the actions and services are intended to achieve by the date the plan will be reviewed, or by another specified date).

The example that follows shows part of a plan developed using the Integrated Children's System planning format:

> This type of planning format makes it easier to review the plan and establish whether each planned action and service has been (and if necessary continues to be) appropriate for the child or young person's developmental needs.
>
> Department of Health, 2002a, p. 26

The agreed plan should be signed by all parties and a copy provided to all those participating in the plan.

For further information on planning, see Department of Health (2000, 2002a).

For further information about child protection plans, see HM Government (2006a, 2006b).

For further information about the Integrated Children's System, see www.everychildmatters.gov.uk/ics.

EXAMPLE

Two-year-old Simon lives with his father, James Weiss. Mr Weiss is a registered heroin addict. There have been concerns about Mr Weiss's care and supervision of Simon, and his name was placed on the child protection register under the category of neglect.

The health section of the child protection plan for Simon included the following:

Child/ young person's identified developmental needs and strengths	How these needs will be responded to: actions and services to be provided	Frequency and length of actions and services: e.g. hours per week	Person/ agency responsible	Dates services to commence/ commenced	Planned outcome: progress to be achieved by next review or other specified date
Simon has suffered a number of accidents in the home and had not been taken for medical treatment for his injuries	Mr Weiss to be provided with advice on structuring Simon's play to prevent accidents	One hour session once a week for 6 weeks	Playgroup		Mr Weiss will be able to structure Simon's play. Simon will be showing appropriate developmental progress as a result of attending play activities arranged by Mr Weiss
	Mr Weiss to supervise Simon in the home	Daily	Mr Weiss		Simon will be protected from accidents in the home
	Mr Weiss to ensure that Simon receives medical treatment for all injuries	As required	Mr Weiss/GP		Simon will receive prompt treatment for any injuries

(*Continued*)

Simon did not receive his immunisations as scheduled	Simon to be taken for developmental checks and immunisations	As required	Mr Weiss	Immunisations will be up to date and his developmental progress will be monitored
There have been concerns that the home environment has posed a risk to Simon's health	Home to be kept clean	Daily	Mr Weiss, health visitor	There will be no concerns about hygiene in the home
	Home conditions to be monitored	At least once a week	Health visitor and social worker	
Simon was not bathed frequently and his clothes were soiled	Simon to be bathed	Daily	Mr Weiss	Simon will be clean with no concerns about his appearance
	Simon's appearance to be monitored	At least once a week	Health visitor and social worker	

INVOLVING FAMILIES IN DECISION MAKING AND PLANNING

The plan forms the basis of future work with children and their families and, therefore, plays a central role in establishing and maintaining effective working relationships between the child, family members and practitioners. Unless their participation would place the child at risk of significant harm, parents/main carers and the child – in accordance with their age and understanding – should always be involved in planning. Family participation in the planning process offers the following benefits to the child, parents and practitioners:

- Clarifies areas of concern and where change is required.
- Establishes the roles and responsibilities of all those involved.
- Ensures that the plan takes account of the knowledge and strengths of family members.
- Provides the foundation for collaborative working between family members and professionals.
- Ensures that family members are involved, have responsibility, and are central to future work.
- Provides a basis for improved outcomes for the child.

Research (Cleaver and Freeman, 1995; Thoburn, Lewis and Shemmings, 1995) has shown that the involvement of children and families in the planning process is not dependent upon the nature and extent of professional concerns. The most significant factors are the commitment of agencies to involve families and the skills of practitioners in engaging families.

The level and extent of preparation required will depend on the needs of the individual child and family members, the complexity of issues or concerns and the nature of the forum where the decisions are being made. For example, if a formal meeting, such as a child protection conference, is being held it is important that the practitioner spends time with the child and family before the meeting to ensure that family members are clear about the purpose of the meeting, the extent of the decisions that can be made at the meeting and the formal and informal 'rules' of the meeting such as how to respond to a comment made by someone else at the meeting. Where written information is being presented at the meeting, family members should have had an opportunity to read and discuss this prior to the meeting.

Following a section 47 enquiry, a child protection conference was called in relation to 12-year-old James Knox. An advocate, Tim Woods, was appointed to support James. Tim met with James, explained his role as an advocate, the purpose of the conference and what would happen at the meeting. Tim discussed with James the social worker's report to the conference and, with Tim's help, James prepared his statement. James decided that he did not want to attend and asked Tim to read out his statement and represent him at the meeting.

Afterwards Tim and the conference chair met with James to explain what had been discussed at the meeting, how his statement had informed their decision making and the outcomes.

Tim explained the plan to James and how it should result in support for him and his family.

Practitioners should be aware that planning may take place in an emotionally charged environment. The child and family members may be hurt, upset or angry with one another and/or professionals. It is important that these emotions do not become the focus of the meeting or deflect attention from the welfare and safety of the child.

In some cases, because of the attitude of a family member or concerns about a child's safety, it may not be possible to fully involve some individuals in decision making and planning. In such circumstances practitioners, together with their managers, will have to decide what information should be given to family members and who will be responsible for this. Unless the child would be at risk of significant harm, the plan should be explained to parents/main carers and the child – in accordance with their age and understanding – and a copy given to them.

For further information on involving and consulting with families, see Chapter 2 and Chapter 3.

See also Cleaver and Freeman (1995), Farmer and Owen (1995), Thoburn, Lewis and Shemmings (1995), Freeman and Hunt (1998), Aldgate and Bradley (1999), Thoburn, Wilding and Watson (2000), Tunstill and Aldgate (2000) and Cleaver, Walker and Meadows (2004).

For further information on working with fathers, see Ryan (2000).

For further information on involving children, see Chapter 1.

See also Butler and Williamson (1994), Scutt (1995) and Modi, Marks and Wattley (1995).

CONCLUSION

Making effective judgements, decisions and plans requires practitioners to use their professional skills, knowledge and expertise. Where children's needs and circumstances are complex, such as when a child has suffered significant harm, it is likely that practitioners from several different organisations will be working with the child and family. In these situations plans provide a mechanism to bring together the evidence base for interventions, provide a framework to coordinate, guide actions and services, and support the involvement of family members. Finally, plans also provide the basis for monitoring whether interventions are improving outcomes for the child.

REFERENCES

Aldgate, J. and Bradley, M. (1999) *Supporting Families through Short Term Fostering*, The Stationery Office, London.

Bentovim, A. (1998) Significant harm in context, in *Significant Harm: Its Management and Outcome*, 2nd edn (eds M. Adcock and R. White), Significant Publications, Surrey.

Butler, I. and Roberts, G. (1997) *Social Work with Children and Families*, Jessica Kingsley, London.

Butler, I. and Williamson, H. (1994) *Children Speak*, Longman, London.

Children Act 1989, Chapter 41, HMSO, London, http://www.opsi.gov.uk/acts/acts1989/Ukpga_19890041_en_1.htm (accessed 22 August 2008).

Cleaver, H. (2001) When parents' issues influence their ability to respond to children's needs, in *The Child's World: Assessing Children in Need* (ed. J. Horwath), Jessica Kingsley, London.

Cleaver, H. and Freeman, P. (1995) *Parental Perspectives in Cases of Suspected Child Abuse*, HMSO, London.

Cleaver, H., Walker, S. and Meadows, P. (2004) *Assessing Children's Needs and Circumstances: The Impact of the Assessment Framework*, Jessica Kingsley, London.

Cm 5730 (2003) *The Victoria Climbié Inquiry. Report of an Inquiry by Lord Laming*, The Stationery Office, London, www.victoria-climbie-inquiry.org.uk (accessed 22 August 2008).

Commission for Health Improvement (2003) *Protecting Children: Results of an Audit of NHS Organisations in England*, CHI, London, http://www.dfes.gov.uk/acpc/pdfs/Audit-findings_report_web.pdf (accessed 22 August 2008).

Department of Health (1991a) *Patterns and Outcomes in Child Placement*, HMSO, London.

Department of Health (1991b) *Child Abuse: A Study of Inquiry Reports 1980–1989*, HMSO, London.

Department of Health (1995) *The Challenge of Partnership in Child Protection: Practice Guide*, HMSO, London.

Department of Health (2000) *Assessing Children in Need and Their Families: Practice Guidance*, The Stationery Office, London, http://www.dh.gov.uk/PublicationsAndStatistics/Publications/PublicationsPolicyAndGuidance/PublicationsPolicyAndGuidanceArticle/fs/en?CONTENT_ID=4008144&chk=CwTP%2Bc (accessed 22 August 2008).

Department of Health (2002a) *Integrated Children's System: Working with Children in Need and Their Families, Consultation Document*, Department of Health, London, http://www.everychildmatters.gov.uk/socialcare/ics (accessed 22 August 2008).

Department of Health (2002b) *The Exemplar Records for the Integrated Children's System*, Department of Health, London, http://www.everychildmatters.gov.uk/socialcare/ics (accessed 22 August 2008).

Department of Health, Department for Education and Employment and Home Office (2000) *Framework for the Assessment of Children in Need and Their Families*, The Stationery Office, London, http://www.dh.gov.uk/assetRoot/04/01/44/30/04014430.pdf (accessed 22 August 2008).

Department of Health and Social Security (1985) *Social Work Decisions in Child Care*, HMSO, London.

Farmer, E. and Owen, M. (1995) *Child Protection Practice: Private Risks and Public Remedies*, The Stationery Office, London.

Fowler, J. (2003) *A Practitioners' Tool for Child Protection and the Assessment of Parents*, Jessica Kingsley, London.

Freeman, P. and Hunt, J. (1998) *Parental Perspectives on Care Proceedings*, The Stationery Office, London.

Grimshaw, R. and Sinclair, R. (1997) *Planning to Care*, National Children's Bureau, London.

HM Government (2006a) *Working Together to Safeguard Children*, The Stationery Office, London, http://www.everychildmatters.gov.uk/safeguarding (accessed 22 August 2008).

HM Government (2006b) *What To Do If You're Worried a Child Is Being Abused*, Department for Education and Skills, London, http://www.everychildmatters.gov.uk/socialcare/safeguarding (accessed 22 August 2008).

Jones, D.P.H. (2001) The assessment of parental capacity, in *The Child's World: Assessing Children in Need* (ed. J. Horwath), Jessica Kingsley, London.

Kluger, M., Alexander, G. and Curtis, P. (2000) *What Works in Child Welfare*, Child Welfare League of America, Washington, DC.

Macdonald, G. (2001) *Effective Interventions for Child Abuse and Neglect: An Evidence-Based Approach to Planning and Evaluating Interventions*, John Wiley & Sons, Ltd, Chichester.

McAuley, C., Pecora, P.J. and Rose, W. (eds) (2006) *Enhancing the Well-being of Children and Families through Effective Interventions. International Evidence for Practice*, Jessica Kingsley, London.

Modi, P., Marks, C. and Wattley, R. (1995) From the margin to the centre: empowering the black child, in *Participation and Empowerment in Child Protection* (eds C. Cloke and M. Davies), Pitman, London.

Monnickendam, M., Yaniv, H. and Geva, N. (1984) Practitioners and the case record: patterns of use. *Administration in Social Work*, **18**, 73–87.

Munro, E. (1998) Improving social workers' knowledge base in child protection work. *British Journal of Social Work*, **28** (1), 89–105.

Munro, E. (2002) *Effective Child Protection*, Sage, London.

Reder, P. and Duncan, S. (1999) *Lost Innocents: A Follow-Up Study of Fatal Child Abuse*, Routledge, London.

Ryan, M. (2000) *Working with Fathers*, Radcliffe Medical Press, Oxford.

Scott, J. and Ward, H. (eds) (2005) *Safeguarding and Promoting the Well-Being of Children, Families and Communities*, Jessica Kingsley, London.

Scutt, N. (1995) Child advocacy – getting the child's voice heard, in *Participation and Empowerment in Child Protection* (eds C. Cloke and M. Davies), Pitman, London.

Social Services Inspectorate (1999) *Planning to Deliver: Inspection of Children's Services Planning*, Department of Health, London.

Thoburn, J., Lewis, A. and Shemmings, D. (1995) *Paternalism or Partnership? Family Involvement in the Child Protection Process*, The Stationery Office, London.

Thoburn, J., Wilding, J. and Watson, J. (2000) *Family Support in Cases of Emotional Maltreatment and Neglect*, The Stationery Office, London.

Tunstill, J. and Aldgate, J. (2000) *From Policy to Practice: Services for Children in Need*, The Stationery Office, London.

Walker, S., Shemmings, D. and Cleaver, H. (2003) *Write Enough: A Training and Resource Pack on Recording in Children's Services*, www.writeenough.org.uk (accessed 22 August 2008).

10 Intervention

ARNON BENTOVIM

The ultimate goal of intervening in the lives of children whose welfare requires safeguarding is prevention. The aim is to prevent harm in the future, ensure that children are wanted and cared for adequately, are protected and exposed to as few risks to their health and development as possible, and that they live in a context where their needs are met. Adequate safeguards will assist them to achieve their developmental potential. Through this approach, the emotional and physical health of the present generation and future generations is assured.

This chapter explores

- levels of intervention when children and young people have suffered abuse or neglect;
- specific ways of helping children and young people recover from the effects of abuse or neglect;
- which families, under which circumstances, might benefit from particular interventions when a child or children in the family have been abused or neglected.

CORE KNOWLEDGE

- Successful intervention to safeguard and promote children's welfare relies on a thorough assessment of the child's needs, parenting capacity, and family and environmental factors. It also relies on an understanding of what has resulted in the child suffering harm and the changes required to ensure the child is adequately protected and cared for.
- The process of assessing the child's needs, parenting capacity, and the family and environmental context is the initial phase of intervention. The assessment itself can lead to parents gaining insights into their behaviour. The family's response to the assessment helps ascertain not only the needs of the child and family, but also the capacity of the child and family to respond to interventions. A key task in planning longer term intervention in a family is to assess the likelihood of change and response to specific interventions in

Safeguarding Children Edited by Hedy Cleaver, Pat Cawson, Sarah Gorin and Steve Walker
Copyright © 2009 by John Wiley & Sons, Ltd

the context of the level of harm, and the capacity of the parent(s) to protect and safeguard their child in the future.

- Different types of harm, and differing levels of severity of harm, require different approaches to intervention. Some types of abuse and neglect may occur singly and others may be part of a pattern of multiple physical, sexual and emotional abuse and neglect. Although some approaches are more effective, what is known is that approaches that have been shown to be effective have to be applied through the extensive engagement of children and parents, and to be delivered by competent practitioners.
- Successful intervention requires that the child is adequately protected from harm whilst these interventions are taking place. The level of protection required depends on the level of harm and the extensiveness of risk of harm within the family context. A variety of approaches will be helpful, ranging from voluntary agreements between the family and professional agencies to the use of court orders.

Although the focus of this chapter is on interventions with children and families where abuse or neglect has been identified, the abuse or neglect of many children is not known about by statutory agencies. For this group, it is important that interventions are developed and maintained to help them talk about their abuse. The chapter therefore begins by considering the kinds of services that can enable children to seek help in order that their abusive experiences might stop. Once the abuse or neglect has been recognised, interventions are provided at different levels and include services available to all children as well as targeted and specialist interventions (as outlined below). This chapter begins by summarising the role of the local safeguarding children board (LSCB) in preventing maltreatment as well as helping those children who have been abused or neglected. It explores the choices and decisions to be made about interventions when providing services to children whose abuse or neglect is not continuing but for whom a child in need plan is in place, or to children where a child protection plan is in place.

THE ROLE OF THE LOCAL SAFEGUARDING CHILDREN BOARD IN INTERVENTION

Ensuring agencies intervene effectively to safeguard and promote the welfare of children is a key responsibility of LSCBs. Three broad areas of activity are set out in *Working Together to Safeguard Children* (HM Government, 2006, Paragraphs 3.12–3.14):

- Activity that affects all children and aims to prevent maltreatment, or impairment of health or development, and ensures children grow up in circumstances consistent with safe and effective care – for example, ensuring that children know who they can contact when they have concerns about their own or others' safety and welfare.

- Proactive work that aims to target particular groups – for example, work to safeguard and promote the welfare of groups of children who are potentially more vulnerable than the general population such as children living away from home or disabled children.
- Reactive work to protect children who are suffering or at risk of suffering maltreatment – for example children abused and neglected within their families.

Where particular children are the subject of interventions to safeguard and promote their welfare, that work should aim to help them achieve their developmental potential – that is, to have optimum life chances.

LEVEL 1 – UNIVERSAL SERVICES

Universal services are available for all children and families. These are provided by professionals, such as health visitors, general practitioners, early years staff or teachers. In interventions where a child has been abused or neglected, it is important that they have access to the full range of universal services appropriate to their age and stage of development. These services should help ensure that, where necessary, family and environmental factors are modified and parenting is supported. It is essential that these services work together and are aware of each other's contribution.

The cooperation of the many practitioners who can be involved in supporting families and preventing abuse is discussed in detail in Chapter 5.

There are children who are not known to children's social care or the police and where family members do not report what they know about abuse perpetrated against a child, or where there is absolute secrecy and only the perpetrator and child are aware of the abuse. For these children, it is helpful to think about interventions that will enable them and their families to recognise and talk about the abuse or neglect, and then to receive help. It is, therefore, essential that there are accessible channels through which children and family members can report the presence of abuse or neglect so that the appropriate actions can be initiated.

Children are clear about the conditions that enable them to talk to adults and ask for help – see Chapter 1 for more discussion of children's perspectives. Children's accounts are found in Gorin (2004) and in Schofield and Thoburn (1996).

The following are examples of initiatives to help children and families talk in confidence about their experiences:

- ChildLine (0800 1111) – the availability of a free helpline for children has been valuable for children who have not been able to speak in other contexts. ChildLine can actively take protective steps to mobilise help for a child, encourage the child to seek a protective figure and maintain contact with the child.

- The Stop It Now campaign (www.stopitnow.org.uk) is a public health initiative to inform the public about the nature of sexual abuse and help family members who are concerned about sexual abuse to seek assistance, irrespective of whether they are partners or parents, or are themselves the abuser.

Such initiatives aim to assist children and parents to begin to talk about abuse that occurs in secret. In addition, educational programmes in schools and the community about the nature of abusive behaviour inform children and parents about both the nature of harm and ways of seeking safety.

For further information on anti-bullying initiatives, see, for example, www.nspcc.org.uk; www.dfes.gov.uk/bullying; www.parentlineplus.org.uk.

While helplines offer one form of easily accessible help, they can be effective only if complemented by services in the community able to offer accessible, face-to-face help. Services such as drop-in centres, community-based family centres and other help to parents and children are discussed in Chapter 2 and in Gardner (2003).

The contribution made by the wider family and the neighbourhood to supporting vulnerable families and preventing harm is discussed in Chapter 3 and in Jack and Gill (2003).

Issues in family support and safeguarding for children and families from minority ethnic communities are discussed in Thoburn, Chand and Procter (2004).

For disabled children and their families, see the report of the National Working Group on Child Protection and Disability (2003).

LEVEL 2 – TARGETED SERVICES FOR VULNERABLE CHILDREN

Targeted interventions include services for children who are considered to be at risk of having their development impaired, and children who may require safeguarding from harm. Targeted parenting programmes are important because they promote positive relationships between parents and their children.

Whilst well-established negative parent–child interaction patterns are difficult to change, promoting positive parent–child relationships is a viable and valid abuse prevention strategy (Wolfe, 1994). A variety of effective targeted parenting programmes have been developed. Targeted interventions are provided by social care, health, the voluntary sector and multi-agency services such as Sure Start, which offers integrated services focused on geographical areas of high need. Targeted parenting programmes teach parental skills in managing children's behaviour without resort to punitive and aggressive discipline.

For further information, see the promoting positive parenting approach (Sanders and Cann, 2002), the Webster-Stratton approach (Webster-Stratton,

1989, 1997) and the Mellow Parenting Approach (Puckering, 2003; Mills and Puckering, 1995). For information on Sure Start, see Tunstill *et al.* (2005).

LEVEL 3 – SPECIALIST SERVICES FOR CHILDREN AT RISK OF HARM

Some specialist interventions are intended to protect children at risk of being harmed. These may be provided by social care, the police, health and other statutory services as well as independent agencies.

LEVEL 4 – SPECIALIST SERVICES FOR CHILDREN WHO HAVE SUFFERED ABUSE OR NEGLECT

Other specialist therapeutic interventions are focused on helping children who are recognised as having suffered abuse or neglect. They aim to ensure that this does not cause lasting harm to the child and that the child and other children in the sibship are effectively protected from further episodes of harm. In Children and Adolescent Mental Health Services, these are categorised as level 4 interventions (Department of Health and Department for Education and Skills, 2004). They are also provided by a range of agencies such as health, social care (adult and children's), education, schools and independent agencies.

Practical interventions at levels 3 and 4 can include specialist group work and individual therapy or counselling. Some examples can be found in Gilligan (2000, 2001) and in Daniel and Wassell (2002).

There is further information on the role of neighbourhood services in Chapter 3 and on collaborative agency working in Chapter 5. Planning coherent strategies for working with children at these levels is discussed in Chapter 9.

EVIDENCE-BASED INTERVENTIONS

The challenge for practitioners and managers is to know which interventions are effective and should therefore be used for a particular child and family. This section summarises what is known in specific areas of abuse or neglect in order to inform decision making and reviewing the effectiveness of the plan for each child. It is usually possible to intervene to safeguard a child within the family home; for only a small proportion of children is it necessary to move to alternative care.

Interventions for specific forms of abuse or neglect have been the subject of research which has used a variety of methods to assess their effectiveness. Methods include

- following up a group of children who have been worked with using a particular approach;

- using well-validated methods of assessing children before intervention and at follow-up;
- comparing groups of abused children receiving specific types of interventions with those who are receiving the usual services in the community;
- randomly assigning children who have suffered a particular form of abuse to contrasting types of interventions.

There are a number of excellent reviews of this body of research which explore the value of different interventions for various forms of abuse, and the quality of these interventions. See, for example, Jones (1998), Stevenson (1999), Macdonald (2001) and Jones, Hindley and Ramchandani (2006).

Stevenson (1999), reviewing international evidence on the short- and long-term consequences of abuse, emphasises that stopping re-abuse is essential for both short- and long-term well-being. Physical abuse was found to be as traumagenic as sexual abuse in the long term.

The following sections summarise the research findings on effective interventions concerning the main types of abuse or neglect.

INTERVENING WITH CHILDREN AND PARENTS WHEN PHYSICAL ABUSE OCCURS

The consensus on what is effective when physical abuse occurs is that it depends on

- making good judgements about the likely outcomes for the child and family;
- ensuring that an extensive, focused parenting programme is put in place;
- the child living in a safe context, during which time therapeutic work is undertaken in an appropriate setting.

An essential part of the judgement is whether the abuse results from temporary loss of self-control by loving parents who are themselves stressed, or is part of a more entrenched pattern of family violence, possibly including violence between parents. Different ways have been developed to help parents avoid punitive responses when they inappropriately perceive children to be defiant or are overwhelmed with anger attributed to the child. An effective approach to such physical abuse is described by Kolko (1996), who assessed the helpfulness of two contrasting methods – cognitive behavioural and family therapy. His work found that the consistent provision of a particular therapeutic programme was more important than the specific theoretical orientation, a finding noted in many well-conducted studies. Whatever the approach, it is essential that practitioners

- make positive relationships with parents and with children;
- are consistent in their approach (are basically accepting and positive);
- are accurate in their empathic responses.

When such therapeutic work is commissioned from non-statutory agencies, it is important that it is undertaken by therapists in accordance with the agreed inter-agency plan.

See Chapter 5 on multi-agency working and Chapter 9 on planning services.

For these professionals, the therapeutic task is not only working with and providing services to the child and family, but also working with the statutory agencies that have responsibility for the child's welfare and, where appropriate, the day-to-day care of the child. During the course of the work, there needs to be an emphasis on openness and not attempting to hide abusive incidents – the considerable difficulties faced by the family must be acknowledged.

All approaches should focus on ensuring that the child's emotional life is enhanced, symptoms are dealt with, attachments become more secure, and the child's sense of self and relationship to others becomes more positive.

The Ward family

The Ward family illustrate a family situation in which there were considerable difficulties. The mother, Moira, had made a new relationship with Ian who had a son by a former partner. She had two children – Michael, aged 9, and Laura, aged 14. It was evident that there were considerable differences between the mother and her new partner. He had, for example, far stricter views about the children's behaviour. As a result of these differences, there was a phase of considerable conflict between the parents, including a period of domestic violence which had led to Moira insisting on Ian leaving the home, although they did subsequently reunite.

With some reluctance, Moira went along with Ian's insistence on appropriate discipline for Michael and Laura, although Laura was increasingly in conflict with her stepfather, staying out late with her friends. Michael was becoming more withdrawn and was unable to respond to the demands for increasing independence expected by Ian and supported reluctantly by Moira. In school, Michael started to look neglected and tired and was arriving late. On one occasion, it was noted that there were bruises on his face. With some reluctance he indicated that Ian had smacked him for being slow to get up that morning.

Following a strategy meeting involving the school, GP, children's social care and the police, a core assessment (under section 47 of the Children Act 1989) took place, which included interviewing Michael and his mother to evaluate the extensiveness of the physical abuse, the quality of the family environment and basic parenting capacity. A family meeting, held as part of the core assessment, revealed an atmosphere of much tension and conflict within the family. Ian acknowledged becoming angry with Michael, justifying the punishment on the grounds that Moira failed to discipline Michael effectively. Laura attacked Ian, pointing out that relationships had been good in the past. Laura also revealed the previous episode of domestic violence. Moira struggled to maintain her relationship with Ian, agreeing with his approach whilst ineffectively trying to support Michael and Laura. She acknowledged that she had begun to drink excessively as a consequence of the increasing family tension.

A child protection conference was held. Moira and Ian accepted that Michael's name needed to be put on the child protection register and they agreed with a child protection plan based on Michael and Laura's needs, their parenting difficulties and the considerable stress on their family relationships.

Either of the approaches – that is, cognitive behavioural or family therapy – described by Kolko (1996) would be effective with the family given their positive motivation for help, and acknowledgement of difficulties, and the fact that the problems were relatively recent.

A family therapy approach involving all family members or a cognitive behavioural approach for individuals provided by a specialist CAMH service in close liaison with children's social care would provide an appropriate way to meet each of the children's needs more effectively, help family members manage conflict in a more appropriate way, and help the mother and stepfather find a unified approach to parenting. It would be important to support the strengths which reinforced the family's identity and were associated with the mother's previous positive pattern of care, and also to recognise where Ian's approach could have value. Moira and Ian would need help to deal with their relationship as partners as well as parents, which could help Moira avoid problem drinking.

In addition, Moira may need to attend local drug and alcohol services to obtain some additional individual help with her problem drinking. The children, particularly Michael, would need help to cope with the traumatic effects of abuse, and Ian would need help to acknowledge the harm he caused.

This case has been adapted from one of the training scenarios in the training video describing *The Family Assessment* (Bentovim and Bingley Miller, 2001). These materials are part of a range of resources commissioned to support use of the *Framework for the Assessment of Children in Need and their Families* (Department of Health, Department for Education and Employment and Home Office, 2000).

SITUATIONS WHERE SERIOUS PHYSICAL ABUSE AND RE-ABUSE HAVE OCCURRED

The major concern for practitioners intervening in family situations where severe physical abuse has occurred is the risk of re-abuse and tragedy. There have been a number of studies intended to identify factors associated with serious re-abuse and these are described below.

Reder and Duncan (1993, 1999, 2002) carried out two studies of fatal child abuse. In 1987 they reviewed information from all the available public inquiry reports, and in 1991 they reviewed local Part 8 reviews of deaths or serious injury as a result of harm to a child. They concluded that

- there is a risk of harm to children when families withdraw from contact with the outside world and practitioners;
- there are frequently disguised warnings given about a critical escalation of the situation, which need to be understood – for example requests for children to be taken into care;
- the emergence of mental health difficulties, violent threats and irrational behaviour, which lead to considerable professional anxiety, are of concern;
- a failure to be aware of previous deaths, which were considered to be explicable by natural causes, may lead to a failure to appreciate the seriousness of a child's current situation (see also Falkov, 1996; Dale, Green and Fellows, 2002).

Such difficulties can be avoided when intervening in the cases of physical abuse:

- By ensuring there is a thorough assessment, which provides a full understanding not only of the child's needs but of parenting capacities and family and environmental factors – for example identifying domestic violence, which is often hidden, and understanding that it is a potent factor associated with violence against children.
- By exploring earlier records regularly when unexplained severe abuse is presented. Examination of the compiled chronology can often reveal patterns in situations – for example where physical harm may have been caused by induced illness. The pattern of seeking care by a medical pathway has often occurred both for the adult and for the child (Gray and Bentovim, 1996).
- By being aware that therapeutic approaches cannot be divorced from the care context. The network of practitioners concerned with the family need to maintain an appropriate level of information sharing, altering the usual confidential nature of therapeutic work. Children's social care has a statutory responsibility for children's welfare and should be kept up to date with any new developments or information.

In working with a family where abuse has occurred, whether in a disciplinary or other context, practitioners need to be sensitive to any cultural issues that may affect the family's approach to childrearing and relationships between parents. However, this must not lead to an acceptance of lower standards of safety for the child. A feature of some child deaths has been that practitioners held stereotypes of black and minority ethnic cultures which led them to misinterpret the family situation, or to accept behaviour towards the child which would have been considered unacceptable for a child from the majority white community.

For some examples, see Chapter 1 and the report of the inquiry into the death of Victoria Climbié (Cm 5730, 2003). For further discussion of evidence on safeguarding with minority ethnic children and families, see Dutt and Phillips (2000) and Thoburn, Chand and Procter (2004).

For further information on interventions with physically abused children, see Nicol *et al.* (1988) and Hamilton and Browne (2002).

INTERVENING IN CASES OF EMOTIONAL ABUSE AND NEGLECT

Intervening effectively in cases of emotional abuse and neglect is a challenging task, not least because of the difficulties in defining the entity. Glaser and Prior (2002) point out that neglect and emotional abuse describe interactions which cause harm, rather than a single abusive event associated with physical abuse. In fact, physical abuse usually occurs against a background of emotional abuse and neglect.

Glaser and Prior (2002) categorise the different forms of emotional abuse and neglect as

- emotional unavailability, unresponsiveness and neglect of care;
- negative attributions such as rejection, denigration, misperceptions of a child's behaviour as hostile and deserving punishment;
- inappropriate or inconsistent interactions – expectations beyond capability, or over-protection, or exposure to highly traumatic and damaging events such as domestic violence or disruptive separations;
- failure to recognise the individuality of the child;
- failure to promote a child's adaptation to social contexts.

INTERVENING IN CASES OF EMOTIONAL ABUSE

In cases of emotional abuse, there is no one approach to intervention which has been demonstrated to be the preferred option. In accordance with basic good practice principles, what is required is a thorough assessment and the use of approaches which have been demonstrated to be generally successful when intervening with the emotional and behavioural difficulties of children and families. Stevenson (1999) reviewed such approaches as well as those demonstrated as being helpful in contexts where abuse had occurred. The following case example describes a child subject to emotional abuse and the possible approaches likely to be effective.

The Bradshaw family

The Bradshaw family consists of the parents Frank and Gina, and their children Ben, aged 5, and Annie, aged 6 months. In this family, there has been a long-standing negative relationship between Ben and his mother since his birth. Frank has provided most of the positive parenting for Ben.

After Annie's birth, the relationship between Gina and Ben became much worse. Gina complained increasingly about what she perceived as his continuous oppositional, attention-seeking behaviour. She became increasingly angry and negative towards him, rejecting his attempts (positive and negative) to gain her attention, and she was increasingly distant from him. The health visitor became very concerned about the emotional atmosphere in the home. She was worried that Ben would be emotionally and perhaps physically harmed, and was concerned about the effect of this atmosphere on Annie. She initiated a referral to children's social care.

During an initial assessment, carried out using *The Home Inventory* (Cox and Walker, 2002), limited responsiveness and emotional acceptance were observed. At one point, Gina asked Ben whether he wanted to be put in a home and he said that he did. These observations were reinforced during the core assessment, carried out in a family centre, involving Annie and Frank. Little positive interaction was observed between Gina and Ben. There was a pervasive atmosphere of rejection and blaming, particularly when Ben sought his mother's attention by taking his sister's toys during the Family Assessment conducted as part of the core assessment. Frank was more sympathetic and warm with Ben, and gently persuaded him to return the toys to Annie. However, the more Frank supported Ben, the more Gina became angry and rejecting of him. It was evident that the parents avoided discussing their different attitudes to parenting. Ben was blamed and, as a result, was being subjected to conflicting emotions, increasing his sense of frustration and the degree of emotional rejection and abuse of him.

During the family history component of the Family Assessment, it was revealed that the parents' early experiences had played an important role in the development of the mother's emotionally rejecting attitude towards Ben and his father's rescuing and protection of him, which paradoxically had the effect of reinforcing the mother's rejection. Frank revealed that his brother was sent away at an early stage, because of oppositional behaviour, to live with grandparents. He feared a repetition of Ben being 'sent away' unless he tried to reduce the tension. For the first time Gina revealed, with considerable distress, that she had been sexually abused in childhood by an uncle. This had made her intolerant of Ben as a male child, experience difficulties in responding to his needs, and developing a fiercely protective attitude to Annie – 'It will never happen to her.'

Depending on the findings from further in-depth work, including specialist mental health assessments of the impact of sexual abuse on Gina, a number of possible interventions may be indicated:

- Frank may be able to provide sufficient protection to ensure that Ben's needs for emotional support are met in the short term, and his mother may be able to step back sufficiently until she has dealt with her own emotional difficulties. Alternatively, it may become evident that there is such a pervasive negative atmosphere that Ben needs a period of care outside the family.
- A family therapy approach with the parents and children together would be effective in rebalancing the relationship between the parents, by helping them make a distinction between past anxieties and the present. They would need to manage their conflicting attitudes in a different way and build on their strengths to work together to manage Ben rather than undermine each other. It would then be possible to improve the relationship between Ben and his mother, and Annie and her father.
- Depending on the mental health assessment of the impact of Gina's sexual abuse on her, she may need abuse-focused therapeutic help to deal with her history of abuse.
- An intensive parenting programme could help Gina develop a more positive response to Ben, and focus and ameliorate Ben's oppositional, negative responses to his mother. The Webster-Stratton (1989, 1997) approach, which works with parents in groups, could help Gina develop a more positive approach by reinforcing Ben's positive behaviour, ignoring any opposition and helping to develop alternatives to conflict.
- Ben may need some individual therapeutic help from a CAMH service to process his own experiences of rejection. There is a risk that he may continue to seek attention from his mother through opposing her wishes even when his mother attempts to develop a positive approach to parenting.
- It is essential that the selected interventions are clearly set out in the plans for Annie and for Ben based on the core assessment findings, and that there is an appropriate level of openness between family members and practitioners. These plans may have been made following a child protection conference or alternatively may have been made because it had been decided the children were children in need, but not at 'continuing risk of significant harm' (HM Government, 2006).

This case is adapted from a scenario in the training video describing *The Family Assessment* (Bentovim and Bingley Miller, 2001).

INTERVENING IN CASES OF PHYSICAL NEGLECT

Neglect is not a unitary concept but a range of administrative categories characterised by the omission of care.

Stevenson, 1998, p. 14

Neglect may have many different manifestations, but will usually involve an absence of age-appropriate physical care and supervision: inadequate nutrition, clothing and health care, and children left alone in dangerous conditions. Neglect is often associated with recent family histories of very stressful life events such as bereavement and divorce, and with economic pressures on the parents. Parental illness or disability, especially depression in mothers, also seems a common contributing factor (Cleaver, Unell and Aldgate, 1999; Dearden and Becker, 2000). Choice of intervention strategy must be based on thorough assessment of possible contributory factors (see Chapter 8). Stevenson (1998) identifies the keys to successful intervention as

- multi-service intervention to support the family in dealing with external difficulties that reduce the capacity to parent;
- intervention focused on the family as a whole;
- family preservation services;
- group approaches to supporting both parents and children.

Stevenson emphasises the importance of strengthening informal support networks in the extended family and the local community. Direct services for children may require supplementary care, especially pre-school day care and respite care, provided in ways that do not pathologise families. Family aides and help from volunteers may be particularly valuable when working with neglect.

Possible support for parents is discussed in Chapter 2 and in Quinton (2004). On support for disabled parents, see Morris (2003). Dwivedi (2002) considers practical support to minority ethnic children and families. Support through the family and neighbourhood is discussed in Chapter 3 and a more detailed discussion of the contribution of kinship care can be found in Broad, Hayes and Rushforth (2001).

NON-ORGANIC FAILURE TO THRIVE

Iwaniec, Herbert and Sluckin (2002) focus on a particularly severe form of neglect – non-organic failure to thrive. This condition is recognised by a serious failure to grow in height or in weight, and is sometimes associated with little growth in the head circumference and signs of neglect. It is the result of a combination of emotional abuse and neglect, poor parenting style, inadequate food intake, feeding difficulties, and a problematic relationship and interaction between parents and children, insecure attachments and weak bonding.

The consequences of such failure to thrive are serious; there can be poor outcomes concerning mental abilities, cognitive development, emotional stability and academic attainment.

The major therapeutic task is to change unresponsive and, often, emotionally abusive or neglectful parenting into better informed and sensitive caregiving. The planned interventions should relate to both the immediate and the longer term.

The immediate intervention (i.e. crisis intervention) should focus on the child's safety, neglected developmental attainments and urgent family needs. The child's development may be seriously delayed, and it is therefore necessary to provide day care or a foster care placement to ensure that they are safe and receive social stimulation and the opportunity to develop cognitively and catch up.

The longer term therapeutic work should focus on the child and family when an in-depth assessment indicates that they require considerable longer term help and support. Such interventions are often required to

- target difficulties in parenting skills;
- target aggressive and rejecting behaviour by the parents;
- enable parents to use positive management strategies, and improve communication and stress management.

Stages when working with severe non-organic failure to thrive

Stage one

Feeding is tackled in a highly structured and directive manner. Mealtimes are made more relaxed, the primary carer is asked to desist from screaming, shouting and threatening the child over meals. Eating is made quiet and calm, the primary carer is asked to talk soothingly and pleasantly to the child. The therapist assists, models, reassures, observes and prompts. The primary carer's partner, usually the father, is encouraged to play a part in child care and feeding activities.

Stage two

To create positive interactions and reduce negative interactions, there is a requirement to desensitise the child's anxiety and fear of the primary carer's feeding and caregiving activities, and to desensitise the primary carer's tension, anger and resentment. There is encouragement to play on a regular basis, encouragement to smile, stroke hair and praise, developing proximity to promote more secure attachment behaviours. Considerable support is required to reinforce the programme.

Stage three

This is a phase of deliberate, intensified primary carer/child interaction, where the mother takes the child everywhere – to chat, make eye contact, smile, cuddle and hug. Considerable support is required during this phase.

Stage four

Some older children presenting with a longer history of failure to thrive, associated with extreme emotional arousal, may require development of pro-social behaviour in other areas.

Stage five

This broadens the primary carer's social context as those with children who fail to thrive tend to be socially isolated and to have little support. Structured parenting training and parent self-help groups can be supportive, as can approaches which resolve issues in family and environmental factors – for example issues with wider family and family history.

Iwaniec, Herbert and Sluckin, 2002

INTERVENTIONS WITH CHILDREN AND PARENTS WHERE ILLNESS HAS BEEN FABRICATED OR INDUCED

Understandably, a key focus in considering this unusual form of abuse has been the identification and initial management of the abuse within a child protection framework. There has been little research on the longer term outcomes for children in these circumstances, but the available evidence suggests that outcomes have been poor for many children who have had illness fabricated or induced (Department of Health *et al.*, 2001, Paragraph 2.35).

Key studies that have addressed this area are summarised in the government guidance on safeguarding children in whom illness is fabricated or induced (Department of Health *et al.*, 2001, Chapter 2), Bools, Neale and Meadow (1993), Davis *et al.* (1998), Berg and Jones (1999) and Gray, Bentovim and Milla (1995).

Gray, Bentovim and Milla (1995) describe 41 children at Great Ormond Street Children's Hospital in whom illness had been fabricated or induced and were then followed up. It was possible to identify the following outcomes:

- whether the child's health and developmental milestones had progressed well;
- whether there were further episodes of fabricated or induced illness;
- what intervention had taken place.

Four children had died – two at the time when induced illness was identified. For the other two, the causes of death were complex and induced illness was not the only factor. Of the remaining 37 children, 21 were found to have poor outcomes and 16 to have good outcomes. The key question was – what were the factors that, and what form of intervention, led to a successful outcome? The sample included children who were failing to thrive as a result of the withholding of food or where the parents held beliefs that the child had severe allergic states. A variety of symptoms were described and medical investigations requested, and some of these children were made ill through the ingestion of substances such as salt or other inappropriate medication.

The following interventions were found to be associated with successful outcomes for the child:

- It was essential that the initial suspicion of abuse and its identification were successfully managed. Team members needed to be aware that a parent who presented as deeply caring could also induce harm. It was essential to understand the nature of the deeply ambivalent feelings that parents can have about children, and the way help could be sought for care and support through a medical route. It was also important that there was a multi-disciplinary/multi-agency approach to management, bringing together the child protection, child mental health and child health teams.
- It was essential that a high standard of information was obtained to explain the child's signs and symptoms, and an in-depth understanding of the child's needs and family situation gained through effective teamwork.
- Protecting children from further harm had to be an essential focus. There was a poor outcome if the intervention was short term, not adequately coordinated, and there was inadequate assessment and understanding of what needed to change in order for the child to be able to thrive within the family.
- There was a better outcome if the assessment was comprehensive, well coordinated and therapeutic intervention occurred over a reasonable period of time within the context of a child protection plan. The focus of therapeutic work should include both individual (child and parent) and family factors.

For further information on intervention with emotionally abused and neglected children, see Iwaniec, Herbert and Sluckin (2002), and Glaser (2002).

INTERVENTIONS WITH CHILDREN AND PARENTS WHEN SEXUAL ABUSE OCCURS

Research on what helps children who have been sexually abused indicates that although parenting is important, as are improving family relationships, the children themselves require focused interventions. This is because the complexity of the impact of sexual abuse on children's development is such that they need help to assist them in recovering from the experience and to deal with the resulting impact on their emotional lives, attachments and sense of self (Bentovim, 2002). Children show differing levels of resilience to sexual abuse. Paradoxically, the impact of sexual abuse does not depend on the severity and extensiveness of sexual abuse alone, but also on whether a non-abusive parent supports the child. In the Great Ormond Street research (Monck *et al.*, 1994; Bentovim *et al.*, 1988) children who were believed and supported were less symptomatic than children who were rejected and disbelieved.

Children who have been sexually abused must be cared for in a context where they are supported and believed; otherwise any therapeutic interventions will be ineffective. It is essential that interventions take account of the following findings:

- They should address the traumatically stressful impact of sexual abuse. Children and young people need to be helped to cope with the intensity of emotional symptoms of a traumatic nature, sleeping difficulties, and the high levels of arousal, anxiety and fearfulness which are evoked by reminders of their abusive experience.
- Although there is an understandable inclination to allow children to speak about their experiences in their own time, recent evidence has demonstrated that a systematic, planned programme of cognitive behavioural work which helps children expose and speak about their experiences (the creation of a narrative of trauma) individually, or in groups, using a variety of different approaches (e.g. art work, music, poetry, group sharing) is a more effective way of reducing the traumatic impact on children than allowing them to address issues in their own time (Cohen *et al.*, 2000).
- It has also been demonstrated by Trowell *et al.* (2002) that a programme of individual psychodynamic work is more effective than group work for reducing the traumatic nature of sexual abuse, flashbacks, memories and sexualised behaviour. On other parameters – particularly of general emotional well-being, mental health measures and relationships – group work and individual psychodynamic therapy were equally effective. The key issue is the focus on the child's experience and the need for the child to speak about the experience of abuse in a safe context, so that the experience is processed and put into memory rather than left and felt to be an ever-present threat.
- Extensive work also needs to be focused on the child's beliefs which result in a negative sense of self. These beliefs arise as children become convinced that the abuse must be their fault. If they have shown severe symptoms, such as intense sexualised behaviour, this is an indication that the child believes that what has happened is their fault. Children have to be helped to understand that their responses are all part of an understandable reaction to abuse and are a sign of their capacities to survive rather than a weakness.
- It has also been demonstrated that having a protective parent working in parallel to understand the impact of abuse on the child, and beginning to

support the child through sharing feelings, repairing attachments and supporting the sense of belonging and identity for the child assists the therapeutic process.

- A further support for the child's recovery is where there is an abusive parent or family member who can make use of therapeutic work. This work requires them to confront their abusive action, understand the negative impact of the abuse on the child (their victim), and begin to make an appropriate apology and reparation to both their partner and the child.

- The results of the Great Ormond Street study (Monck *et al.*, 1994; Bentovim *et al.*, 1988) demonstrate that integrating family and group approaches helps children to be rehabilitated to their families through work with the child and the protective parent. Achieving full rehabilitation for the family, including the perpetrator, requires considerable work with the abusive individual and family and this occurred less frequently.

- It is also important to stress that when boys and some girls are exposed to high levels of violence, rejection, emotional abuse and neglect, and are also victims of sexual abuse, they are at risk of becoming perpetrators themselves during adolescence (Skuse *et al.*, 1998, Salter *et al.*, 2003; Bentovim, 2002). These children require work both to assist them to take responsibility and deal with their abusive behavioural patterns and to be aware of their needs as victims of abuse (see also Borduin and Schaeffer (2001), who successfully used an intensive individual and family intervention – multi-systemic therapy).

Having undertaken a systematic review of the literature on child sexual abuse, Jones and Ramchandani (1999, p. 65) and Ramchandani and Jones (2003, p. 490) conclude:

> All the children who have been sexually abused, whether symptomatic or not, require basic education concerning sexuality, sexual roles and the nature of abuse and maltreatment adapted to their age and developmental stage. Symptomatic treatment requiring a specialised treatment focus will need to be integrated with general care in the family system.

The Green family

Sarah (aged 8) had three brothers – Charlie, David and John (aged 13, 10 and 4, respectively). When Charlie was aged 5, children's social care were involved because of reports of excessive physical chastisement. Recent concerns arose because of both Charlie and David's poor school attendance. An initial assessment revealed extensive and long-standing conflict between the parents, with the father spending increasing time at the home of his own family. The mother was not coping. She could not persuade the boys to go to school. There was an atmosphere of neglect in the home, poor boundaries and a sense of hopelessness as the mother withdrew and left the children to fend for themselves.

A core assessment of Sarah's needs (undertaken during section 47 enquiries in respect of each of the four children) brought to light that Sarah had been sexually abused by Charlie, her eldest brother. When the abuse became known, children's social care arranged for Charlie to live with relatives. It was also recognised that John had poor language development and was in conflict with his mother. Following a child protection conference, a child protection plan was drawn up for each child. These plans addressed each child's identified needs but they were also interrelated to take account of shared issues, such as contact between the siblings.

As part of the plan, the father agreed to live away from home in order to assess whether the mother could care more adequately for the three younger children without the negative impact of her husband's criticism of her. It was then revealed that David, Sarah and John were also involved in sexualised activity. David was still not attending school so it was agreed he would be placed with foster carers whilst further assessment was undertaken of the extensiveness of Charlie's sexualised behaviour and its impact on his siblings.

Whilst immediate steps were taken to address the safety of the children, a thorough knowledge of all the factors that led to the abuse was necessary in order to make decisions about appropriate levels of protection and services to meet each of the children's needs. The extensiveness of the abuse perpetrated by Charlie and involving all three of his siblings, the failure of the parents to intervene effectively despite knowing about the abuse for some time, their neglect of the children and the complexity of the children's needs resulted in care proceedings being initiated. Specialist assessments of the children's needs, including ones by a child and family psychiatrist, were ordered as part of the care proceedings. The capacity of the parents to parent each of the children and work together was also assessed. The assessments resulted in an understanding of the family relationships. The consequences of the parents focusing on their own conflict and a failure to meet each other's needs were such that they became depressed, did not work together as parents and failed to supervise their children. In turn, Charlie's growing adolescent needs were not being met, there was a failure to ensure he attended school regularly, and an expectation that he would take on the parental role with his three younger siblings in the absence of parental supervision or provision of basic care. The parents' failure to act when they were aware of the sexual activities meant the abuse continued, the intensity of Charlie's responses increased, and the traumatic and behavioural impact on the younger siblings increased. The children's difficulties in attending school and in managing their emotional states in turn impacted further on the parents' ability to be responsive, so that an increasingly complex interaction between impairment to the children's development and harm continued in a downward spiral.

Outcomes of intervention

Sarah

Sarah benefited from an extensive sexual abuse treatment programme, which focused on her experiences in considerable detail using a variety of approaches, including play, drawing, artwork and building a trusting relationship with her therapist. She learnt a variety of anxiety management 'stress inoculation' skills, such as relaxation and self-calming, and more appropriate social skills with other children, managing to develop trust of others rather than responding automatically with fear and attack.

Through a parallel programme, her mother was helped to be open to hearing about Sarah's abusive experiences rather than minimising them and finding it hard to believe their extent.

Sarah was helped to develop a meaningful narrative, or account, and to understand that the sexual activities were not her responsibility but Charlie's. She was also helped to develop more appropriate social ways of relating to others in order to reduce the risk of her continuing the sexualised mode of relating learnt as a result of her extensive involvement in abusive activities.

Charlie

In parallel, Charlie was helped to understand that responsibility for the abusive action was his. He attributed a degree of responsibility to Sarah, believing that because she was responsive sexually, this justified his further abusive action. Charlie was helped to understand that he was responsible for inducing this response in Sarah – she was significantly younger than him, and her response did not justify continuing the sexual activity. Charlie had convinced himself that his sexual interest was a form of affection in compensation for failures of care within the family. With therapy, he became aware that his actions were abusive and potentially damaging to Sarah's future well-being.

Charlie took seriously the task of preventing such sexual actions in the future, participating in a 'relapse prevention programme' using cognitive behavioural approaches. He was helped to take part in a session where he fully apologised to Sarah and answered the questions which she raised – Was it her fault? Would it happen in the future? Could he assure her that she would be safe and that he would do everything to protect her? The family, who cared for him, was also helped to reinforce and to motivate him to achieve his objectives in life, as well as to become a safe individual in the future. It was not appropriate for him to return to his mother's care, but contact with Sarah could develop in the longer term.

David

David was helped by his foster carer to get back to full-time schooling and he, along with his other three siblings, was provided with a programme of therapeutic work. David needed help with his emotional difficulties and to ensure he did not behave abusively. His foster carer required considerable support to help manage his extreme distress at his separation from his family where he saw himself as a key supporter of his mother.

David began to thrive in school and catch up educationally, becoming more independent, showing less immature responses and beginning to move into adolescence.

John

John attended a programme of work at a specialist voluntary agency. His mother needed considerable support in helping him benefit from the programme and in managing his stormy behaviour. He was able to continue living with his mother and sister Sarah, as his mother was able to meet his needs.

The parents

The parents attended counselling to help them resolve their considerable differences and concluded that their marriage had been at an end for some time and there was no prospect of it improving. The mother's psychological state improved; she benefited from the parenting programme, was less depressed and was able to achieve more stability for her two younger children. There remained concerns about whether she would also be able to meet the needs of David and Charlie who continued to do well with their respective carers. The father played an increasingly peripheral role, absenting himself from the family.

The Green family illustrate the different stages in therapeutic work in the context of child maltreatment. These include

- planning to ensure the victim(s) is/are protected from abuse whilst therapeutic work is progressing;
- working with perpetrators and protective parents in a context where the child/children is/are protected;

- the development and planning of a variety of different interventions to meet the needs of individual family members;
- considering a rehabilitative phase of therapeutic intervention on the basis of the following assessment:
  - an understanding of the child's development;
  - an assessment of parenting capacity;
  - modifications in the family and environmental factors, looking at family structures which could provide safe contexts;
- provision of alternative long-term care when reunification cannot be achieved.

Following a period of assessment and interventions, such as those described above for the Green family, the following prognostic factors need to be evaluated in each domain of the *Framework for Assessment of Children in Need and Their Families* (Department of Health, Department for Education and Employment and Home Office, 2000) in order to aid the making of professional judgements and decisions.

For further information on interventions with sexually abused children, see Finkelhor and Berliner (1995), and Jones and Ramchandani (1999).

For interventions with adult sexual offenders, see Fisher and Beech (2002) and for children and young people who are sexual offenders, see Vizard, Monck and Misch (1995).

FACTORS RELATED TO LONG-TERM OUTCOMES FOR THE CHILD

The following factors should be carefully considered when considering reuniting children where they have been removed from the family for a period because of concerns about their safety (Bentovim, Elton and Tranter, 1987; Jones, Hindley and Ramchandani, 2006; Silvester *et al.*, 1995).

CHILD DEVELOPMENTAL NEEDS DOMAIN

- The level and severity of abuse perpetrated, and the extensiveness of traumatic damage or delay caused to the child's physical and emotional health and development.
- The level of care and therapeutic work the child will require to recover from the effects of abuse or neglect.
- The specific nature of therapeutic work required to assist the child to recover from the effects of abuse or neglect.
- The level of parenting capacities required to meet the child's needs within the child's timeframe.

PARENTING CAPACITY DOMAIN

- The degree of responsibility for the state of the child taken by the parents, from initial denial through to contemplation and acknowledgement (Bentovim, 2003).
- The degree to which the capacity of the parent will be required to change to meet the child's needs.
- The general attitude of the parents to members of the professional network – is there a prospect of a reasonable collaborative approach, or is there a negative stance of denial and a persisting sense of grievance?

FAMILY AND ENVIRONMENTAL DOMAIN

- The level of parental psychopathology, personality problems, learning disabilities and the motivation of the parent to undertake the necessary therapeutic work to reverse the personal attributes which have contributed to creating an abusive family context.
- Issues such as parental drug addiction, mental health problems, parental domestic violence and availability of treatment which affect the likelihood of modification within the child's timeframe.
- The availability of a supportive family network, neighbourhood and social support.
- The availability of an integrated community approach to ensure a broad-based approach to intervention to include a focus on children's needs, parenting capacities and family and environmental factors (Bentovim, Elton and Tranter, 1987).
- The availability of settings which can provide intensive therapeutic work, whether in a family/day centre or on a residential basis.

A judgement on whether a child can be reunited with the family will be based on information gained during an assessment and subsequent intervention which relates to each of the following three domains – child development, parental capacity and family and environmental factors.

ACHIEVING A GOOD OUTCOME

The following features have been identified in those cases where there are better prospects for achieving good outcomes for children.

Child development domain

- The child's state – for example, the level of abuse, emotional state, attachments and sense of self are modifiable within the family context so that less severe forms of abuse are present and the child is generally healthy.

Parenting capacity domain

- Parents take adequate responsibility for their abusive action or neglect where appropriate.
- The parents can provide for the child's identified needs within a reasonable period of time, there is adequate potential for attachment and empathy and some areas of parental competence.
- There is a protective capacity within the family or family network – for example, a non-abusive parent who recognises that his or her partner has abused or neglected the child and is prepared to protect the child over and above his or her relationship with the partner, or members of the extended family who acknowledge abuse or neglect and will act protectively.
- There is potential for the development of a reasonable attachment and relationship between the parents and each child, and a reasonable degree of flexibility in the way in which the family functions.

Family and environmental domain

- Based on salient family factors, there is a capacity for modification and change in parents who have been abusive or neglectful, and a recognition of the relevance of their own childhood abusive experiences; domestic violence is not present.
- A willingness to work reasonably cooperatively with children's services practitioners, to accept the need for change even if this is initially with the motivation of maintaining children within the family context, and a likelihood of change achievable within the child's timeframe.
- Appropriate therapeutic settings need to be available – a family/day centre setting or a residential resource, depending on the severity of abuse, and the nature of family's strengths and difficulties.
- Environmental factors – for example, housing, neighbourhood and financial issues are modifiable within the child's and family's timeframe, and social support, local facilities and volunteer networks are adequate.

A CASE WHERE A GOOD OUTCOME IS LIKELY

A case where there are prospects for achieving a good outcome would be the Bradshaw family described earlier, where Ben was experiencing emotional abuse.

The Bradshaws – a potentially good outcome

Child development needs domain

Although Ben was highly challenging and oppositional to his mother, he was far more cooperative with his father. He had a good capacity to relate to family members in the wider social context. The protective response from his father and his positive attachment suggested that he did not show severe traumatic effects and had developed sufficient resilience to cope with the stressful impact of his mother's rejection.

Parenting capacity domain

Frank showed an excellent capacity to respond to meet Ben's needs. Although at the time of the referral, Frank's positive supportive responses were having a negative reinforcing effect on Gina's hostile relationship with Ben, this appeared modifiable within Ben's timeframe.

Gina took an appropriate degree of responsibility for her emotionally abusive attitude towards Ben. It was possible to understand her long-standing response to him on the basis of her own childhood history and experiences.

Family and environmental domain

Frank had a positive understanding of Gina's responses once she revealed her history of sexual abuse and was able to understand his role as rescuer and peacemaker on the basis of his own history.

Both parents showed positive motivation to make good use of therapeutic help. This suggested there was potential for the development of positive relationship patterns and a more secure attachment. There was a possibility of an improvement in Gina's emotionally abusive attitudes and her negative perceptions of Ben, as well as a less oppositional response from Ben to his mother.

Despite Gina's history of abuse, she had a capacity to function well outside her specific relationship with Ben. Frank was protective towards both Gina and Ben as a consequence of his own history. This meant that the parents had the potential to resolve the experiences of their own childhoods within a reasonable period of time and were likely to respond to therapeutic work based on an assessment and understanding of their individual and relationship needs.

Other factors such as employment, housing and geographical area were satisfactory, and there were the resources to provide an integrated plan to ensure adequate protection, care arrangements and therapeutic services from children's social care and community health services.

A LIKELY POOR OUTCOME

The likelihood of children being reunited with their birth family is extremely poor when none of these criteria are fulfilled – when:

Child development domain

- There is severe multiple physical, sexual, emotional abuse, which has had a pervasive impact on the child's physical and emotional health, contact causes severe regression in the child's behaviour, and the child is rejected.
- The child is developmentally delayed with special needs, mental health difficulties or is very young and requires rapid parental change.

Parenting capacity domain

- The parents fail to take responsibility for the state of the child.
- The needs of the parents take primacy over the needs of their children.
- A combative oppositional stance to working with practitioners emerges.

Family and environmental domain

- Severe psychopathology in parents becomes known – for example drug abuse, serious marital violence or long-standing personality problems, with anti-social, sadistic or aggressive problems which may not be amenable to therapeutic work within the child's timeframe, or there is an unwillingness to accept that there are problems, and a failure to acknowledge the role of childhood abuse.
- Parents demonstrate disordered attachments, lack empathy, have poor capacities to care, or have learning disabilities, difficulties with power and high levels of family stress.
- There is a lack of resources, social isolation, and violent and unsupportive neighbourhoods.

A case of likely poor outcome

Josie (aged 5 years) is an example of where there is a very doubtful outcome. Josie had first come to the notice of children's social care before her birth, when her young mother said she wanted her placed for adoption because she could not envisage herself as a parent at the age of 18. Josie's mother had grown up in a family where she had been exposed to considerable domestic violence and her father had had alcohol problems. Her older brothers showed evidence of oppositional, severe conduct disorder, and she herself had coped in adulthood through developing a career rather than wanting to consider herself as a parent. She had made allegations of sexual interference against her father but had then withdrawn the complaint.

At the last moment, following Josie's birth, her mother decided to keep her. However, her mother found she could not manage to meet Josie's needs. Despite her childhood experiences, she placed Josie with her own parents and later became concerned when Josie said that her grandfather had been touching her. She then asked for Josie to be accommodated in foster care.

The assessment of Josie, her mother and grandparents whilst she was in foster care revealed that it was unlikely that Josie would be able to return to the care of any of her immediate family members. The information obtained during the assessment was analysed and the judgements reached are summarised below.

Child developmental needs domain

Josie herself showed evidence of a severe attachment disorder, with indiscriminate sexualised behaviour, as well as challenging, aggressive behaviour.

Josie's behaviour regressed after family contact, and it was thought that she would require a lengthy period of therapeutic work in a protective context before a new family placement could be considered with a view to adoption.

Parenting capacity domain

Josie's grandfather refused to consider that he could have been responsible for the abuse of Josie, and her grandmother totally supported the grandfather. They could not contemplate that they could have been responsible for the disruption of Josie's attachment patterns and a failure to provide stability.

Josie's mother and grandparents were not able to meet her needs successfully when observed at contact or in other contexts.

Family and environment domain

There were multiple factors in the family history of Josie's mother and the wider family which were not acknowledged. There was little awareness of a need to change, and there was limited likelihood of change given the extensiveness of family conflict and alcohol misuse.

AN UNCERTAIN OUTCOME

The possibility of children being reunited with their family is uncertain where

- practitioners are not yet clear from the early therapeutic interventions with the family whether the situation is hopeful or very doubtful;
- there is uncertainty about the nature of the child's state and whether there is adequate capacity for the child's recovery, about parents taking

responsibility and whether parental pathology is changeable, whether there is a willingness to work with statutory authorities and other independent agencies, whether resources will be available to meet the extensiveness of the problem, or whether there will be change within the child's timeframe.

In these situations, further work needs to be undertaken to clarify the needs of the child and the capacity of the parents to respond to their child's needs appropriately and within the child's timeframe.

The Green family described earlier was an example of a family context where there was a considerable level of uncertainty about whether any of the four children could return home to live with their mother.

The Green family – a case of uncertain outcome

Child developmental needs domain

Each of the four children showed considerable needs in every area of their development as a result of physical abuse, neglect and sexual abuse. Each child was found to have unmet needs in relation to his or her health, education, emotional and behavioural development, identity, family and social relationships, self-presentation and self-care skills. They each had considerable therapeutic and parenting needs.

Parenting capacity domain

The parents had provided a long period of poor, punitive and neglectful care, had failed to supervise their children's activities and had exposed them to high levels of parental conflict.

Although the parents could acknowledge their difficulties and take a limited amount of responsibility, there was considerable doubt about their capacity to change within the older children's timeframe. There was a possibility that the mother would be able to meet the two younger children's needs on her own with the help of an intensive parenting programme.

Before this decision could be made, the mother needed to demonstrate a capacity to provide adequate basic care, stimulation, emotional support, set boundaries and be consistent.

Family and environmental domain

There was a background of low income, poorly maintained housing, social isolation and long-standing conflict within the wider family. These factors maintained a negative conflictual relationship between the parents, which in turn triggered mental health difficulties.

Relationships were positive with the practitioners and a plan for each child involving children's social care, their respective schools, health and a specialist voluntary agency was developed. However, there remained considerable doubt about what change could be achieved by the mother and whether the two older children could ever return home to live with her.

CONCLUSIONS

If we are to successfully safeguard and promote children's welfare by intervening to prevent abuse or neglect, to protect those children who come to the attention of the statutory authorities and to provide adequate therapeutic work for children who have been abused and for their parents, we need to build up integrated services and approaches to intervention. Each local authority will differ in its profile, the levels of privation and need, the extensiveness of negative family and environmental factors, the availability of services and the development of different approaches to intervention. Successful prevention and intervention in relation to children's safety and welfare require the following:

- Each local authority to have an accurate profile of the children and families living within its boundary.
- (Depending on local needs for targeted interventions) programmes which can target, follow and support children and parents who are vulnerable because of extensive family and environmental difficulties.
- Provision, for families where there are extensive difficulties, of supportive targeted services to ensure that parenting capacity is developed and children with considerable needs are helped to achieve good outcomes.
- The use of evidence-based approaches to assessing the needs of children, parenting capacity, and family and environmental factors so that when children are identified as being in need of protection from harm, action can be taken in the light of a full understanding of their developmental needs.
- Good-quality decision making to ensure that children are protected from harm and an in-depth assessment of their needs at all levels informs decisions.
- Focused therapeutic interventions (informed by evidence-based knowledge and based on an understanding of the child's needs within the family context) from agencies which can provide the appropriate intensity, consistency and extensiveness of intervention programmes. Such services need to be delivered in a context of protection to test whether rehabilitation is feasible, or whether a new family context is required for those children with the greatest need for safeguarding.
- The availability of multiple pathways to encourage children and their parents to find a voice and be protected from harm.

REFERENCES

Bentovim, A. (2002) Preventing sexually abused young people from becoming abusers, and treating the victimisation experiences of young people who offend sexually. *Child Abuse and Neglect*, **26**, 661–78.

Bentovim, A. (2003) Is it possible to work with parental denial? in *Studies in the Assessment of Parenting* (eds P. Reder, S. Duncan and C. Luceig), Brunner-Routledge, New York.

Bentovim, A. and Bingley Miller, L. (2001) *The Family Assessment: Assessment of Family Competence, Strengths and Difficulties*, Pavilion, Brighton.

Bentovim, A., Elton, A. and Tranter, M. (1987) Prognosis for rehabilitation after abuse. *Adoption and Fostering*, **11**, 26–31.

Bentovim, A., Elton, A., Hildebrand, J. *et al.* (eds) (1988) Child sexual abuse within the family: assessment and treatment, in *The Work of the Great Ormond Street Sexual Abuse Team*, John Wright, Bristol,

Berg, B. and Jones, D.P.H. (1999) Outcome of psychiatric intervention in factitious illness by proxy (Munchausen's syndrome by proxy). *Archives of Disease in Childhood*, **81**, 465–72.

Bools, C., Neale, B.A. and Meadow, S.R. (1993) Follow-up of victims of fabricated illness (Munchausen syndrome by proxy). *Archives of Disease in Childhood*, **69**, 625–30.

Borduin, C. and Schaeffer, C. (2001) Multisystemic treatment of juvenile sexual offenders. A progress report. *Journal of Psychology and Human Sexuality*, **13**, 25–42.

Broad, B., Hayes, R. and Rushforth, C. (2001) *Kith and Kin: Kinship Care for Vulnerable Young People*, NCB and Joseph Rowntree Foundation, London.

Cleaver, H., Unell, I. and Aldgate, J. (1999) *Children's Needs – Parenting Capacity: The Impact of Parental Mental Illness, Problem Alcohol and Drug Use, and Domestic Violence on Children's Development*, The Stationery Office, London.

Cm 5730 (2003) *The Victoria Climbié Inquiry: Report of an Inquiry by Lord Laming*, The Stationery Office, London, www.victoria-climbie-inquiry.org.uk (accessed 22 August 2008).

Cohen, J.A., Mannarino, A.P., Berliner, L. and Deblinger, E. (2000) Trauma-focused cognitive behavioural therapy for children and adolescents: an empirical update. *Journal of Interpersonal Violence*, **15**, 1202–223.

Cox, A. and Walker, S. (2002) *The Home Inventory. A Training Approach for the UK*, Pavilion, Brighton.

Dale, P., Green, R. and Fellows, R. (2002) *What Really Happened? Child Protection Case Management of Infants with Serious Injuries and Discrepant Parental Explanations*, NSPCC, London.

Daniel, B. and Wassell, S. (2002) *The School Years: Assessing and Promoting Resilience in Vulnerable Children 2*, Jessica Kingsley, London.

Davis, P., McClure, R.J., Rolfe, K. *et al.* (1998) Procedures, placement and risks of further abuse after Munchausen syndrome by proxy, non-accidental poisoning and non-accidental suffocation. *Archives of Disease in Childhood*, **78**, 217–21.

Dearden, C. and Becker, S. (2000) *Growing Up Caring: Vulnerability and Transition to Adulthood – Young Carers' Experiences*, Youth Work Press, Leicester.

Department of Health, Department for Education and Employment and Home Office (2000) *Framework for the Assessment of Children in Need and Their Families*, The Stationery Office, London, http://www.dh.gov.uk/PublicationsAndStatistics/ Publications/PublicationsPolicyAndGuidance/PublicationsPolicyAndGuidance Article/fs/en?CONTENT_ID=4008144&chk=CwTP%2Bc (accessed 22 August 2008).

Department of Health and Department for Education and Skills (2004) *National Service Framework for Children and Young People and Maternity Services: The Mental Health and Psychological Well-Being of Children and Young People*, Department of Health, London, www.dh.gov.uk/en/Publicationsandstatistics/ Publications/PublicationsPolicyAndGuidance/DH_4089114 (accessed 22 August 2008).

Department of Health, Home Office, Department for Education and Skills and Welsh Assembly Government (2001) *Safeguarding Children in Whom Illness is Fabricated or Induced*, Department of Health, London, http://www.dh.gov.uk/Consultations/ ResponsesToConsultations/ResponsesToConsultationsDocumentSummary/fs/ en?CONTENT_ID=4017163&chk=Ekjq8h (accessed 22 August 2008).

Dutt, R. and Phillips, M. (Department of Health) (2000) Assessing black children in need and their families, in *Assessing Children in Need and their Families: Practice Guidance*, The Stationery Office, London, http://www.dh.gov.uk/assetRoot/ 04/07/93/83/04079383.pdf (accessed 22 August 2008).

Dwivedi, K.N. (2002) *Meeting the Needs of Ethnic Minority Children – Including Refugee, Black and Mixed Parentage Children: A Handbook for Professionals*, 2nd edn, Jessica Kingsley, London.

Falkov, A. (1996) *Study of Working Together "Part 8" Reports: Fatal Child Abuse and Parental Psychiatric Disorder*, Department of Health, London.

Finkelhor, D. and Berliner, L. (1995) Research on treatment of sexually abused children. *Journal of the American Academy of Child and Adolescent Psychiatry*, **34** (11), 1408–423.

Fisher, D. and Beech, A. (2002) Treating adult sexual offenders, in *Early Prediction and Prevention of Child Abuse* (eds K.D. Browne, H. Hanks, P. Stratton and C. Hamilton), John Wiley & Sons, Ltd, Chichester.

Gardner, R. (2003) *Supporting Families: Child Protection in the Community*, John Wiley & Sons, Ltd, Chichester.

Gilligan, R. (2000) Adversity, resilience and young people: the value of positive school and spare time experiences. *Children and Society*, **14**, 37–47.

Gilligan, R. (2001) *Promoting Resilience: A Resource Guide on Working with Children in the Care System*, British Association for Adoption and Fostering, London.

Glaser, D. (2002) Emotional abuse and neglect – a conceptual framework. *Child Abuse and Neglect*, **67**, 697–714.

Glaser, D. and Prior, V. (2002) Predicting emotional child abuse and neglect, in *Early Prediction and Prevention of Child Abuse* (eds K.D. Browne, H. Hanks, P. Stratton and C. Hamilton), John Wiley & Sons, Ltd, Chichester.

Gorin S. (2004) *Understanding What Children Say. Children's Experiences of Domestic Violence, Parental Substance Misuse and Parental Health Problems*, National Children's Bureau, London.

Gray, J. and Bentovim, A. (1996) Illness induction syndrome: paper 1 – a series of 41 children from 37 families identified at The Great Ormond Street Hospital for Children NHS Trust. *Child Abuse and Neglect*, **20** (8), 655–73.

Gray, J., Bentovim, A. and Milla, P. (1995) The treatment of children and their families where induced illness has been identified, in *Trust Betrayed? Munchausen Syndrome by Proxy: Inter-Agency Child Protection Work and Partnership with Families* (eds J. Horwath and B. Lawson), National Children's Bureau, London.

Hamilton, C. and Browne, K.D. (2002). Predicting physical maltreatment, in *Early Prediction and Prevention of Child Abuse* (eds K.D. Browne, H. Hanks and P. Stratton), John Wiley & Sons, Ltd, Chichester.

HM Government (2006) *Working Together to Safeguard Children*, The Stationery Office, London, http://www.everychildmatters.gov.uk/safeguarding (accessed 22 August 2008).

Iwaniec, D., Herbert, M. and Sluckin, A. (2002) Helping emotionally abused and neglected children and abusive carers, in *Early Prediction and Prevention of Child Abuse* (eds K.D. Browne, H. Hanks and P. Stratton), John Wiley & Sons, Ltd, Chichester.

Jack, G. and Gill, O. (2003) *The Missing Side of the Triangle: Assessing the Importance of Family and Environmental Factors in the Lives of Children*, Barnardo's, Ilford.

Jones, D.P.H. (1998) The effectiveness of intervention, in *Significant Harm: Its Management and Outcome* (eds M. Adcock and R. White), Significant Publications, Croydon.

Jones, D.P.H. and Ramchandani, P. (1999) *Child Sexual Abuse: Informing Practice from Research*, Radcliffe, Abingdon.

Jones, D.P.H., Hindley, N. and Ramchandani, P. (2006) Making plans: assessment, intervention and evaluating outcomes, in *The Developing World of the Child* (eds J. Aldgate, D.P.H. Jones, W. Rose and C. Jeffery), Jessica Kingsley, London.

Kolko, D.J. (1996) Individual cognitive behavioural treatment and family therapy for physically abused children and their offending parents: the comparison of clinical outcomes. *Child Maltreatment*, **1**, 322–42.

Macdonald, G. (2001) *Effective Interventions for Child Abuse and Neglect*, John Wiley & Sons, Ltd, Chichester.

Mills, M. and Puckering, C. (1995) Bringing about change in parent – child relationships, in *The Emotional Needs of Young Children and their Families: Using Psychoanalytic Ideas in the Community* (eds J. Trowell and M. Bower), Routledge, London.

Monck, E., Sharland, E., Bentovim, A. *et al.* (1994) *Child Sexual Abuse: A Descriptive and Treatment Outcome Study*, HMSO, London.

Morris, J. (2003) *The Right Support: Report on the Task Force on Supporting Disabled Adults in Their Parenting Role*, Joseph Rowntree Foundation, York.

National Working Group on Child Protection and Disability (2003) *'It Doesn't Happen to Disabled Children': Child Protection and Disabled Children*, NSPCC, London.

Nicol, A.R., Smith, J., Kay, B. *et al.* (1988) A focused casework approach to the treatment of child abuse: a controlled comparison. *Journal of Child Psychology and Psychiatry*, **29**, 703–11.

Puckering, C. (2003) Parenting in social and economic adversity, in *The Handbook of Parenting* (ed. M. Hoghugi), Sage, London.

Quinton, D. (2004) *Supporting Parents: Messages from Research*, Jessica Kingsley, London.

Ramchandani, P. and Jones, D.P.H. (2003) Treating psychological symptoms in sexually abused children. From research findings to service provision. *British Journal of Psychiatry*, **183**, 484–90.

Reder, P. and Duncan, S. (1993) *Beyond Blame: Child Abuse Tragedies Revisited*, Routledge, London.

Reder, P. and Duncan, S. (1999) *Lost Innocents: A Follow-Up Study of Fatal Child Abuse*, Routledge, London.

Reder, P. and Duncan, S. (2002) Predicting fatal child abuse and neglect, in *Early Prediction and Prevention of Child Abuse* (eds K.D. Browne, H. Hanks and P. Stratton), John Wiley & Sons, Ltd, Chichester.

Salter, D., McMillan, D., Richards, M. *et al.* (2003) Development of sexually abusive behaviour in sexually victimised males: a longitudinal study. *The Lancet*, **361**, 471–76.

Sanders, M. and Cann, W. (2002) Promoting positive parenting as an abuse prevention strategy, in *Early Prediction and Prevention of Child Abuse* (eds K.D. Browne, H. Hanks and P. Stratton), John Wiley & Sons, Ltd, Chichester.

Schofield, G. and Thoburn, J. (1996) *Child Protection: The Voice of the Child in Decision-Making*, Institute for Public Policy Research, London.

Silvester, J., Bentovim, A., Stratton, P. and Hanks, H.G. (1995) Using spoken attributions to classify abusive families. *Child Abuse and Neglect*, **19** (10), 1221–232.

Skuse, D., Bentovim, A., Hodges, J. *et al.* (1998) Risk factors for development of sexually abusive behaviour in sexually victimised adolescent boys: cross sectional study. *British Medical Journal*, **317**, 175–79.

Stevenson, J. (1999) The treatment of the long-term sequelae of child abuse. *Journal of Child Psychology and Psychiatry*, **40**, 89–111.

Stevenson, O. (1998) *Neglected Children: Issues and Dilemmas*, Blackwell Science, Oxford.

Thoburn, J., Chand, A. and Procter, J. (2004) *Child Welfare Services for Minority Ethnic Families: The Research Reviewed*, Jessica Kingsley, London.

Trowell, J., Kolvin, I., Weeramanthri, T. *et al.* (2002) Psychotherapy for sexually abused girls: psychopathological outcome findings and patterns of change. *British Journal of Psychiatry*, **180**, 234–47.

Tunstill, J., Allnock, D., Akhurst, S. and Garbers, C. (2005) Sure Start local programmes: implications of case study data from the National Evaluation of Sure Start. *Children and Society*, **19**, 158–71.

Vizard, E., Monck, E. and Misch, P. (1995) Child and adolescent sex abuse perpetrators: a review of the research literature. *Journal of Child Psychology and Psychiatry*, **36**, 731–56.

Webster-Stratton, C. (1989) Systematic comparison of consumer satisfaction of three cost-effective parent training programs for conduct-problem children. *Behaviour Therapy*, **20**, 103–15.

Webster-Stratton, C. (1997) From parent training to community building. *Families in Society*, **78** (2), 156–71.

Wolfe, D.A. (1994) The role of intervention and treatment services in the prevention of child abuse and neglect, in *Protecting Children from Abuse and Neglect: Foundations for a New National Strategy* (eds G. Melton and F.D. Barry), Guilford Press, London.

FURTHER READING

Bentovim, A. (1992) *Trauma Organised Systems: Physical and Sexual Abuse in Families*, Karnac, London.

11 Reviewing and Ending Intervention: Achieving the Best Possible Outcomes for Children

WENDY ROSE

> The reviewing of the child's progress and the effectiveness of interventions are critical to achieving the best possible outcomes for the child.
>
> HM Government, 2006a, Paragraph 66

This chapter explores the importance of monitoring and reviewing a child's progress and the effectiveness of the actions being taken. The process of monitoring and reviewing starts as soon as there is contact with a child about whom there are concerns and for whom a child protection plan is put in place. It continues until work with the child and family is brought to a close. It is important to make a distinction between this continuing process of monitoring and reviewing and the formal points at which plans for a child require professional review under legislative regulations and guidance. Emphasis is placed on the process as a collaborative activity with the child and family and with other professionals involved, and includes consideration of the perspectives of children and their parents about their experiences. Finally, the chapter addresses how work with the child and other family members may be brought to a close, the significance of good enough endings to the well-being of the child and family, and how the ending of work can be used positively even in difficult circumstances.

CORE KNOWLEDGE

- Monitoring a child's progress in the context of a child protection plan requires knowledgeable and skilled engagement with a child and family, and reflective and critical supervised practice, where the focus is firmly maintained on the child.
- Monitoring in order to safeguard a child's welfare is an inter-agency activity which requires a high level of coordination and information sharing with the child, family and other professionals.

Safeguarding Children   Edited by Hedy Cleaver, Pat Cawson, Sarah Gorin and Steve Walker
Copyright © 2009 by John Wiley & Sons, Ltd

- Reviewing the child protection plan is required by regulations and guidance but is integral to working with the child and family. The review conference is a formal process in which the child, parents or carers and the professionals working with them should be fully involved, and which should be conducted with great sensitivity in order to reach agreement about how well the plan is working and what needs to change.
- Ending work with a child and other family members by statutory agencies requires careful preparation and management to ensure the child continues to be safeguarded and work with the family, whatever the outcome, is affirmed. Disengagement should be conducted in a manner which recognises the meaning of change, transitions and loss, and the impact of endings in relationships on children, parents and practitioners.

MONITORING AND REVIEWING

Monitoring and reviewing what is happening to a child in need in the context of his or her family and community is fundamental to ensuring the child's welfare is being safeguarded and promoted. The significance of monitoring and reviewing is heightened where there are concerns about harm to a child and a child protection plan is in place. However, this process of work with children and families is the least well defined and discussed. The processes of assessment, planning and intervention have more clearly identified frameworks and guidance to help the practitioner. Although acknowledged as an important aspect of work with children, there is little written about monitoring and reviewing (or *evaluating*, as it is referred to by some writers). In an important publication by Margaret Bryer in 1988, she incorporated the process of monitoring and evaluating into the heart of her model of Planning in Child Care, observing that

> Monitoring is a continuous process and it is surprising how much work is involved.... The purpose of the monitoring will be twofold: first to collect and organise the material on which the subsequent evaluation will be based, and second, to identify as quickly as possible any problems or misunderstandings, in order to deal with them before they escalate into major difficulties.
>
> Bryer, 1988, pp. 38–39

There are key points where the plan for a child requires formal review as required under regulations and guidance, but this is not the same as the continuous process of keeping a child in mind, engagement with the child and family, watching and reflecting on the child's progress, checking whether the plan is working out as intended and taking action as required in the interests of the child. However, the review is an integral part of the work between professionals and the child and family, and should not be regarded as an unnecessary or unwelcome imposition on families and professionals. The formal reviews of children's plans are important times when information about a child's progress and the implementation of the plan are considered by all those with responsibility for the child, together with the family, and critical decisions are made about the future direction of work.

As the result of so little attention to monitoring and reviewing in the literature, it is easy to see how it can become a diffuse, unstructured activity lacking in clarity, focus and purpose. It is hardly surprising that monitoring becomes undifferentiated from other activities such as organising and auditing the delivery of services according to the child's plan, and it can be (or perceived to be) a rubber-stamping exercise in agencies' work with a family. Parents' perspectives and understanding of the activity can be crucial to their trust and cooperation with professionals. As one parent, in a study of parents' views on social work interventions, remarked about the home visits they received:

> [The social worker] is not interested in us – not interested in Hugh. I felt she was out, just to be out for the sake of being out – just to mark it down in her diary – just to keep her job – to get the visit done.
>
> Spratt and Callan, 2004, p. 216

MONITORING AND REVIEWING AS A CONTINUOUS PROCESS OF CONCERN ABOUT A CHILD

Monitoring and reviewing is therefore best understood as a continuous process of concern about a child. The key questions being asked throughout this process are:

- Is this child safe enough – that is have they achieved the planned outcomes?
- How well is this child doing?
- How well is the child protection plan working?
- What changes are occurring in this family and its circumstances?
- What is the impact of these changes on the child or other family members?
- How is the family being kept involved and prepared for the future?

These questions start from the first contact with the family when there are issues as to whether a child is at risk of, or is suffering, harm and should continue through a process of engagement between the child, family and practitioners until work is brought to a close.

Just as assessment requires seeing the child and gathering information to understand what is happening to him or her, which continues throughout intervention, so there is a parallel process which requires the practitioner to monitor how the child is doing and how far his or her needs are being met in the current circumstances. There can, however, be great variation as to how well this is understood and carried out in practice. As a social services manager says:

We're not bad at the investigation, we're not bad at coming up with a plan to
protect the child, what we are bad at is following it up.

Hallett, 1995, p. 235

The following example illustrates why this is important.

Chloe and Tom

Chloe, aged 10, and Tom, aged 8, were difficult to manage and unhappy in
school. They were known to children's social care as their mother, Sandra,
was a single parent suffering from periods of depression when she found it
hard to cope and she neglected her children as a result. There were sufficient concerns and evidence of neglect for the child protection conference
to decide the children were at continuing risk of harm and should be the
subject of a child protection plan with the children's mother. As part of
this plan, the family was referred to a project with programmes for both
children and parents. Sandra attended regularly and participated fully in
the group parenting programme. Chloe and Tom attended the children's
programme; Chloe quickly flourished but Tom remained sad and withdrawn. Project workers were visiting Sandra at home to review the children's progress, and they found she was coping better with Chloe but using
excessive physical punishment on Tom when he would not cooperate. She
had not been able to admit it in the parenting group, although she desper-
ately wanted to be able to be a better parent and not to harm Tom. Chloe
and Tom were admitted on a voluntary basis to foster care, and Sandra
chose to continue attending the group parenting programme as well as having individual help with her problems and so work towards her children's
safe return home.

Monitoring is therefore an active and not a passive activity. Fresh information constantly requires noting, considering for its implications and incorpo-
rating into work with the family. It should also be carefully recorded. Change,
which is intended as part of the child's plan, may require positive action to reinforce progress and encourage the family. On the other hand, change which
is not in the child's interests and not in the child protection plan requires early
identification and action, however hard that may be for the family. In her book
on helping families with troubled children, Carole Sutton notes that 'sometimes reviewing progress throws up other factors which are impeding progress
and about which something must be done' (Sutton, 1999, p. 139). These factors may include changes in circumstances outside the immediate family that
may have an impact on how they function, such as a new adult member join-
ing the household, or the family experiencing harassment in the local community or illness in the family of a neighbour who provides regular out-of-school
care for a child. Relatively minor incidents can have major consequences and,

where there is a child protection plan in place, vigilance by the named key worker is required and careful decisions about the level and frequency of professionals' availability to the family have to be made as a consequence. Cleaver and Freeman (1995) warn us that 'long exposure to a case can raise [professionals'] threshold of tolerance' and, as a result, significant factors such as 'inadequate control, marital discord and the lack of affection can be missed' (p. 138).

Such changes may require a range of responses, including moving to contingency plans in situations of urgency, bringing forward core group discussions or the multi-agency review of the child protection plan and, following discussion between agency partners, agreeing with the family:

- action on behalf of the child or other family members;
- review or revision of the assessment conclusions and decisions;
- changes in the child protection plan;
- changes in the services being provided.

Sutton suggests the changes that have occurred may sometimes require a re-assessment 'to consider what has been overlooked in the first assessment, or what has happened to throw an initially good programme off course' (Sutton, 1999, p. 142).

MONITORING AND REVIEWING IN PRACTICE

A framework for monitoring and reviewing is provided by the developmental/ecological approach of the Assessment Framework (Department of Health et al., 2000). This assists core group members to structure their monitoring work with the child and family so that they can focus on what is happening in relation to

- the child's developmental needs;
- the parents' or caregivers' capacity to respond to those needs;
- the impact of wider family, family history and environmental factors.

At the same time, its use ensures consistency between the assessment, planning and monitoring processes (as Bentovim has demonstrated in Chapter 10).

Sally Holland (2004), in her study of two neighbouring coastal cities, found that using the Assessment Framework assisted practitioners in their tasks of monitoring and evaluation. Edna, a social worker from the Hillside Family Centre, commented:

> I think the ... framework is asking you to evaluate all the time, which is much more helpful.

p. 137

Holland concludes that the model is 'one of constant critical and reflective enquiry, where emerging conclusions are opened up to scrutiny and amendment by ourselves and others' (Holland, 2004, p. 137).

Key features in the practice of monitoring and reviewing

The process of monitoring and reviewing requires the following:

- Having clarity about who is responsible for undertaking the activities of monitoring, gathering together information and taking action.
- Being clear about the purpose of the activity and the timescales with the child and family and with other agencies.
- Keeping the focus on the child or children, and keeping them in mind during other work with the family.
- Engaging with, informing and involving the child/children and family.
- Selecting the methods of direct work (such as observation, individual and family sessions, shared activities with the child, using questionnaires and scales) in order to monitor progress.
- Liaising with staff (such as childminders, children's centre staff, health visitors or teachers) in other agencies who may have daily or significant contact with the child and family.
- Noting changes and relating them to the objectives and detail of the child's plan.
- Having time to think and reflect on what is happening to the child and family, and to weigh the relative significance of change.
- Keeping the Assessment Framework in mind as a tool to stimulate reflective and critical analysis.
- Having access to supervision and support to assist both critical reflection and management of the work.
- Recording what is happening, particularly evidence of progress and change.
- Ensuring that findings from monitoring are communicated to core group members and other agencies as appropriate.
- Considering the implications for the objectives and action detailed in the child's plan.
- Taking effective action as required, for which the child and family are informed and prepared.
- Gathering information together and preparing for formal reviews of the child's plan.

It is important for practitioners to ensure, with their supervisors, that they have the necessary skills, experience, knowledge, training and resources to fulfil these requirements.

ISSUES ABOUT MONITORING AND REVIEWING TO SAFEGUARD CHILDREN

As we have seen in other chapters, safeguarding children is complex and demanding work. Cooper and others observe that 'beyond a certain point, there is nothing straightforward about most child protection work' (Cooper 2005, p. 4).

A feature of such work is that, although there will be a named key worker appointed, it may well involve a number of different workers from both children's and adults' services, such as health visitors, teachers, youth workers, children's centre staff and community psychiatric nurses. Families where there are safeguarding concerns have complicated and difficult lives, and the range of services involved may be extensive and include adult services working with the parents.

The Children Act 1989 recognises that to promote the welfare of children, services may need to be provided to address the difficulties their parents are experiencing. All those workers, therefore, who have continuing contact with the child and family will have a role in identifying progress and change as part of the child protection plan. They will be members of the core group who have responsibility 'for developing the child protection plan as a detailed working tool, and implementing it, within the outline plan agreed at the initial child protection conference' (HM Government, 2006b, Paragraph 5.118). As already noted, one of the important responsibilities of the key worker is to liaise with members of the core group who are in contact with the child and family, and coordinate the information that arises. The effective operation of core groups can be influenced by difficulties arising from issues of inter-agency working, professional discretion and accountability, and they require careful management and oversight (helpfully discussed by Harlow and Shardlow, 2006). Monitoring and reviewing is therefore not a single-agency responsibility, and effective practice must respond to the challenges of multi-agency and inter-professional collaboration.

Particular issues about safeguarding work, identified by researchers and practitioners, may influence how the process of monitoring and reviewing is undertaken and will require attention through training and supervision. One of the most commonly noted issues is that once a view is formed about what is happening it becomes fixed and endures, often from the initial child protection conference (Cleaver and Freeman, 1995; Farmer and Owen, 1995; Munro, 2002). New information is subjected to 'selective interpretation' according to pre-formed views, or treated in isolation 'instead of within the context of the history of the case' (Reder and Duncan 1999, p. 17). Reder and Duncan conclude, from their study, that a coherent overview did not therefore emerge and, 'in many cases, this meant that persistent abuse was not recognised or considered severe enough to warrant a protective intervention'

(p. 17). This underlines the importance of reviewing and re-evaluating initial perspectives.

Turnell and Edwards (1999) remind us that work with some families may become 'bogged down and stuck' (p. 168), losing its sense of purpose and direction, often because the family and professionals are 'stuck in a cycle of repeatedly doing something that is not working' (p. 169) or they are limited in what they can do by the services available to them. This can be a crucial time when frustrated practitioners may become less vigilant and rigorous in their monitoring of the family's circumstances and listening to what the child and family members are saying to them. Work may tail off and the child or children become less visible. At this point, it may require trying different approaches or undertaking an early review of the overall objectives.

Keeping the focus on the child is not always easy. Parental problems may divert attention away from the child (see, e.g., Cleaver, Unell and Aldgate, 1999; Tanner and Turney, 2003). This has implications for the practitioner in monitoring and reviewing. Tanner and Turney (2003) highlight the issue in their review of the literature on child neglect. They identify that in cases of neglectful families, intervention may require long-term intensive support to bring about parental change by 'a blend of concrete services and therapeutic interventions ... delivered to families for a lengthy period of time' (p. 28). However, such work should also be accompanied by a parallel process of work with the child, to assess the impact on the child and ensure the child's needs are addressed. Reviewing is not just about whether parental change has occurred but whether it is having any positive impact on the child's welfare.

Writers who draw on their extensive clinical experience of working with maltreated children alert us to the difficulties children may experience in talking about their situations and their abuse, and the time it may take to disclose past experiences (discussed by Jones, 2003, 2006; Rustin, 2005). Thus, throughout the process of monitoring work with the child and family, 'it will be important for the practitioner to ensure that the scope of continuing enquiry and assessment is kept sufficiently broad to meet the needs of the child' (Jones, 2003, p. 144) and to be able to respond appropriately as the child overcomes the inevitable problems of being able to trust an unfamiliar adult (Rustin, 2005, p. 16). A young person in McGee's study (2000) describes with insight the importance of the process of building a relationship over time. Children will then choose their time when they feel ready to talk:

I think with the social worker and them, like they talk about stuff, other things at first so I grow to trust them and then we would start talking about stuff like that [the sexual abuse].

Fiona, aged 15, p. 126

Gorin (2004) emphasises the value that children place on professionals providing them with information about what is going on and not focusing exclusively on the parent(s). As Shirley in McGee's study (2000) reports:

> I don't think I had any security, any knowledge of what was going on. I needed to be told everything. I didn't realise that there was a chance that I might have been taken away.
>
> Shirley, aged 16, p. 124

The appropriate time for providing such information may only become clear as a relationship with a child is established with a worker who is consistent and trusted.

Sustaining work with children and families in circumstances of child maltreatment requires a very particular combination of professional skills and personal qualities. The emotional impact on the worker should not be overlooked. It can have a subtle and pervasive influence on the practitioner's perceptions and management of practice while working with a family and monitoring a child's progress. Cooper (2005) sets out the challenge:

> I would say this means the capacity to both endure intensity of emotional pain and turmoil, and exercise measured thought, analysis and judgement. The answer lies not in one or the other, but in both.
>
> p. 5

The culture of the organisation, the provision of high quality supervision and relevant training and an approach which values openness and collaboration are powerful contributory factors to the confidence and expertise with which the practitioner will undertake the task of monitoring and reviewing.

REVIEWING THE CHILD'S PLAN

The principle which underpins reviewing the child protection plan is that any inter-agency plan which sets out objectives for securing a child's safety requires regular and formal review by the participating agencies and the family. For half a century there has been a requirement enshrined in the UK legislative framework for some form of monitoring and reviewing of children's cases, which started with the Boarding-Out Regulations of children in foster care in 1955 (discussed in Department of Health, 1995a). Although the requirements were gradually broadened to include children in other circumstances, in the absence of detailed regulations and guidance, there was increasing concern about the understanding and effectiveness with which such responsibilities were being carried out (Sinclair, 1984). In particular, there was uncertainty and confusion about how children and their parents could expect to be involved and participate in the formal inter-agency meetings where critical decisions were being made about them. The situation has become much clearer since the Children

Act 1989 and subsequent government guidance (Grimshaw and Sinclair, 1997; HM Government, 2006b).

Following the initial child protection conference, the purpose of subsequent conferences is

> to review the safety, health and development of the child against the planned objectives set out in the child protection plan; to ensure that the child continues to be safeguarded; and to consider whether the child protection plan should continue to be in place or changed.
>
> HM Government, 2006a, Paragraph 66

After an initial child protection conference has been held and the child protection plan is in place, it is the responsibility of the children's social care manager to ensure that the first review conference is planned to take place within 3 months. It is a requirement that further review conferences are then held on a regular basis at intervals of not more than 6 months, unless there are changes in circumstances as discussed earlier in the chapter, which mean that the next review conference should be brought forward. The task of convening a review conference at a time and place that will facilitate the attendance of the agencies involved will always be fraught with difficulties. It ought to be easier when a date for review has been set at the initial or previous child protection review conference. Even so, Farmer and Owen (1995) found a tailing off in attendance by other professionals as time went by, except in those circumstances where concerns continued to be high (p. 248), a feature also noted by Hallett (1995).

The same care should be taken in arranging the review conference at a time that is suitable for the child or young person subject to a child protection plan and for other family members who wish to attend. Walker's findings (1999), from interviews with young people about their attendance at statutory reviews, are revealing. One young person described his experiences:

> … at the end of the review everybody gets their diary out to arrange the next meeting; but I haven't got a diary, so nobody asks me!
>
> p. 38

Similarly, young people who wanted to attend reviews thought adults should bear in mind that doing so may not always be the most important thing in a child's life at that particular time:

> I was chosen to play for the school team, but I couldn't because they told me that the review was more important.
>
> p. 39

These comments illustrate how difficult participation in formal processes is for children and for their parents. There will always be an imbalance of power between professionals and family members, which may be exacerbated by lack of understanding and confusion about the purpose of review conferences, about how to contribute appropriately in such a meeting and uncertainty as to whether they will be listened to. It is not easy to respond honestly and openly in such circumstances. This is where the way in which work is undertaken with children and parents from the start is critically important, and includes all contact by professionals and others providing services, who may well then be attending the review conference with the family. It also places a particular responsibility on the chair of review conferences to ensure that participating family members have had appropriate information and preparation, and to anticipate and respond to their needs during the conference (see Calder, 2003).

In preparing for the review conference, the contribution from other professionals who have been in contact with the child and family is critical. Maintaining the involvement and commitment of core group members is a challenging task for the named key worker and for the relevant children's social care manager. Very often the quality of liaison and information sharing during the intervening period between review conferences is a critical factor in reinforcing the role each professional is playing. The work put into the preparation for the review conference, including the gathering of reports from practitioners across the agencies to provide an evidence-based overview, is equally important. Preparation involves consideration between the key worker and the chair of the conference of how best to arrange and facilitate the participation of children and young people and/or their family members or carers, according to their individual circumstances, and to ensure they feel as confident and well briefed as possible. It also requires considering the participation of other professionals. It has to be acknowledged that sometimes practitioners are as anxious about the formal review as the child and family. There should be no surprises for any of those participating in the review conference – child, family or professionals – and the information and its implications should have been shared and discussed well in advance of the meeting.

However well prepared, the review conference can on occasions be a tense and difficult experience. When attending reviews, children and young people report that they feel, variously, too anxious to concentrate, embarrassed (particularly when attending with parents or foster carers), bored by the style of the meeting and their contributions listened to but not heard or taken into account (Walker, 1999). These responses suggest the importance of making the review as *human* as possible, allowing it to be sensitive and creatively responsive to circumstances, and not bureaucratic or mechanistic.

For a copy of the child/young person's child protection review – social worker's report, see http://www.everychildmatters.gov.uk/socialcare/integratedchildrenssystem/resources/exemplars/?asset=document&id=33994.

CHAIRING REVIEW CONFERENCES

Much rests on how the conference is chaired and the degree to which the chair has been involved in its preparation. Equally critical is the way the review conference is conducted – for example, ensuring that the child, parents and all the professionals are encouraged to have their say, holding the conference in an appropriately non-stigmatising environment, and orchestrating the meeting so that it 'becomes more impartial, fair and unbiased and less prejudiced' for all taking part (Calder, 2003, p. 47). The chair needs to pay particular attention to those children and families for whom English is not their first language. Some of them may require an interpreter working with them or, because of disability or other circumstances, may require additional support in their communication.

The practice guidance about assessment of black children in need and their families (Dutt and Phillips, 2000) and disabled children (Marchant and Jones, 2000) is helpful in this respect.

Children's services vary in their practice about chairing: some designate off-line managers as chairs of child protection conferences, others employ independent chairs or independent reviewing officers (IROs) who may also be chairing reviews of care plans for looked after children.

The guidance for IROs on looked after children provides a detailed outline of the role and responsibilities, which is of relevance to those chairing child protection review conferences (Department for Education and Skills, 2004).

Farmer and Owen's study (1995) is a valuable reminder of the importance of the chair in ensuring that the review conference is effective and exerts appropriate influence on the work with the child and family – for example, ensuring that areas of risk of harm to children are not overlooked and that there is a reappraisal of the management of the case if required; and that professionals other than the key worker contribute effectively and that the review conference does not simply continue to endorse the pattern of case management previously agreed, even when it is clearly deficient (pp. 253–261). The absence of dissent at child protection conferences has concerned a number of researchers (Farmer and Owen, 1995; Hallett, 1995) and suggests the special responsibility the chair of the conference has to elicit potentially differing or conflicting perspectives and to manage the process of weighing up their significance to assist the conference to reach agreement about the way forward. Calder (2003), taking account of these research findings, gives valuable advice to those who chair child protection conferences about ways to address their tasks effectively so they can be well prepared and manage the conference to ensure the outcomes reached are understood by all the participants. He pays particular attention to the group processes, which may come into play during the conference and the leadership role required of the chair.

Calder (2003) provides the following summary of 'tips' for improving practice (p. 47):

- preparation is necessary;
- evidence should be substantiated;
- clarification by summarising and checking is important;
- agreement by the whole conference on risk of harm, registration and recommendation should be sought;

- dissent and emotional undertones need to be brought out, acknowledged and dealt with;
- creativity should be a priority.

THE REVIEW CONFERENCE

Every review conference is required to consider explicitly whether the child continues to be at risk of significant harm, and hence continues to require safeguarding through adherence to a formal child protection plan (HM Government, 2006a, p. 33, Paragraph 67). This requirement emphasises that the focus of the review is on the child. Each child needs to be considered individually (even if there are siblings from the same family who are the subject of a child protection plan), and a view reached about how well each child is doing and whether he or she should continue to be the subject of a child protection plan. As in the process of monitoring a child's progress between child protection conferences, it is sometimes easy to lose the focus on the child by starting with a more general review of how the family is doing. Parental crises and difficulties can then dominate, and attention drifts away from what has happened to the individual child or the impact on the child of other events and circumstances in the family.

The review conference is, therefore, an important tool in work with the family, and a balance has to be found between formality and flexibility in the process of engagement between the family and professionals, so that the conference can be a positive aid in building on work done and agreeing work to be done. Key issues to be addressed in the course of the review conference, and for which preparation is required, are listed below:

- Have the objectives of the plan been achieved, partially achieved or not at all?
- What may have contributed to the objectives being achieved/not being achieved?
- What is the difference that has been made as a result of the planned interventions?
- What has been the impact of interventions on the child?
- Are more of the same services required or fewer, or different services or can services cease?
- Is the child safe and, if not what has to be done to ensure the child's safety?
- How should the child protection plan be updated as a result of the review?
- What will be the impact of the change of plan on other family members or caregivers?
- Is the plan practical and achievable or are adjustments required?
- Does the child need to remain the subject of a child protection plan and, if not, does there need to be a different type of child's plan?
- Who will take which actions forward?
- Who will communicate the outcome of the review to the child and family (if not present) and to other agencies as required?

- Have all the relevant people at the conference been heard and their views considered carefully?
- What are the particular tasks of the core group before the next review and how are they to be carried out?
- When is a further review conference required?

Having reviewed the child's current experience, the review conference may need to step back and take a longer view but, again, there should be no surprises to those participating in the review conference. Are the child's developmental needs and outcomes being sufficiently addressed? Is the overall direction hopeful? If the parents are being required to change, are they making sufficient changes within the child's timescales?

See Chapter 10 and Jones, Hindley and Ramchandani (2006) for an exploration of these critical issues.

In some situations, there are families unable or unwilling to work cooperatively with professionals who are, however, making sufficient changes to safeguard their children adequately. In other circumstances, it may be found that change has not been achieved or that change is possible but 'the timescale is simply too extended for the child's needs' (Jones, Hindley and Ramchandani, 2006, p. 286). As Jones and his colleagues comment:

> It goes against the grain for those working in children's services to conclude that some families are beyond our abilities to facilitate change. It can even be seen as offensive to consider some families beyond help ... no matter what resources we have or skills we bring to bear, sometimes families seem unable to change sufficiently to render their child safe in their care.
>
> p. 285

The review conference may have to reconsider the overall aims of the intervention and the implications for the longer term plan, timescales and action. For example, is the aim still reunification or should it become achieving permanence in another family situation through care proceedings? A difficult and painful part of the review may then be planning for the separation of parent and child. For these reasons, Jones and colleagues emphasise the importance of openness in the decision-making and care planning process from the beginning (Jones, Hindley and Ramchandani, 2006) and throughout work with the family.

The conclusions of the review conference will require detailed recording, including any revisions to the child protection plan, and they will need to be produced in an accessible and age appropriate form for the children concerned, as well as for their parents, caregivers and professionals.

See Chapter 9 on recording.

For a copy of the child/young person's child protection review conference – chair's report, see http://www.everychildmatters.gov.uk/socialcare/integrated-childrenssystem/resources/exemplars/?asset=document&id=33994.

WHAT CHILDREN AND PARENTS VALUE FROM PROFESSIONALS

Emphasis has been placed in this chapter on the importance of children's and families' participation in any decisions and plans which may affect them, and their review. It is critically important, therefore, that professionals (whether practitioners, managers or chairs of child protection conferences) consider children's and parents' individual circumstances to ensure appropriate involvement at all stages of work – particularly, in the context of this chapter, in review conferences. Researchers and those championing children's participation are increasingly addressing children's perspectives and providing compelling accounts of their views and experiences of working with professionals. See, for example, Gorin (2004).

These accounts should inform the work of practitioners and managers with responsibility for monitoring and reviewing children's progress. For example, in thinking about whether a child's plan is working or not, practitioners may want to consider some of the views of parents and children on what they value from professionals and reflect on how far these may be having an impact on the current situation.

The overview of the Children Act 1989 research studies (Department of Health, 2001) identified the qualities children valued in professionals. They were remarkably consistent with other findings about children's views. See, for example, Butler and Williamson (1994) and findings summarised by Gorin (2004) and Rose (2006).

Qualities in professionals important to children:

- reliability – keeping promises
- practical help
- the ability to give support
- time to listen and respond
- seeing children's lives in the round, not just the problems.

Department of Health, 2001, p. 93

The same overview of research also examined the findings of the Children Act 1989 research studies about parental perspectives and summarised the features of services that were important to parents (Department of Health, 2001).

Key factors that delineated a good service from parents' perspectives

Parents were very clear on what they valued:

- services that were targeted at the whole family, not just the child;

- interagency services that were well coordinated by social services;
- services that offered a combination of practical and emotional help;
- services that were offered in a welcoming, non-stigmatising manner;
- family centres that combined referred and non-referred cases and offered open access to a range of services or activities;
- transparency about the purpose and expected outcomes of services;
- seeing the same social worker over time.

Department of Health, 2001, p. 79

Knowing what children and parents value from practitioners and services is one thing. Putting these messages into practice is far harder. It requires commitment from practitioners and their managers to give the space and time required by children and other family members as part of the child protection plan, and to ensure that their views and concerns are heard throughout the process of work with them.

ENDING INTERVENTION

Ending intervention should mark the completion of work with a child and family and the achievement of objectives set out in the child protection plan. The reality may be very different in practice, particularly when all the objectives in the child protection plan have not been achieved and when it requires agencies to be satisfied that a child is being safeguarded. Writers identify a number of issues about this stage of intervention:

- Closing a case can be a valuable and productive phase of the helping process, if its particular challenges are recognised and met by worker and client (Maluccio, Pine and Tracy, 2002, p. 170).
- Closing a case appropriately can be difficult to achieve and requires skilled, competent practitioners supported by focused, thoughtful and sensitive supervision (Trevithick, 2000, p. 110).
- Case closure is a judgement call and, as with all other assessment points in child protection work, it may not always be clear. It is also not unusual for professionals to disagree with the decision (Turnell and Edwards, 1999, p. 173–174).

Maluccio, Pine and Tracy (2002, p. 170) offer some useful examples of indicators for considering bringing work to a close:

- problems or needs that contributed to the initial requirement for services have been reduced or ameliorated;
- basic needs are met;
- children are no longer in danger;

- family members have learned new skills conducive to safe and healthy family functioning;
- family communication is effective.

Trevithick (2000) and others point to the importance of timing and appropriateness. Trevithick (2000) suggests that

> under ideal circumstances, cases should be terminated at a point that has been mutually agreed: when goals have been reached or the time allocated for the work has come to an end and the service user feels ready to end the contact.
>
> p. 110

However, in circumstances where there are concerns about a child's safety, agencies involved in the child protection plan may have differing perceptions about whether the child is now adequately safeguarded, and whether sufficient progress has been made by family members to ensure the child's welfare. As Turnell and Edwards (1999) observe:

> ... we know of cases that have been closed although we were uneasy about the situation and, conversely, cases held open with no constructive purpose for continued involvement.
>
> p. 174

This places particular importance on, first, the acquisition of evidence of positive or negative changes and weighing the relative significance of those changes (Jones, Hindley and Ramchandani, 2006) and, second, the quality of inter-agency communication and sharing of information.

Evaluation of change by the child and family with the practitioner is critical at this stage, especially the impact that parental change has had on the child or children. Particularly important will be the evaluation of the parents' sensitivity and responsiveness to their child's developmental needs. There are various means by which changes in the family's functioning and situation can be measured, including the use of questionnaires and scales which may already have been an important part of the assessment process. *The Family Pack of Questionnaires and Scales* (Department of Health, Cox and Bentovim, 2000), *Home Inventory* (Cox and Walker, 2002) and *Family Assessment* (Bentovim and Bingley Miller, 2001) may all be used to evaluate change, according to the circumstances of the child and family. These may have an important part to play in assisting the family and professionals to make confident and agreed decisions about the timing of ending intervention as well as deciding what other services may be helpful.

There are other sound reasons for engaging families in evaluating their progress. It offers children and families a valuable opportunity to consider for themselves their own achievements and wishes for the future. Maluccio, Pine and Tracy (2002) stress that

... workers should strive to help clients appreciate the progress they have made, solidify their gains, and strengthen skills for anticipating and coping with future life challenges and crises.

p. 170

Part of strengthening the family's coping skills will be helping them extend their social support networks, so that they have made connections with formal and informal support services, and they know where to find additional help or information when needed. Trevithick (2000) describes this as

... encouraging people to bring other people into their lives to replace us, by helping them to turn to others who can provide the care, concern, guidance and support that they need.

p. 110

However, it has to be recognised that some families will have great difficulty in finding support from within their local community, such as refugee families with little or no knowledge of English or families whose past behaviour has alienated their neighbours. For some families, the wider family may not be an appropriate source of support where there is a known history of child abuse. For these families, continuing professional support is likely to be required to ensure their children's welfare is promoted and safeguarded within their families. Gauging the extent to which families are confident about asking for help and their knowing whether and how to seek help and support is critically important in determining readiness either to end intervention or to continue to offer services, albeit outside the framework of a child protection plan.

Endings that are mutually agreed with the family or other agencies take time and preparation, even in a negative context, and may not always be a feature of child protection work – for example, because cooperation between the practitioner and the family may never have been satisfactorily established or may have broken down; or because families sometimes precipitate closure by moving from one area to another without informing their key worker or other agencies; or because there may be disagreement about the need for continuing work with a family when one of the key agencies cannot sustain its involvement in view of pressing resource constraints or other priorities. Such endings are unsatisfactory as well as worrying for all concerned and can be a cause of local inter-agency anxiety, dispute and tension. The child and family can quickly become lost from view. It is in these situations that contingency arrangements (as outlined in local safeguarding children procedures) may need to be mobilised immediately across all agencies – for instance, if a family subject to a child protection plan has suddenly moved out of the area, if access to the child or children is denied to the key worker, or the child stops attending school or primary health care services. The child protection plan may require urgent review if the agreed resources from one agency have not materialised or have been withdrawn. These are inevitably sensitive circumstances and can quickly escalate to involve senior agency managers. Practitioners will need to engage with their supervisors, managers and other agency colleagues in a process of evaluation and reflection, to learn from these situations when they arise, and rebuild appropriate trust and confidence for future work together.

Child protection work is distinguished, as we have seen throughout this reader, by the high level of multi-agency collaboration which is required. It has to be remembered, therefore, that closure of work with a family may also bring to an end close collaborative partnerships between workers of different agencies, either through their membership of the core group or as a network of practitioners and managers working together across the statutory and voluntary sectors. These partnerships may have lasted over a considerable period and through many trying times. In preparing for ending work, they should not be overlooked but their impact on workers acknowledged and valued. They should be used as the basis for both learning from the experience and 'saluting the positives and leaving behind the negatives' (Harrison *et al.*, 2003, p. 89) so as to ensure a sound foundation for future collaboration.

ENDINGS AND THEIR IMPACT ON CHILDREN AND THEIR FAMILIES

Ending intervention usually incurs changes or endings in relationships between practitioners and children and their families. We have seen from the accounts of children and their caregivers the significance they attach to their relationships with practitioners working with them, even in adverse circumstances.

See, for example, Jones and Ramchandani (1999), Department of Health (2001) and Tanner and Turney (2003).

Jones and Ramchandani (1999), in their review of key research findings on intervening with sexually abused children and their families, highlight the crucial importance of 'the quality of the helping alliance' that can develop between practitioners and their patients and clients even in one of the most difficult areas of safeguarding work. They conclude that 'treatments cannot work in isolation, but require direct social casework support to enable them to be effective' (p. 65). Furthermore, as Jones (1998) writes:

> ... it is probable that professional factors exert an effect on outcome over and above that which is attributable to the abuse and the context within which this occurs.
>
> p. 110

This is echoed by Trotter (2004) who argues that the relationship with child protection workers 'can often make a real difference' (p. 27). Farmer and Owen (1995), in their study of child protection practice, found that even after initially unhappy experiences of parents, matters did tend to improve and

... those social workers who kept in constructive contact with both the child and other family members were highly valued, and this kind of co-operation contributed greatly to a good outcome.

Department of Health, 1995b, p. 62

If the relationship between child, carer or family members and practitioners is so important, both in its impact on the child and family and in its contribution to the effectiveness of intervention, then it follows that the relationship has to be carefully nurtured and supported, and great care given to the manner and management of its ending. However, there is a marked absence of attention given to the impact of endings on clients in the literature on practice.

For some exceptions, see Turnell and Edwards (1999), Trevithick (2000) and Maluccio, Pine and Tracy (2002); a still relevant earlier work by Jones *et al.* (1987) (with a valuable chapter on disengagement) and, more recently, Seden (2005).

Huntley (2002, p. 61) is one of those who have explored these issues, observing that

Even in well-known texts there is little noted in the index under 'termination' or 'case closure'. Sometimes there is a brief reference to the transfer to another worker but the termination is rarely addressed. Yet in related fields, such as psychotherapy, ends and endings are more fully faced.

The messages from therapy and counselling, helpfully drawn out by Jacobs (1998), Huntley (2002) and Seden (2005), are relevant to those working in children's services:

- The importance of preparation and planning for the endings of work together – Jacobs (1998, p. 206) cites as a rule of thumb allowing 'a further quarter of the time already spent in therapy for working through to its finish'.
- The significance of the ending in its link to earlier experiences of separation and loss which, without due care, 'may result in the reinforcement of previous negative separation experiences for the client and may undo much of the positive work that has been achieved' (Huntley 2002, p. 59).
- The process that anticipates the end has obvious parallels with many of the stages of grief, including disbelief, sadness, relief and the recognition of unfinished business (Jacobs, 1998).
- The opportunity that the ending provides to evaluate what has taken place during therapy or counselling, and to consolidate what has been achieved (Jacobs, 1998; Seden, 2005).
- Acknowledgement that there can be real sadness on both sides with the finality of the ending (Jacobs, 1998).

Applying these messages to child protection work emphasises the importance that should be attached, for example, to managing changes of practitioners or the ending of work by agencies with children and families. In some cases, strong dependency on practitioners' support may have developed, particularly if there has been sustained work over a period of time (Jones *et al.*, 1987). It is critical to effective practice that there is an understanding of the implications of transitions and loss and that, for children and adults, handling constant changes and interventions can have an immobilising and overwhelming effect. It may result in behaviours and distress that can be misinterpreted as lack of cooperation or hostility, and which can contribute to a deterioration in participation and partnership to the detriment of the child's and family's welfare.

Children and young people who are subject to child protection procedures in order to safeguard their welfare are more likely than most of their peers to undergo additional and traumatic changes in their lives. Some measure of stability and certainty becomes a priority for them, and keeping the same social worker or other trusted adult worker might be critical to their welfare (Rustin, 2005). This may similarly be the experience of parents for whom separation, loss and rejection have been significant in their lives (Jones *et al.*, 1987). On the other hand, some parents may view a change of worker with relief (Cleaver and Freeman, 1995; Farmer and Owen, 1995). As discussed, relationships may end during work with a child or family members for a plethora of positive and negative reasons, initiated by either party or in circumstances completely outside their control.

However, all too often, changes of practitioner are due to staffing difficulties in the statutory child welfare services. The current attention being directed by government to the children's workforce and to issues of recruitment and retention are indicative of some deep-seated problems in children's social care, manifested in high levels of staff turnover and increasing use of agency and overseas staff to cover vacancies (Chief Inspector of Social Services *et al.*, 2002; HM Government, 2005, 2006c; and for information on the Options for Excellence social care workforce review see http://www.everychildmatters. gov.uk/optionsforexcellence). The result of this constant state of staff movement in some local authorities, combined with the impact of organisational boundaries around different functional responsibilities, can mean that children and families experience many unwanted changes of practitioners. A pattern of abrupt beginnings and endings in their relationships with practitioners may occur. The consequences of what may be a series of unplanned or administratively required endings may have a damaging effect on the child or family, and impair their trust in the agency and their willingness to transfer to another worker, as well as undermine the effectiveness of other aspects of the child protection plan.

It is, therefore, critically important for practitioners and their managers to approach closure of work with a family, especially where the work has been difficult and complex, as a process which requires planning, preparation and sufficient time. If other professionals will continue to be in contact with the family – from agencies such as health, education, youth services or even perhaps youth justice – then closure needs to be achieved without undermining the roles, responsibilities and relationships of others. Whether closure is planned or a change or transfer of worker is required, the implications for the child, parents or carers need to be given proper and sensitive consideration as an integral part of achieving good outcomes for children.

Planning and preparation in these circumstances require careful distinction between the needs of the adults involved (parents, carers, perhaps grandparents and other extended family) and children. Different family members may have very different responses to the ending of work with some of the child welfare agencies, which need to be tested out and taken into account. Children may require sufficient time with a practitioner who has become a trusted adult in their lives to understand what will be happening and why, and multiple forms of communication used creatively to affirm messages about endings and goodbyes. It will also be important for the child to think about and feel confident about getting help or assistance in the future, should it be required. This may be by identifying other trusted adults in their lives or, for older children or teenagers, by being given contact numbers or written information for future reference (Jones, 2003). Other issues may re-emerge, such as about future confidentiality and information sharing, especially if a new worker is becoming involved, which will require exploration and agreement. Whatever the pressures under which they are working, professionals should not underestimate the significance of their practice at the point of ending their work with a family. Last memories are as important as first impressions, and effective work at this stage may help to create a more positive model for coping with loss and change in the future.

CONCLUSION

The importance of active engagement with the child who is the subject of a child protection plan, keeping the child in view and at the centre of concern, has been emphasised throughout the chapter. The process of monitoring and reviewing requires continuously asking 'how well is this child doing?' and 'is this child safe?' This cannot be achieved without direct contact and communication with the child and other family members or caregivers, and attention being given to any changes as they occur, weighing them up for the significance of their impact on the child. Monitoring is an active, not a passive, activity and clarity of purpose is essential, and needs to be shared and understood by the family. It requires a high level of multi-agency and inter-professional collaboration and communication between the key worker and other members of the core group. The opportunity for critical reflection by practitioners, with the support of skilled supervision, is fundamental to effective monitoring of a child's progress, and the emotional impact of safeguarding work on staff should always be kept under review by supervisors and managers. Child protection review conferences are integral and not peripheral to the overall process of monitoring and reviewing and are potentially positive vehicles for formal consideration by professionals and the family. The review needs to evaluate how the plan is working and whether changes should be made in the child's best interests, including taking a longer view of the direction of change and its impact on the child's development. However difficult it may be, preparation is important so that there are no surprises at the conference for the child, family or professionals. The quality of chairing of review conferences is critical to ensure their effectiveness for all participating.

Work with a child and family who have been subject to a child protection plan may come to an end for a variety of planned and unplanned reasons, and not always in optimal circumstances. The timing of ending engagement by professional agencies with the child and family may be a difficult decision. It may result in a change of workers who have been important to the child or other family members. This requires as much judgement and preparation as other aspects of child protection work. The impact of ending relationships on the child and family must be given proper consideration, and sufficient time and resources allocated for the purpose. The child's and parents' views should always be sought and taken into account, in order to achieve the best possible outcomes for that child.

REFERENCES

Bentovim, A. and Bingley Miller, L. (2001) *Family Assessment*, Child and Family Training, London.

Bryer, M. (1988) *Planning in Child Care: A Guide for Team Leaders and Their Teams*, British Agencies for Adoption and Fostering, London.

Butler, I. and Williamson, H. (1994) *Children Speak: Children, Trauma and Social Work*, Longman, London.

Calder, M.C. (2003) Child protection conferences: a framework for chairperson preparation. *Child Care in Practice*, **9**, 32–48.

Chief Inspector of Social Services, Director for Health Improvement, Commission for Health Improvement, Her Majesty's Chief Inspector of Constabulary, Her Majesty's Chief Inspector of the Crown Prosecution Service, Her Majesty's Chief Inspector of the Magistrates' Courts Service, Her Majesty's Chief Inspector of Schools, Her Majesty's Chief Inspector of Prisons and Her Majesty's Chief Inspector of Probation (2002) *Safeguarding Children: A Joint Chief Inspectors' Report on Arrangements to Safeguard Children*, Department of Health, London, http://www.dh.gov.uk/assetRoot/04/06/08/33/04060833.pdf (accessed 22 August 2008).

Children Act 1989, Chapter 41, HMSO, London.

Cleaver, H. and Freeman, P. (1995) *Parental Perspectives in Cases of Suspected Child Abuse*, HMSO, London.

Cleaver, H., Unell, I. and Aldgate, J. (1999) *Children's Needs – Parenting Capacity. The Impact of Parental Mental Illness, Problem Alcohol and Drug Use, and Domestic Violence on Children's Development*, The Stationery Office, London.

Cooper, A. (2005) Surface and depth in the Victoria Climbié Inquiry Report. *Child and Family Social Work*, **10**, 1–9.

Cox, A. and Walker, S. (2002) *Home Inventory*, Child and Family Training, London.

Department for Education and Skills (2004) *Independent Reviewing Officers Guidance, Adoption and Children Act 2002*, Department for Education and Skills, London, http://www.everychildmatters.gov.uk/resources-and-practice/search/IG00007 (accessed 22 August 2008).

Department of Health (1995a) *Looking After Children: Good Parenting, Good Outcomes. Training Guide*, HMSO, London.

Department of Health (1995b) *Child Protection: Messages from Research*, HMSO, London.

Department of Health (2001) *The Children Act Now: Messages from Research*, The Stationery Office, London, http://www.dh.gov.uk/PublicationsAndStatistics/Publications/PublicationsPolicyAndGuidance/PublicationsPolicyAndGuidance Article/fs/en?CONTENT_ID=4006258&chk=Ko0nZX (accessed 22 August 2008).

Department of Health, Cox, A. and Bentovim, A. (2000) *The Family Assessment Pack of Questionnaires and Scales*, The Stationery Office, London, http://www.dh.gov.uk/PublicationsAndStatistics/Publications/PublicationsPolicyAndGuidance/PublicationsPolicyAndGuidanceArticle/fs/en?CONTENT_ID=4008144&chk=CwTP%2Bc (accessed 22 August 2008).

Department of Health, Department for Education and Employment and Home Office (2000) *Framework for the Assessment of Children in Need and Their Families*, The Stationery Office, London, http://www.dh.gov.uk/PublicationsAndStatistics/Publications/PublicationsPolicyAndGuidance/PublicationsPolicyAndGuidance Article/fs/en?CONTENT_ID=4003256&chk=Fss1ka (accessed 22 August 2008).

Dutt, R. and Phillips, M. (Department of Health) (2000) Assessing black children in need and their families, in *Assessing Children in Need and Their Families: Practice Guidance*, The Stationery Office, London, http://www.dh.gov.uk/PublicationsAnd Statistics/Publications/PublicationsPolicyAndGuidance/PublicationsPolicyAnd GuidanceArticle/fs/en?CONTENT_ID=4006576&chk=M3Qrpp   (accessed   22 August 2008).

Farmer, E. and Owen, M. (1995) *Child Protection Practice: Private Risks and Public Remedies*, HMSO, London.

Gorin, S. (2004) *Understanding What Children Say. Children's Experiences of Domestic Violence, Parental Substance Misuse and Parental Health Problems*, National Children's Bureau, London.

Grimshaw, R. and Sinclair, R. (1997) *Planning to Care*, National Children's Bureau, London.

Hallett, C. (1995) *Interagency Coordination in Child Protection*, HMSO, London.

Harlow, E. and Shardlow, S.M. (2006) Safeguarding children: challenges to effective operation of core groups. *Child and Family Social Work*, **11** (1), 65–72.

Harrison, R., Mann, G., Murphy, M. *et al.* (2003) *Partnership Made Painless*, Russell House, Lyme Regis.

HM Government (2005) *Children's Workforce Strategy: A Strategy to Build a World-Class Workforce for Children and Young People*, http://www.everychildmatters.gov.uk/deliveringservices/workforcereform/childrensworkforcestrategy (accessed 22 August 2008).

HM Government (2006a) *What to Do If You're Worried a Child Is Being Abused*, Department for Education and Skills, London, http://www.everychild-matters.gov.uk/safeguarding (accessed 22 August 2008).

HM Government (2006b) *Working Together to Safeguard Children: A Guide to Inter-Agency Working to Safeguard and Promote the Welfare of Children*, The Stationery Office, London, http://www.everychildmatters.gov.uk/safeguarding (accessed 22 August 2008).

HM Government (2006c) *Children's Workforce Strategy: Building a World-Class Workforce for Children, Young People and Families. The Government's Response to the Consultation*, Department for Education and Skills, London, http://www.dcsf. gov.uk/consultations/downloadableDocs/CWS%20update%20PDF%20version.pdf (accessed 22 August 2008).

Holland, S. (2004) *Child and Family Assessment in Social Work Practice*, Sage, London.

Huntley, M. (2002) Relationship based social work – how do endings impact on the client? *Practice*, **14** (2), 59–66.

Jacobs, M. (1998) *The Presenting Past. The Core of Psychodynamic Counselling and Therapy*, Open University Press, Buckingham.

Jones, D.N., Pickett, J., Oates, M. and Barbor, P. (1987) *Understanding Child Abuse*, 2nd edn, MacMillan Education, Basingstoke.

Jones, D.P.H. (1998) The effectiveness of intervention, in *Significant Harm: Its Management and Outcome*, 2nd edn (eds M. Adcock and R. White), Significant Harm Publications, Croydon.

Jones, D.P.H. (2003) *Communicating with Vulnerable Children*, Gaskell, London.

Jones, D.P.H. (2006) Communicating with children in adverse circumstances, in *The Developing World of the Child* (eds J. Aldgate, D.P.H. Jones, W. Rose and C. Jeffery), Jessica Kingsley, London.

Jones, D.P.H., Hindley, N. and Ramchandani, P. (2006) Making plans, assessment, intervention and evaluating outcomes, in *The Developing World of the Child* (eds J. Aldgate, D.P.H. Jones, W. Rose and C. Jeffery), Jessica Kingsley, London.

Jones, D.P.H. and Ramchandani, P. (1999) *Child Sexual Abuse: Informing Practice from Research*, Radcliffe Medical Press, Abingdon.

Maluccio, A.N., Pine, B. and Tracy, E.M. (2002) *Social Work Practice with Families and Children*, Columbia University Press, New York.

Marchant, R. and Jones, M. (Department of Health) (2000) Assessing the needs of disabled children and their families, in *Assessing Children in Need and Their Families: Practice Guidance*, The Stationery Office, London, http://www.dh.gov.uk/ PublicationsAndStatistics/Publications/PublicationsPolicyAndGuidance/ PublicationsPolicyAndGuidanceArticle/fs/en?CONTENT_ID=4006576&chk= M3Qrpp (accessed 22 August 2008).

McGee, C. (2000) *Childhood Experiences of Domestic Violence*, Jessica Kingsley, London.

Munro, E. (2002) *Effective Child Protection*, Sage, London.

Reder, P. and Duncan, S. (1999) *Lost Innocents: A Follow-Up Study of Fatal Child Abuse*, Routledge, London.

Rose, W. (2006) The developing world of the child: children's perspectives, in *The Developing World of the Child* (eds J. Aldgate, D.P.H. Jones, W. Rose and C. Jeffery), Jessica Kingsley, London.

Rustin, M. (2005) Conceptual analysis of critical moments in Victoria Climbié's life. *Child and Family Social Work*, **10**, 11–19.

Seden, J. (2005) *Counselling Skills in Social Work Practice*, 2nd edn, Open University Press, Maidenhead.

Sinclair, R. (1984) *Decision-making in Statutory Reviews on Children in Care*, Gower, London.

Spratt, T. and Callan, J. (2004) Parents' views on social work interventions in child welfare cases. *British Journal of Social Work*, **34** (2), 199–224.

Sutton, C. (1999) *Helping Families with Troubled Children: A Preventive Approach*, John Wiley & Sons, Ltd, Chichester.

Tanner, K. and Turney, D. (2003) What do we know about child neglect? A critical review of the literature and its application to social work practice. *Child and Family Social Work*, **8**, 25–34.

Trevithick, P. (2000) *Social Work Skills*, Open University Press, Maidenhead.

Trotter, C. (2004) *Helping Abused Children and Their Families*, Sage, London.

Turnell, A. and Edwards, S. (1999) *Signs of Safety: A Solution and Safety Oriented Approach to Child Protection Casework*, Norton, London.

Walker, S. (1999) Children's perspectives on attending statutory reviews, in *Involving Children in Family Support and Child Protection* (ed. D. Shemmings), The Stationery Office, London.

FURTHER READING

Children Act 2004, Chapter 31, The Stationery Office, London, http://www.opsi.gov.uk/ACTS/acts2004/20040031.htm (accessed 22 August 2008).

Department of Health (2002) *Exemplar Records for the Integrated Children's System*, Department of Health, London, http://www.everychildmatters.gov.uk/socialcare/integratedchildrenssystem (accessed 22 August 2008).

Index

Safeguarding Children   Edited by Hedy Cleaver, Pat Cawson, Sarah Gorin and Steve Walker
Copyright © 2009 by John Wiley & Sons, Ltd